ANNA KENT is a huma   nidwife.
After receiving a Nur   rsity of
Nottingham, she comp   ____pioma in Tropical Nursing in London
and joined Médecins Sans Frontières (Doctors Without Borders) in
2007. She gained her First Degree in Midwifery in 2010 and has
worked as a midwife across the world, including in South Sudan, Haiti,
Bangladesh and the UK.

FRONTLINE MIDWIFE

Finding hope in life, death and birth

Anna Kent

with Julia Gregson

BLOOMSBURY PUBLISHING

LONDON · OXFORD · NEW YORK · NEW DELHI · SYDNEY

BLOOMSBURY PUBLISHING
Bloomsbury Publishing Plc
50 Bedford Square, London, WC1B 3DP, UK
29 Earlsfort Terrace, Dublin 2, Ireland

BLOOMSBURY, BLOOMSBURY PUBLISHING and the Diana logo are trademarks
of Bloomsbury Publishing Plc

First published in Great Britain 2022
This edition published in 2023

2 4 6 8 10 9 7 5 3 1

Typeset by Newgen KnowledgeWorks Pvt. Ltd., Chennai, India
Printed and bound in Great Britain by CPI Group (UK) Ltd, Croydon CR0 4YY

To find out more about our authors and books visit www.bloomsbury.com
and sign up for our newsletters

For Aisha

PREFACE

When I talk about aid work, most listeners expect a feel-good, inspiring story, where good inevitably wins over evil. This was the narrative I naively imagined as a twenty-something-year-old, heading out on my first intrepid adventure. And sometimes wonderful things do happen. But the reality of humanitarian crises is that they are always complicated, often harrowing, and there is certainly no simple fix.

I fervently hope that by speaking out on behalf of the women I've been honoured to meet – sometimes in the most amazing, and the most horrific, of circumstances – that somehow their lives may be improved. Their stories deserve to be told, and to protect them, all patients have been anonymised. Every extraordinary birth described in this book has happened in real life and many of the scenes are graphic.

Trigger warnings are given for: baby loss, gender-based violence, birth-related injuries and maternal death. I have a duty to protect you, rather than harm you with my words. But equally, I want you to share the joy, laughter and heroism of the many extraordinary women and families I have met through my frontline work as a nurse and midwife.

CHAPTER ONE

April 2007. I haven't met the woman on the plane yet, but our paths will cross in a matter of days, and one day the smell of her will haunt me. It's the smell of the mothers you can't save, and their babies. When we do meet, we'll both be juddering on the floor of an old cargo plane in South Sudan, where she'll be at the extreme point of her suffering. Her intravenous (IV) infusion will be tied by a sad piece of fraying string to a ripped seat. She will be alone – abandoned by her family and unable to tell us who she is – and the sight of her will change me forever.

Right now, I'm standing half dressed – sensible knickers, new T-shirt – in an airy, high-ceilinged bedroom in Nottingham that smells of furniture polish and candles. I'm staring at a mound of stuff piled on the hoovered carpet, trying to talk to myself in a relaxed, sensible voice.

Do your packing. Calm down, this is what you've been waiting for.

In a few hours' time, I'll start the long journey to South Sudan and my first assignment as a nurse with Médecins Sans Frontières (MSF) – Doctors without Borders – a medical organisation that sends doctors, nurses and other professionals to conflict zones, natural disasters and epidemics. On one side of the bed sits my backpack, half full already with the essentials: stethoscope, headtorch, multitool, diary and insect repellent. T-shirts, trousers, sarongs and vests sit in a toppling pile next to it. Although I've checked the list endlessly, I know they won't all fit in, but how do you pack everything for nine months into one bag?

Jack, my boyfriend, is still asleep on the other side of the bed, and the sight of his brown hair flopped over his eyes makes me feel like I've been punched in the stomach. Soon he'll drop me off at the airport, we'll cry and talk of our commitment to each other, before I start the first leg of my journey. He'll come back to this place alone.

There's been no word of reproach from Jack about me leaving. He supports my decision to be an aid worker with MSF, and even says he's proud of me. We're sure we've talked it through from every angle, and are dedicated to staying together – both looking forward to when I return and we can build our lives together. But I'm so far from knowing myself, I can only give him a partial explanation of my motives.

My yearning to be an aid worker ignited when I was a child in the 1980s, aghast to see TV news footage of starving children in Ethiopia. Those skinny arms and wide vacant eyes shocked me, as I realised for the first time that such suffering existed in the world. *How does this happen?* Within my comfortable and loving family home in a small Shropshire village, I hadn't realised inhumane things like starvation could happen, especially to children. I wanted to help. Simple as that, or so I thought. That feeling grew stronger every time the next tsunami or earthquake filled our TV screen with images of suffering people. But now I'm twenty-six. I have other darker, complicated reasons for wanting to go, buried inside me like thorns. I can't talk about them yet, even to myself.

Flying MSF workers to remote areas costs a lot, and because the work is tough, and often scary, the dropout rate is high, so MSF tries not to throw you in at the deep end. It's not possible, but they try. For nurses, the minimum requirement is three years' experience in acute areas of nursing, either an emergency department (ED), surgery or intensive care, plus some overseas work experience. In my case, I have a master's degree in nursing from the University of Nottingham, and following this, spent three years as an ED nurse at Queen's Medical Centre, a massive teaching hospital said to have one of the busiest EDs in Europe, where I coordinated the major trauma unit. This, incidentally, was where I saw my first birth – a young, scared, fifteen-year old, who'd concealed her pregnancy and told us her abdominal pain was from a fall. She surprised us all by bearing down in a side room, before we'd had a chance to fully triage her, shouting fearfully, 'Don't call me dad, he'll kill me!'

The baby's head was crowning before she'd even pulled her jeans past her knees, and this chaotic and disturbing arrival into the world showed me how much I still had to learn. I wasn't a midwife, so while they were wheeling her off, at speed, to the maternity department, baby already in her arms, I decided to do some voluntary shifts in the maternity unit on my annual leave before joining MSF.

Next, I did a diploma in tropical nursing from the London School of Hygiene and Tropical Medicine, then a short voluntary stint at a rural Zambian hospital, and finally an MSF pre-departure preparation course in Germany.

I'm trained and ready for this, I try to reassure myself as I zip up the stuffed backpack, taking comfort that my UK colleagues often describe me as cheerful, or calm in a crisis. I'm hoping like hell I can stay this person with MSF. *It'll be an adventure too*, I silently muse, wondering if I'll want to get an MSF logo tattoo on my return home, as I've seen successful Olympians do.

When Jack stirs, I move the backpack, sit down beside him and stroke his hair. Jack is more than I'd hoped for in a partner – beautiful, kind and talented – a non-nerdy computer analyst, who plays the guitar to professional standard. He loves children and loves me. I'll miss him and our home dreadfully, with its carefully chosen artwork and lazy Sunday mornings in a big comfy bed, the light filtering through the gaps in the shutters. Sometimes, though, in the middle of the night if I can't sleep, I'm also silently perplexed, *why isn't this enough for me?*

We've talked about marriage and children, but in my mind's eye it's always far in the future, not here and now. Through a crack in the door to the living room, I can see the grand piano, a recent gift from Jack. It was so thoughtful – I'd once made a passing comment that I missed our family's battered old piano, and he'd bought one. It was an insanely expensive present by our standards, and he'd stayed up most of the night to be eBay's last bidder for it.

But something about it makes me feel uneasy and sad. For him, it's a symbol of our permanence, but I'm secretly thinking, *I'm leaving and I can't use it*. Part of me wishes he'd given me something small, something useful I could take with me, but that seems awfully ungrateful.

Now isn't the time for this, I remind myself, reciting the plan, which is for me to go, 'do my bit', enjoy the adventure, and come home happier because I've done it. How simple it seemed then, how little I knew what a crossroads I was at, though precipice is probably a better word.

*

By the time I've landed in Lokichoggio, north-west Kenya, I've been travelling for six days. On my way here I've been briefed in Amsterdam and Nairobi. 'Loki' is a haphazard town of mud roads, bare brick buildings and aid tents, surrounded by the arid land of the Turkana people. MSF has a large operational base here, from which several different medical facilities in South Sudan are coordinated. My week-long training in Loki leaves me in no doubt that South Sudan is a scary place to be. Team briefings, held around a long wooden table under a ceiling fan and thatch roof, discuss the long and bloody civil war that has raged, on and off, for fifty years. Although the war has officially ended, its legacy is appalling. At least 2 million people have been killed, more than 4 million have become refugees or internally displaced people, there are still severe food shortages and outbreaks of conflict.

I'm handed a sky-blue security card during the briefing. It states I have permission from the Sudanese People's Liberation Army to enter South Sudan and that I'm not bearing arms – MSF is an unarmed organisation. Next is training for the event of kidnapping, which leaves me feeling winded. Then discussion of evacuation procedures and 'bush runs' (grabbing what we can and running for as far as we can), should we need to. From now on, in case it might save my life, I must carry $100 in cash in a grab bag to hand over to my captors.

I'm told to be hyper-aware of landmine fields and warned that some local people carry AK-47s for protection. I'm shown pictures of Sudanese snakes – including red cobras and black mambas – some of them deadly, and scorpions, which are everywhere and can cause excruciating and incapacitating stings. Maybe it will seem more exciting when I can email family and friends about it, create a picture that I'm more Carrie in *Homeland* than Anna nauseated from nerves.

Shell-shocked and jet-lagged, I'm shown next how to work in isolation to prepare me for Tam and Koch, the two small Sudanese towns where I'll be based for the next nine months, running basic health-care units. In Tam, I'm warned, there's no internet signal (the heat is such that computers simply melt), no telephone and no nearby hospital. Although I might get sent to other projects, most of the time I'll have only one other international person to work with, a nurse called James. That's all I know about him, except he's sixty-one years old and eccentric.

In the clinics I must expect to see everything from infected thorn injuries to complicated pregnancies, and it's the last bit that alarms me most. I've seen babies being born at the Nottingham maternity unit, I'd marvelled as an onlooker when heroic women cried tears of happiness as their new babies were lifted into their awaiting arms, but I've had no formal midwifery training.

*

So much information is hurled at me in Loki, I start to feel like Bambi on ice. Or, more accurately, a Bambi covered in flies, lying in a bunk bed of a concrete building surrounded by barbed wire. On my last night, a few of us new recruits try to relax before our flight into South Sudan, and head to Trackmark, a nearby bar in town.

Loki, with its mishmash of aid organisations and tented warehouses, isn't an obviously romantic place, but I'm told it's a party hotspot for many aid workers coming out of the field: the place to let off steam after long, stressful and lonely months of aid work in South Sudan.

Sipping my first drink at Trackmark, politely declining the bartender's offer of ice, I meet Jaan. He looks a bit like Prince Harry, but with a suntan. Jaan, nursing a whisky over ice, leans over the red and white checked tablecloth and explains in a South African accent that he and several other pilots work for a private aviation company in Loki. He's been doing it for years, apparently. When he tells me about a rescue mission he'd previously undertaken in Somalia, I'm girlishly impressed. With his battered panama hat and cotton short-sleeved shirt tight on his upper arms, he doesn't look like any of the men I grew up with in that sleepy Shropshire village of my childhood, which feels exciting.

'So is there someone missing you at home?' he asks nonchalantly, as he downs the rest of his drink and orders another. He shoots me a look to see if I want one; I shake my head and ask for a Coke, keen to be bright-eyed for the flight to Tam tomorrow morning.

'That's great,' he says when I tell him about Jack, his eyebrows raised in a look I can't read, before he turns to chat to someone else. Jack's love letter is in my pocket, wilted from heat and sweat, but so close I can feel it.

*

I'm on my way. This is it – the final leg of my journey to Tam, flying over some of the flattest, driest earth I've ever seen. I want to drink it all in, this astonishing barren scene, and although the adventure feels thrilling, my mind's reeling with all the new information. The large cargo plane, with its roars and snorts and tumbling aid boxes, feels like something outlaws might use. Half of the seats don't even have seatbelts, and the voices around me are speaking in Dutch, French, Arabic, Swahili... everything, it seems, but my own language. I'm trying to act relaxed, and ahead of me, in the cockpit, is Jaan, now wearing his pilot epaulettes, who occasionally turns round to give me an encouraging smile.

*

An hour into the flight and my nervous breath catches in my throat as the unpressurised plane bounces up and down in turbulence. Big black flies that flew into the cabin in Kenya cling to my bright white MSFT-shirt - so pristine – displaying I'm the inexperienced newcomer. Across the aisle, two men are deep in conversation in English about troop movements. One is wearing faded khaki trousers and muddied walking boots, the other linen trousers and creased shirt, but I don't recognise any of the place names they're talking about. Shrinking back in my seat, I fold up the tattered remnants of Jack's letter (in the flurry of leaving Loki, I'd nearly left it under my pillow) and take out the security briefing again, like I'm cramming for an exam that I know I'm unprepared for.

Fifty years of civil war broken only by failed peace agreements. There has been fighting over land, fighting between tribes, fighting in Darfur, fighting between North and South, fighting for oil, fighting against corruption and fighting for survival. Now those images from the news – child soldiers, villages burnt to ashes – feel horribly real.

Suddenly our plane plummets towards the ground like a shot bird. Down and up, down and up, like a fairground ride. The two men across the aisle smile at my sudden yell.

'It's called a buzz,' one explains patiently. The 'buzz' is a planned dive in order to get herded cattle off the mud runway. Up again, down again, *don't let me throw up.*

As we fall, I see, on the patted earth of the makeshift runway, a shot-down plane lying like a dead carcass on its side, and then, bump, wallop, we land at last. When the plane doors burst open the heat is extraordinary.

How am I going to breathe in this heat, let alone work? Khaki-pants man tells me this is a brief stop to unload supplies and take on patients to be dropped at a place called Leer. There's no time to lose. The plane must go on to land in five of the twenty-two MSF projects in this area before sunset, when the skies get too dangerous.

It's impressive to see the team leap into action: everyone busy, everyone, except me, knowing exactly what to do. Outside the plane, the team joins lines of tall and graceful Nuer people; they're all lifting heavy aid boxes along a human chain. From here, I can easily see the burnt-out plane. It's an aid plane. *Who shot it down? Who was on board?*

Suddenly I stop, because this is the moment when I smell the worst smell I've ever smelt: a nightmare stink of infected flesh and excrement that makes my eyes water.

Frowning, nose puckered, I look for its source. A bundle of rags on a splintered stretcher is put down in the aisle beside me. When a limp hand flops from under the sheet I'm mortified by my own disgust – my first sighting of a patient and I feel like throwing up.

I'm trying to put the stretcher on a more even part of the floor when I see her face for the first time. Dull waxy skin. Whites of her eyes flickering as the pupils roll back in their sockets. A gaping mouth, flies scrabbling over dried saliva. She is dying. No special training needed to see that. A cloth has been thrown over her to protect her dignity; underneath it she wears a clean T-shirt, a long skirt. The rows of traditional beads around her neck are vibrant against the black of her skin, and rock in time with her shallow, rapid breaths.

A nurse, arms full of equipment, bustles past me to get to the woman. Her MSF T-shirt is thick with mud-dust and has a hole in the collar. An IV line is deftly connected to the woman's arm and attached with string to the edge of the seat. Sponging the woman's forehead, the nurse is whispering encouraging words in Nuer that I can't understand.

There's a fire burning in her eyes that says, *You will live!*

'What's wrong with her?' I ask the nurse when we're airborne again.

'Obstetric fistula,' she says in a French accent, giving me a look of disdain. I'm disturbing her.

Obstetric fistula? My mind flips back to my notes. The nurse still looks pissed off. Over the growing roar in the cabin, she explains in a sharp tone.

'This woman had no midwife. The civil war took it all from her, so her baby died inside her. The dead body didn't deliver; it became rotten, made a hole in her uterus until it finally passed out of her. The hole goes to her bladder and bowel, so she constantly leaks urine and faeces. She can't stop it. The bad smell means her family deserted her. Maybe two years she's been like this, but she's unable to tell us who she is and where she's from. Now she's septic and maybe she will die.'

Two years! Like this! To live every day with horrific injuries from your own dead baby? The nurse, defensive, says the unidentified woman was washed and clothed before they got on the plane, but the smell is unstoppable.

My superficial air of confidence is all gone in a moment. I've seen for the first time what war does to innocent women. There was no midwife for this woman, no hospital for her to go to, and because of her smell, she's been ostracised by her family. For the first time in my life, I'm up close to the most extreme form of suffering, and I feel totally useless.

The French nurse is still working hard. She's changed the IV drip, set up IV antibiotics. I'm allowed to take over sponging the clammy forehead, the woman's eyes now tightly closed. Dusty light coming in sideways from the porthole windows highlight her tribal markings: concentric circles made from scars and dots that begin at her mouth and cover her entire face.

I wish I knew her name. I wish I knew her language. I wish I could speak to her. Back in the UK, she would be hooked up to drips and bleeping monitors, and here she is, bundled under a few shitty sheets, her IV attached to a fraying string. Access to medical care should not be denied because of geographical or political borders.

*

Around lunchtime, the plane lands in Leer, the capital town of the state. The plan is to drop the woman off at the region's only safe place for surgery – an MSF hospital with wards, a theatre, a team of international surgeons and doctors. Plane doors fly open. A spray of mud as an MSF 4 x 4 ambulance arrives to take the French nurse and stretchered woman to the hospital. Other patients with bandaged arms and legs are led off the plane, each escorted by a family member as a caregiver. Only the woman is alone.

That unidentified woman has stayed with me ever since: her suffering and her loneliness haunt me. Years later I will think of her, remembering how at the time I'd silently vowed to find out what happened to her, whether she'd survived. But then, because of all the dreadful, unbearable and wonderful things that came to claim my time, to my shame I never did.

I watch them load the woman into the 4 x 4. Jaan is firing up the propellers to fly me on to Tam, and I wonder if I'm going to be strong enough for what lies ahead. The ambulance has a prominent red symbol on the back of its white door. 'Don't shoot us,' is its message, 'we're the good guys.'

Red tail lights move off and disappear in a cloud of dust.

CHAPTER TWO

I arrive in Tam on a Saturday afternoon. Having been away from home for two weeks, I'm trying with all my might not to look back or feel homesick. This trip has already been a wake-up call about all the things I took for granted. Love, for instance. Comfort. On a typical weekend at home, I'd have been woken up by Jack in a comfy bed in the flat he owned in a converted lace mill in Nottingham.

If I'd been on a night shift, which was often, Jack would bring me tea in bed. After a lie-in, I'd take a power shower, often to the sound of Jack playing guitar on the sofa, probably rehearsing for a gig. Maybe we'd watch a film, or have friends round for a Sunday roast – he was a great cook – or Saturday tea in my parents' lovely garden in Shropshire.

But this Saturday, I'm stepping off the plane, part of me wishing already I was back home. This is hands-down the hottest and most barren place I've ever seen. On one side of the mud runway there's a scattering of thatched mud huts, with the main town of Tam just behind them. On the other side is an enclosure surrounded by a flimsy stick fence, which is, apparently, the MSF clinic.

I'd expected something more official-looking, more secure, but these man-made structures plonked in the middle of mile upon mile of baked brown earth remind me of tumbleweed, so fragile-looking, yet able to withstand the most hostile of environments. There is one lone tree here, no other structures, just this clear view through to the horizon, a sight that on a glass half-full day you might see as awesome and beautiful and strange, and on a glass half-empty day, as unending nothingness.

A man steps out of the dust, a big white grin underneath the Stetson hat that he tips at me.

'Howdy, partner!' he says. 'I'm James. Welcome to Tam!'

I very much want to like James. He will be my nursing partner and main non-Sudanese colleague for the next nine months. But James is sixty-one – old enough to be my father, or even grandfather – and, sorry to say (but I have promised to tell the truth as I see it), does not impress me at first sight. With his extravagant handlebar moustache, his rose-coloured John Lennon glasses, the faded tattoos of an old biker, his shaved head and his sparkly white Californian teeth, he looks like a bit of a dick.

James waves cheerfully to the old guard outside the clinic, greeting him in the local language. Probably, or so I imagine, saying something like, 'Hey baby what's happenin'?' like the extra in *Easy Rider* he seems to have modelled himself on. The old guy cackles happily, showing lots of empty spaces in his mouth, as you have to be your own dentist in South Sudan.

James, bouncing on the soles of his feet, says we'll have the proper clinic tour tomorrow, but today we'll set up my quarters in the living compound, just a few feet away. At the stick fence entrance to the small compound is Nicole, a Welsh nurse just finishing her nine-month placement in South Sudan. She greets me with kind, tired eyes and a cup of tea in a plastic camping cup.

'So let's get you settled. That's my tent,' says James, looking towards a blue sun-bleached shape beside a scrubby bush.

'When Nicole leaves, you can sleep there.' His tattooed arm points at a spot about two feet away from his tent.

'We need to be close,' he says, seeing my startled expression. 'Not so's you can hear me fart in the morning, but 'cos it's safer that way. I'll also need to know where you are when we get called in the night, which we will be.'

He grins his blindingly white grin as if this is a great treat: 'Trust me.'

'Want a hand with the tent?' asks Nicole in a gentle accent that feels familiar and comforting. Shaking my head, I'm keen to show them I'm no tenderfoot, and my tent (the kind of cheap plastic thing you buy for Glastonbury) looks pretty foolproof. When it's up, I crawl in on my hands and knees leaving grubby sweat prints behind.

There's just enough room in its mould-smelling interior for my mattress, which is just a yoga mat, and my backpack. While Nicole finishes her handwritten handover information, James shows me the shower block – a cup and a bucket of water that the sun heats up, surrounded by the stick fence. He jokes that the kids who live in the mud huts (tukuls) on the other side of the runway sometimes try to peep through the compound fence to giggle at the sight of a foreign white bottom.

After unpacking, I wash the dust off my face with a wet wipe. It's getting late when I hear James saying, in a head waiter's voice through the tent wall, 'Dinner is served, ma'am.' Nicole laughs gently, kindly. She looks exhausted.

'Lovely! Thank you!' I sound like my mum at a Shropshire tea party.

Joining them in the outdoor 'kitchen' – a tiny metal table, three metal fold-out chairs and a bucket of water – the silence is extraordinary. No birds, wind or traffic. Just me, Nicole and James with the sunset reflected in his rose-coloured specs.

James talks me through supper – what he calls 'a celebration three bean medley' (one can butter beans, one can baked beans, one can chickpeas and a can of tomatoes all heated together on the one-ring camping stove). Between mouthfuls of beans, Nicole, who is roughly my age, with innocent elven features and big dark circles under her eyes, briefly tells me about her last nine months in South Sudan. She sounds tired when she talks of the people she's been honoured to meet, and her awe at the ability of humans to survive in the most hostile conditions. I don't hear a word of her own suffering and she barely mentions how she feels about going home to Wales. Is she excited? Nervous? Or just too tired to explain it to me? Perhaps I see myself in her, not just our physical features, but our desire to care for the people here. But I'm intimidated too – she knows so much of what to me is just a daunting mystery. *Can I ever live up to her legacy? Am I strong enough for this?* As Nicole trails off into thoughtful silence, James, who doesn't seem to do small talk, tells me about his love of Tam and its people, but then jumps into a tale of his former alcoholism, his multiple marriages and three children, his hippy commune days in Israel, where he lived on cabbage for a month because they were penniless. Just one breath, and now we're exploring his twenty-five years of intensive-care nursing, and finally his present Buddhist practice to atone for the sins of his past.

'So don't freak out if you hear me omming in the morning, as well as fartin', haha!'

I'm grateful for his optimism, but secretly am so completely overwhelmed and shocked at the basic facilities of my new home that I'm having difficulty keeping up my look of polite interest.

'You both look beat,' James says suddenly. The skies have gone black around us, sunsets don't mess about here, they go out like a light.

'We'll give you the rest of the grand tour tomorrow.'

Before bed, James says it's a good plan for us to always go to bed at the same time, otherwise, he looks at the tents, 'Those guys are so flimsy you get the full strip show in silhouette. Oh! And zip tight, otherwise you'll get about a million bugs, snakes and scorpions wanting to crawl in to cuddle ya!'

His white teeth flash. He's gone, the black sky around us crazy with stars.

*

James omming in his tent wakes me up the next morning. He winds up a small, screeching hand-held radio. He'd told me over the bean medley last night that the radio can only pick up the BBC World Service and an Arabic station with no music broadcast from Khartoum. The larger, heavy VHF radio is the size of a backpack and has its antenna wire wrapped around the prickly shrub between our tents. Nicole explains it's used only for the morning and night safety communications with the base in Loki, plus emergency distress calls, should we need to make them. The broadcast is done in phonetic code, otherwise there's a risk of the supply plane or cash payroll being hijacked. In Loki, I'd learnt these codes, and my mind grapples to remember the sequences, manically running the phonetic alphabet through my head from alpha to zulu.

7.30 a.m. 40°C. I left my fusty-smelling boots outside overnight, so I check them for scorpions and find two small black ones inside. After squealing and shaking them out, I splat them both with the heel of my boot, my heart pounding in my throat. Next comes a wet-wipe wash – there's no running water here. After breakfast Ryvita, 'Watch out for the weevils' and tea with powdered milk, a startlingly beautiful six-foot-tall Nuer woman arrives. She's carrying, with the grace of a ballet dancer, that day's supply of water in a container balanced on her head. Her name is Angela and she is one of ten Sudanese national staff here; she touches Nicole's shoulder tenderly, giving a shy smile of greeting.

Angela carries this water each day from the end of the runway, a distance of about a mile, but has apparently laughed off attempts to give her a cart to carry it in. Each of the tukul households here in Tam carries its own water from that well, but I feel grossed out by her having to carry it for me, like some awful colonial throwback. 'But if we spend all day carrying water, who will see the patients?' chimes in James, as if he's in my head. Note to self – go easy on water. That container must weigh a ton and it's a long trek in the heat.

Over breakfast, James, Nicole and I listen to news on the wind-up radio of a mass shooting at the University of Virginia in the USA. We muse about how disturbing it is, in a bountiful country like America, that there is still so much suffering and so little gun control.

'I don't believe in borders.' James has switched off the radio and is speaking while spreading jam on his Ryvita. 'If anyone asks me where I'm from, I say, Planet Earth.'

There's laughter in his piercing blue eyes. I want to roll mine like a teenager.

*

On our short walk to work, about ten steps, James tells me that the two basic health-care units we now run are the only medical facilities in an area that is roughly the size of Belgium.

'So how many patients do you see a month?' I ask, trying to keep the 'Oh, bloody hell!' note out of my voice.

'About a thousand a month, over two clinics,' he replies casually. 'It's a great learning curve cos you'll get to see everything: landmine victims, malaria, malnutrition, cholera, gunshot wounds, obstructed labour – that will be your job – I don't do childbirth.'

'But I'm not a midwife, James.' I remind him gently that I have seen a few births but not been responsible for them.

'You will be.'

Nicole adds, 'There are no formally trained Sudanese midwives here.' She goes on to explain that there's only one known trained midwife in the whole of South Sudan, the bleak result of the low status accorded to women plus the war destroying education facilities and hospitals.

'There's a local saying here that pregnant women have one foot in the grave.'

She shakes her head in disbelief.

*

My tour of the clinic doesn't take long. Inside the stick fence, there are four small, cylindrical mud and reed tukuls, which James describes enthusiastically as the pharmacy, the inpatient department (IPD) and two outpatient 'suites'. These battered huts form a small quad, with a patted-down mud courtyard in the middle. Just outside the quad is a large, lone tree, creating shade under its leafy branches. James thinks it's a type of mahogany, he's noticed how it's an evergreen, but explains it's also the waiting room.

'Shade is a big deal in these parts.'

9.00 a.m. Temperature about 45°C. Heatwaves shimmer off the lid of the metal handwashing bucket. Close to a hundred patients have arrived. They sit, or lie, under the Waiting Tree in respectful, calm lines on tarpaulin that covers the mud, waiting to be registered and seen.

James greets everyone with open joyous arms:

'Malee! Ma gua,' Nuer for, 'Hi guys, totally rad to see you,' or so I imagine, as he enters the clinic. But he makes them smile. Nicole goes to the pharmacy tukul to organise the supplies before she leaves. I already feel a pang in my chest at the thought of this – I want her and her reassuring eyes to stay.

Some of the patients have walked for nine days over landmine fields, sand and swamp in the belief that our humble clinic can help them. That's roughly equivalent to the length of time it would take a sporty person to walk from London to Manchester, with only a hope of finding help there. Patients will now wait several more hours, often all day, to be seen.

'We can save the life of most people that come here,' says James, reading my thoughts again. 'That's all we can hope for.'

It's hard not to compare this with the ED waiting room in Nottingham: the teen kicking off at having to wait an hour for his minor wound to be seen; the drunk woman vomiting in the corner; the overweight guy with chest pain because he'd spent his adult life eating and drinking too much.

To cut down on the frustrations that sometimes led to staff being attacked, the National Health Service (NHS) paid millions redesigning that department with comfy chairs, vending machines, digital screens giving up-to-date waiting times. But I'd still had a knife pulled on me there, a few months back, by a patient high on amphetamine. When I'd pressed my personal panic button, security staff came running in seconds. Who'd come here? Earlier, James joked that the old man who guards the compound spends most of the night making rope with his toes from shreds of old plastic.

Back in that busy ED, after each patient left, walls would be wiped down, hands washed in hot water, blood mopped, furniture and equipment restored to pristine condition. Now, as we jackknife 90 degrees to enter another dark and dusty tukul, brushing aside the cobwebs, James can't wait to show me his pride and joy, and my first reaction is *Oh, fuck! What?* It's a 1950s-style dentist's chair where, he explains, patients are examined. Bits of dirty-looking foam sprout from its stained turquoise plastic cover; its metal arms are rusty.

Nothing is ever thrown away in South Sudan, he tells me proudly, and I think James must love this relic because it's the one thing that makes this place look like a medical facility. I don't want to rain on his parade, but I'm appalled: you can't clean rust, so the chair is a breeding ground for infection. In my old hospital, every single metal or plastic implement was sterilised or thrown away after each procedure. True, it was a mountain of waste, but at least everything was clean.

Standing by, also beaming proudly at the chair, is Queth, our registrar. When he smiles, one of the widest, kindest smiles I've ever seen, I'm transfixed by his enormous protruding, almost horizontal top white teeth. Apparently, sticky-out teeth are considered beautiful here and deliberately pulled forward in adolescence. Across his forehead are seven horizontal tribal markings that crease in empathy when he listens to a patient's story. The parallel cuts, made with a knife or glass when he was a boy, identify him as Nuer and are prestigious signs of entry into manhood. Later, I would see many infected tribal markings, from dirty cutting instruments, and adults with bulbous, bulging scars where infections were left untreated and the repairing skin had over-granulated.

Queth tells me that shorter cuts and spots show if a man is Dinka, an opposing tribe. He leans close to gossip: 'Dinka eat monitor lizards,' he informs me in a hushed tone, apparently the most distasteful of accusations he could throw at his rivals.

Queth's never been to school. He's lived most of his twenty-four years during a civil war, which destroyed any chance of formal education. His job here is to record patients' details in a shaky pencil into a large register book, a slow business – Queth allegedly had two fingers blown off by a helicopter gunship – but he makes the entries with great care and dedication.

Keeping good records is an incredibly important part of MSF's work here. Nicole explains part of my job is to make sure medications and prescriptions are accurately dispensed, and every patient registered. Attempts at digitalising the process in Tam have so far failed: laptops crash quickly here in the unbelievable heat. Instead, every month, we must take the handwritten data back to the main base at Leer, where we'll collate it into a spreadsheet for the monthly medical report to be emailed to the operational centre in Amsterdam. This helps to build a bigger picture of the health of the country, spot epidemics early, and decide where to focus future medical programmes. I was already looking forward to that first trip to Leer; it's where I'd be able to email home for the first time.

*

Everyone slowly shuffling forward in the queue is extremely thin. Not starving exactly, but certainly malnourished. The dietary staple of most people, James explains, is sorghum, a millet seed that's ground to make porridge. Local markets have been hit hard by the fighting, and the few scrappy wooden stands that remain in Tam seem to sell only shrunken red onions and salt.

'One source of protein,' he says, 'is a bony mudfish that lives in the Nile, but there's one great big motherfucker of a Nile crocodile waiting for you there too – largest freshwater predator in the world.'

*

When it's time for the first patient to be seen, the crowd under the tree push forward the most deserving. This morning it's Nhial (the name, Queth explains, means 'rain' in Nuer, as he was born in a thunderstorm). He's eight years old, collapsed in his grandma's arms, at least, I think it's his grandma – people look so much older here and estimated life expectancy for women is only around 50. Nhial, who wears a worn-out vest top and no pants, is covered in perspiration; his pale pink tongue looks dry, and both knees are massively swollen and hot. James, assisted by Stephen, a young Sudanese community health worker (CHW), begins in a soft murmur, 'There you are, good buddy, we're gunna help you.'

James looks kindly into Nhial's eyes and smiles as he's lifted into the dentist's chair. First thing James does is a top-to-toe assessment, with a stethoscope and thermometer his only aids.

'Hmmm... swollen lymph, joint pain, fever, swollen liver, see here...?' He touches the boy's abdomen, feeling gently over the right side. He has massive car mechanic hands, but he's gentle with them. James then shows the keen Stephen how to palpate an abdomen for hepatosplenomegaly: basically, feeling gently over the boy's belly for an enlarged liver and spleen, typical of many diseases of the tropics. Back in the UK, I'd have sent for liver function blood tests and ultrasound, but here, in the absence of any electricity or labs, James *is* the lab and blood test.

Fifteen minutes later, James gives the working diagnosis of brucellosis, a serious bacterial infection from drinking unpasteurised milk. It's common in areas without a secure food supply – people are forced to eat and drink whatever's available, even if it's unsafe.

James concludes: Nhial should be admitted, given IV antibiotics and IV fluids. He'll be discharged a few days later back to the cattle camps, where huge numbers of cattle are tended to, and used as trading currency in the absence of banks. This eight-year-old's job is to protect the herds. He'll be armed with a spear to defend against night raiders armed with machetes and AK-47s, who may ride in on pick-up trucks.

By the end of this assessment, I look at James with new respect. He showed such grace with this boy, morphing from a wandering hippy into a dynamic practitioner. Someone I can learn from. Sweat pours down now from under his John Lennon specs, as he turns towards the silent grandma to give her reassurance, and he's still so damn cheerful.

*

We work all morning without a break. Wounds, stomach pains, rashes, fevers, everything you'd see a doctor for back home, but also a multitude of diseases found mainly in the tropics: malaria, schistosomiasis, amoebic dysentery, to name just a few.

When the temperature soars past 50°C at midday, and with my T-shirt and trousers glued to my skin, I'm secretly glad that everyone is forced to throw in the towel. Maybe now we can stop for a drink of water, some lunch. It's at this moment a man comes running into the compound with a woman collapsed in his arms. He's tall and proud, lean muscles taut below a tatty vest, feet bare and covered in dust. There's a holler in Nuer from the other patients, drawing our attention to an emergency. Stephen listens to the man talk hurriedly.

'She's pregnant,' he translates to James, 'very sick.'

'Anna,' James says, 'this one's yours. I told you, I don't do midwifery.'

I look at him, praying he doesn't mean it. This is the worst timing possible: my first morning, and the thing I've been dreading most. I am not a midwife.

There's no way out, and Nicole appears beside me, ready to guide. Other patients help carry the woman into the second tukul, one with solid mud walls so that children can't peek through the gaps. I have to flick my headtorch on to see as we bend in half to get through the small opening, the beam of light picking up spider webs on the straw ceiling, glinting like dew on grass. It's clammy hot in here and smells like the hay scent of a pet shop mixed with bitter sweat.

This woman's name is Nyachoul. Perspiration beads are running from her short, plaited hair as I kneel in the dust and start the top-to-toe assessment James showed me and that I'd covered in MSF preparation lectures. Talking through what I see with Nicole, I note the skin under Nyachoul's eyelids is pale from severe anaemia, and she's taking fast breaths from possible infection. Her soft, concave abdomen and low body weight make it difficult to know if she's even pregnant.

Nyachoul has tribal scars across her belly like large X marks and rows of tiny coloured beads strung together in several belly chains. *Is she scared? Embarrassed?* I don't know – she can't look me in the eye.

Stephen, on the other side of the reed doorway, helps to translate from Nuer to English. He explains that the beads are called a teek and Nyachoul wears them to encourage spirits to protect her health – a small symbol of hope when she has nothing else and pregnancy carries such high stakes. He says she has three young children at home in a village nearby, all completely dependent on her.

We do a finger-prick blood test for malaria. Nyachoul's still silent, staring at the mud wall, I wish I could talk to her directly. Stephen is outside asking questions to the husband. Nicole catches my thoughts.

'Working with women here is hard.'

There are so many barriers between us, the obvious ones being language and men doing the translating. Women don't have much status or protection in South Sudan. It was well publicised that some national leaders exhorted, 'Men should have as many wives as they can afford, and as many children as God gives them.'

'Beye – any pain? Rhiem – any bleeding?' Nicole asks tenderly in Nuer, directly to Nyachoul, who responds by making a clicking sound at the back of her throat to signify 'yes'. *I need to learn Nuer.*

Two lines on the strip test show Nyachoul is positive for falciparum malaria, the most dangerous kind. It's common here and arrives with the swarms of mosquitoes that descend at sunset. But, more worrying, she's eight weeks pregnant and has been bleeding for four days. The husband says the bleeding has stopped now, but from the history it sounds likely that she's had a miscarriage. Our job now is to keep her safe – and alive. Stephen, keenly attentive, explains through the wall that malaria can cause severe anaemia as the parasites rupture the red blood cells. Just one episode of malaria infection in early pregnancy triples the rate of miscarriage.

'Would she have anti-malarials in her village?' I ask, reminding myself to take mine tonight.

'No.'

Stephen warns that even mosquito nets don't fully protect you from the mosquitoes that hide in the straw roof and bite you during the day. He also tells me some people keep fires alight inside their huts so the smoke repels the mosquitoes, but that brings the risk of respiratory conditions and toddlers getting severe burns.

I look at Nyachoul again; she looks away.

I'd worked with many threatened miscarriages back in ED, but my role there was to stabilise the women and transfer them to a gynae ward for ultrasound scans and investigations, knowing the one in four UK women who had a miscarriage would get safe care. A miscarriage in South Sudan, in the middle of nowhere, came with risks of infection or uncontrolled bleeding. It could be fatal. Who would look after Nyachoul's children then? James explains later, there's no social service organisation in South Sudan, just gangs that pick up orphaned children – sell the girls, and recruit boys as gun-wielding child soldiers, sometimes known as 'the Lost Boys'.

I knew enough to understand it was possible for us to arrange an emergency flight for Nyachoul to the surgical hospital in Leer, a so-called 'greenlight medevac' (medical evacuation), but even that hospital had no ultrasound. I was also uncomfortably aware that each additional flight cost thousands of pounds. Advice was available from a doctor in Leer over the satellite-phone, but it's up to Nicole and me to make the final clinical decision, and that feels frightening. MSF had warned me, I'd be working out of my normal scope of practice; I just hadn't realised it would happen this quickly and feel this scary.

After much discussion, and review of the medical guidelines, it's decided to treat the malaria, observe for further bleeding, and 'watch and wait'. If the malaria treatment didn't work, or there were new signs of sepsis or bleeding, then we would greenlight to Leer for further treatment.

Frustration boils in my throat when I hear this. It doesn't seem like a good plan at all! Just *waiting* to see what happens.

'We can't fly out every patient with a fever,' says James patiently. This morning alone he's treated ten patients with fevers, and I can see he's observing what I'm going to do next. Last night he told me about the nurse who arrived in the project, took one look around, and promptly got on the same flight home. Is he thinking the same will happen with me?

'But what if Nyachoul has another bleed?' I ask him. 'What if she deteriorates tonight and we can't get a flight out tomorrow?'

'We use our judgement. And we try our best.'

I close my eyes, hoping to avoid some timely Buddhist quote, while Nicole spreads out a blanket so Nyachoul can sleep on the floor of the inpatient tukul. James connects IV lines filled with paracetamol, antibiotics and malaria treatment to the thatch ceiling with string, Nicole says comforting words in Nuer.

And that's it. We walk back to the living compound; the waiting patients drift away to escape the midday heat, invited to take refuge in nearby homes of strangers. We flop in our tents with the front flaps open. I smell like baking bread; it's too hot to talk, so we'll just wait until the sun gets lower.

*

By the end of the afternoon clinic, the Waiting Tree stands deserted, just a fold-out metal desk and chair underneath it like the ghost of a day. It's then that Queth comes excitedly to us in long gangly strides, making his ankles show from under his too-short trousers, bright teeth glinting and pointing to the sky.

'Nhial madid!' he calls, meaning 'big rains'.

The sky is completely cloudless. Not a hint of wind. It's April and there hasn't been rain yet this year.

But sure enough, an hour later, as Nicole reads in her tent and James and I are finishing up our bowls of bean and tinned runner-bean stew and he's telling me a funny story about his 'bunny boiler' ex-girlfriend (who cut up his bed sheets and slashed his tyres), a warm blast of wind sweeps across us, like the air pushed ahead of a train in an underground station.

Within minutes, dark clouds rumble over and two hours later James and I sit in darkness between the living compound and clinic, watching the most electrifying storm I've ever seen.

Boom! Constant rolling thunder. Fork lightning on every side of us, and fireballs that turn the sky green. We're right at the centre of a storm before the rains arrive.

'What happens if lightning hits us?' I ask.

'We die,' says James simply, fearlessly.

Feeling charged and adventurous, I can't wait to email home about this, if we make it. This feels like the adventure I'd been dreaming of.

And then, out of the darkness, seemingly from nowhere, a lone woman appears, carrying a bundle of cloth in her arms. I don't know where she's come from, there's no one here to translate. When James jumps up to help her, she silently hands him the rags.

There's a dead baby inside. It's already cold. Small, like a premature newborn, perfectly formed with peaceful expression, a bit of reed tied around his umbilicus. James looks at the baby. He looks at the woman. He tenderly rewraps the baby and hands him back, shaking his head. No words are said.

Hanging her head lower, the woman's shoulders slump as if punched in the chest, and she walks back into the dark alone.

I jump up to try and get her to go to the clinic, to holler for Nicole, but the woman's already gone.

'Shouldn't we do something? Help her?' I feel seasick from the sudden jolt out of the storm and into this unexpected emergency.

'Anna, it's death.' James looks at me squarely. 'Death isn't good and it isn't bad. It's our job to keep it away if we can, but we can't save everyone.'

He's right of course, but that night, by the light of my headtorch, I write in my diary: *I am going to be a midwife*.

CHAPTER THREE

My life had started to resemble a surreal and terrifying TV reality show, one in which you're taken to a country you don't know to live in isolation with a strange man more than twice your age. Your job is to perform a series of tasks you feel massively unprepared for on traumatised people whose language you don't speak. The price of failure is the possibility of hurting or killing them.

The first rule of medicine, *do no harm*, was starting to haunt me, and my biggest fear was that I'd make some colossal mistake and someone would die.

James scared me too, at first. After we'd waved Nicole off on her end of mission flight, it was just the two of us.

'So did I ever tell you about the time when I was in prison for marijuana possession?' he said conversationally one night after I'd been there a couple of weeks. We were taking a break from the radio, with only huge silence around us. I'd just opened a tin of Dairylea-like cheese and was cutting it into squares to garnish the bean stew. On the table between us there was a small, wizened red onion I'd looked forward to chopping up. Chopping vegetables was a job we'd agreed to take in turns, as it was one of the few breaks from work. Tonight was my turn. When I saw James pick up a knife, his tattooed arm moving up and down, I felt sulky and cheated, but was too polite to show it. To lighten the atmosphere, he continued with his bedtime story.

'Yep, I was in for six months that time.' This said in the calm tone of a man describing a grocery shop. He gathered up the onion pieces and flung them in the stew.

'Wow, that's a long time.' I nodded and smiled.

'In that jail, I knew I was prime meat for the taking, if you know what I mean.'

He twinkled and winked at me, as if we shared a fun understanding, when I was thinking, *What the hell was MSF doing placing me with an ex-convict?*

'Being an alcoholic, as I was then.'

James, moving the onions around the small fry pan, showed me how he deterred any sexual predators from coming near him by pulling his face into a terrifying grimace. Eyebrows up, eyes wide open so the whites showed all round his sky-blue irises, not a single blink, mouth contorted. He even seemed to be able to flush his white skin to a deep red on demand.

'And I didn't let that look go for six whole months. The bad guys in the worst gangs would nudge each other as they went past me. "Stay away!" I heard them say. "He's really dangerous!"'

When he laughed, his veneered teeth shone, the flush left his cheeks, and his eyes watered a little from the happy memory.

'Gee!' He looked up suddenly. 'What about that sunset! All the colours of the world in one sky. Aren't we the luckiest souls on Earth?'

My face froze in polite assent, but inside all I heard was *alcoholic, prison, danger*. And although that sunset was beautiful, I saw it without feeling it; I was scared.

I hadn't spoken for half an hour now, but James was in full flow, the sunset dappling his face with crimson and amber lights.

'Buddha said, "If a man can control his mind, he can find a way to enlightenment, and all wisdom and virtue will naturally come to him."'

I can't wait to get back to the team in Leer, I was thinking, as James stood up creakily from his metal chair. A new thought had hit him:

'Did I tell you about the time I crashed my car? It rolled over two times and I've got a metal plate in my head to prove it?'

*

Brooding about this later, I tried to focus on his good qualities: James had great skills as a diagnostician, he was kind, he treated everyone as a friend, and realistically, ours was a situation that would test the nerves of the closest of friends. To be forced, for the next nine months, to share every breakfast, lunch and tea with this one person, with only a few short breaks in between, was bound to feel stifling.

But that said, he and I seemed to live in some kind of fractured reality. While he was giving a big thumbs up to the universe, loving the sunsets, celebrating the tiniest of victories with patients, I was desperately worried I wouldn't be able to cope with this white-knuckle medicine, and the ugly decisions that had to be made about who to treat and who to leave to their own fate.

But what frightened me most about James was that he seemed like a person with no boundaries: he was older and yet, unlike most of the adults I'd known, there was nothing about him that seemed settled. At the hint of an adventure his blue eyes would sparkle and he'd remind me of a puppy: restless, curious, always up for a new lark, and this alarmed me tremendously in this remote and dangerous place. Before coming here, I imagined aid workers to be quiet, sober and sandal-wearing types, altruistic, the clear heroes. But both James and the others I'd met in Loki seemed more brooding and complicated than this. True, the motives to be here seemed pure; the desire to help in humanitarian crises united us all. But when I saw people in the bars of Loki, it was like everyone was on fast-forward. Those who smoked didn't seem to have just one cigarette, but lit the next as soon as the first had been stubbed out. Those who drank didn't drink just one, but ordered the next before the glass was even empty. It left me feeling vulnerable, not understanding the boundaries in this new, extreme world.

*

For the first few weeks, I didn't express my feelings. I prided myself on being someone who hid their rawest and most uncomfortable emotions deep, deep down. That way, uncomfortable feelings didn't break the calm status quo of my relationships.

I'd grown up in a tight-knit community in Hinstock, Shropshire – a place so small that everyone knew each other. There were just four pupils in my year at our quaint village primary school. The world I grew up in encouraged sensible behaviour, reticence, clear boundaries. My hardworking, well-organised father had a good job managing a local hospital; my mother was a teacher who'd left her job to take care of me and my older siblings, Helen and Daniel.

In our house, a large white cottage with a pretty garden to play in, I always knew my parents loved me, even though we weren't a particularly 'huggy' family. My parents' parents had served in World War II, endured the Blitz, long separations, the deaths of many friends, and when it was all over, barely mentioned it again.

'No point dwelling on all that,' my granny would say while stirring the gravy. 'Once the war was over, we had to get on with our lives. Make do and mend.'

This very British coping strategy became mine too, so I didn't share my deepest turmoil back then, not with Jack, not now with James, not with anyone. I put my head down, worked hard and kept my fears, failures and fallibility locked deep inside.

I'd witnessed horrific events in ED over the three years I'd nursed there, in an era when stabbings and shootings were regular occurrences in British cities. In particular, I remembered the young kid we treated one night for a stab wound in the chest. He'd been all bravado and shrugged shoulders when he was wheeled in and we examined him. But there was another mark on his neck we'd disregarded because it wasn't bleeding or painful; it looked like a hair-line scratch hidden beneath the dried blood splattered over him. Until suddenly, he'd sat up and vomited bright crimson blood everywhere, and we realised that the mark was another stab wound to the neck and had internally been dripping blood from his carotid artery into his stomach. Red had splashed over my face, my clothes, down the wall, like someone had thrown a bucket of paint. His mother screamed, his blood pressure plummeted, and he'd pleaded like an infant as he was rushed to emergency surgery. Thankfully, he survived, but the surgeons had to remove his voice box to stem the bleeding; he'd never easily talk again.

He was just a kid had echoed guiltily through my thoughts afterwards. *You missed the wound.* I'd talked a little to Jack about it, but kept my fears and self-doubt hidden. Instead, I'd make the growing list of awful-things-that-happened-at-work into amusing anecdotes, not wanting to admit my own sense of failure or alarm. Medical texts classify this as 'avoidance coping', a common strategy in ED nurses who regularly confront traumatic events, but I didn't even realise I was doing it.

One place where I could unburden was my diary, my confessional and confidant. *Next time I'll be more thorough on checking the wounds*, I would scribble at night, but I simply didn't know how to make those words come out of my mouth.

Going to the pub with other ED friends who understood was another coping strategy. Every now and then, we'd meet up on our days off and get completely sloshed on vodka, finding a way in bleak humour to laugh, and purposefully drinking to forget.

*

James had been quick to encourage and praise my organisational skills – the ordering of the drugs, the note-taking, the observance of MSF protocols – but privately, I was sure he saw me as boringly straight. What stories could I offer over a bean medley? I had never bunny-boiled, or skinny-dipped off Mexican yachts, taken drugs, feigned insanity while in prison, or slept with exotic strangers.

My life so far, from studious girlhood with the top A level results in my under-performing comprehensive school, to nursing training, to a young love formed at an age when we were both innocent and sincere, was not the stuff of thrilling anecdotes. It had been shaped and pointed towards coming here, and now I was secretly dismayed because I wasn't sure I could hack it. It's not that I particularly wanted to experience the same messy, disturbing experiences that James revelled in. Although I admired his self-awareness and was even a little envious of his liberty to say just what he wanted, the stories I yearned to tell (much as I'm cringing to admit it) were the happy-ever-after ones. Stories like flying into foreign countries in a beaten-up old plane with the wind in my hair; stories with wholesome happy endings, which probably meant that everybody miraculously survived.

Deep down, there was also a fear that one day I'd wake up, old (like so many patients I'd worked with) and confronting mortality, and would look back at my life and think *was that it*? I wanted depth to my life, colour, raw experiences. Once the adventures were done, or so my naive thinking went, I'd return to safe, cosy suburbia, proud I had *done my bit,* and happy to get on with 'normal' life again.

*

Tensions grew between James and me, and I grew quieter and quieter.

When James told me that he was longing to go and have dinner with Queth at his tukul, to meet his family, to immerse himself in his culture, I bit my lip, but silently fumed.

I'd have liked that too, but MSF's rules about socialising and security are clear and strict. We weren't encouraged to socialise with local people or develop relationships that went beyond professional friendships. If we did, we might be accused of favouritism, or get involved in romantic relationships that might prove dangerous or exploitative.

Breaking the rules with an innocent dinner or even a flirt might risk the ability of the entire project to operate effectively in that area and provide medical aid – the only reason we were there in the first place. Why was it up to me to point this out to him?

When the rains came, my mood darkened further.

The hot, dry season was over, and by May, despite it still being 40°C, so much water fell that it felt as if full bathtubs were being upended from the sky and our tents would billow and lift off the ground. The compound became a brownish-red quagmire, all the tukuls began to leak like sieves, the scorpions and snakes multiplied, and everything felt worse. Clumps of mud stuck to the bottom of our boots, the ground under our feet having become a red glue.

Scorpion avoidance was now part of the daily routine. I slept with my stinky boots beside me inside the tent so the 'critters', as James called them, kept out. Going to the latrine at night had to be done in the dark, otherwise the headtorch attracted massive bluebottles that lived in the poo and would skydive into your face.

More snakes and far fewer patients. People couldn't walk easily to us through the expanding swamps, which was frustrating and worrying as they hadn't stopped getting sick, they just couldn't reach us. When the mosquitoes began to hatch their larvae in the puddles, malaria rates soared.

The runway, too wet for the supply planes to land, became an exotic bird sanctuary with cranes, storks and ibis. But I missed the planes, as they brought a short spell of company from the pilots and letters from Jack, which came in the same old-fashioned blue and red airmail envelopes that my grandparents had used during the war. Jack would often include sweets with his letters, and give me news of his promotion, of a gig he'd played, of parties, and friends he'd seen. *I was an idiot not to appreciate all that when I had it.*

When we couldn't see patients, James, an excellent if unconventional teacher, drew slashing diagrams on a chalkboard, teaching our national staff about the intricacies of the oxygen exchange system, or how blood travelled around the body. I once heard one of James's patients ask, 'Where are you from?'

'The other side of the world,' said James, making a circle with his hands.

'You mean the Earth is round?' The man's eyes were wide and innocent. Stephen translated this with no hint of sarcasm.

*

Bit by bit, I was getting to know three of our national staff better than the others, mainly because I worked closely with them, and they spoke English. Queth, our registrar, was impressive. This gangly 6-foot-plus man had no formal education, but he marvelled at James's teaching; the idea that it was the heart that pumped blood around the body was new and astounding to him. He'd tease James in a good-natured way for being fat, a compliment in South Sudan.

Stephen, our community health worker (CHW), who I had deep respect for, spoke Nuer, Dinka, Arabic and English. Born in the north of Sudan, he was quiet and studious and could easily have been a doctor had life given him the chance. Hungry for knowledge, he asked thoughtful questions and recorded answers in a notebook kept in a plastic bag to stop it getting wet or mouldy. I trusted his clear translations and medical opinions, and was always relieved when he was on the night shift with us.

William, our other CHW, was more reserved. His deep tribal markings were usually furrowed in a frown. There were yellow ridges in the whites of his bulbous eyes formed by years of exposure to wind and sand, and something reluctant about his stare. His monosyllabic translations of long conversations with female patients worried me: he was smart, but I was never quite sure I had the full story. The problem was, when he was on shift, we were completely dependent on him to understand each complex patient.

*

Difficult saturated terrain meant more people arriving unexpectedly at night. We'd often be woken three or four times. I'd been asleep for two hours, when one night, 'Jaaaaames? Anna?'

A voice calling from the compound entrance, above the 'wurr wurr' of the frogs that now lived in the mud. It's William. He sounds apprehensive: like many of the local staff, he hates waking us, frightened if the work gets too much, we'll just leave.

James is up in a flash, unzipping his tent, staggering out to grab the emergency medical boxes, calling to me loudly to hurry. It's hard to dress, face swollen from sleep and slippery with sweat from the night humidity. Fumbling, I know I'm wasting precious time, and from now on, after my evening bucket shower, I'll sleep with my boots by my feet, socks on and headtorch round my neck.

Stumbling out of my tent, drunk with tiredness, I clutch my grab bag. As I switch on my headtorch and run after James towards the clinic, hundreds of crickets, moths, bugs and beetles bombard us from every direction. A cloud of mosquitoes follows us, maybe all carrying malaria.

Having forgotten to put my bra on under my T-shirt, I feel vulnerable out in the fresher air, running through the shadows after William, who's already past the Waiting Tree. When we arrive in the clinic quad, a gruesome scene is unfolding. In a circle of light from a kerosene lamp, a woman lies crumpled on the patch of open ground bordered by the four tukuls, as if on a stage. There's a stream of blood down both of her legs, dripping onto the mud. A man stands over her, one slim arm holding the lamp, the other gripping a swaddled baby. He moves the lamp so we can see, looking at us silently with pleading eyes.

'It's Nyabol. Her baby out. Placenta not out.' William's torch lights up the deep tribal cuts across his face, I wait for more information from him, but nothing comes.

Retained placenta, I whisper to myself. I'd studied this briefly in a classroom lesson and seen it once in the maternity department. I knew just about enough to understand that unless the placenta is delivered, the woman could have a postpartum haemorrhage (PPH), the biggest single cause of maternal death in developing countries, but I've never been in charge of such an emergency.

When I look at James, he says bluntly, 'I'll take the baby. You take the woman.'

He moves his stethoscope to one side, takes the baby in his arms and begins his examination.

Fear boils up in me, but I have to steady my thoughts and think calmly, quickly, or else this woman could bleed to death in minutes. At full term, the placenta has up to 800 ml of blood passing through it every minute, so there's no time to carry her into a tukul, though it feels shockingly public to leave her lying on patted earth with her trail of blood growing muddy at the edges. At least there's no one else to stare in the pitch black of night.

I'm standing in the dark listening to my own ragged breath when some kind of animal recognition jolts me back into myself and I remember that breastfeeding can release the hormones that contract the uterus, aiding a natural placental delivery.

But that scrap of a baby isn't ready to feed. Thinking out loud, I tell William we can simulate the action with nipple tweaking. He looks at me, questioning, silent.

'Do this, Nyabol.' I put my own fingers on my bra-less chest and tweak my nipples through my T-shirt.

'Do this, *please*,' I say urgently. It may sound odd at a moment of such extremis, but I didn't want to do it *to her* without her consent. It would feel as if I was violating her.

A few agonising seconds pass and William says something in Nuer, which I hope is a translation. Fast breaths from Nyabol, her face greying under torchlight, her legs childishly thin. At last, she closes her eyes tightly and tweaks her own nipples.

A few more minutes pass. *Oh, God! Help me!* Nothing has happened, so *now what?* We have no oxygen cylinders out here to help her breathing.

William's watching me from a discreet distance.

Oxytocin! Yes, oxytocin and ergometrine, synthetic drugs used to help placentas deliver as standard practice in UK hospitals. Flinging open the medical chests we've run with, I'm crestfallen to see there are no IVs in either of them. And even if there had been, I couldn't have used them as the vials of liquids have to be kept in the fridge we don't have. I hand over small tablet versions of the drugs, which Nyabol takes.

For a moment, I stand paralysed. All I can hear is the husband praying and my own heart thumping, when my mind ropes up a stray fact from an MSF lecture several months before. *Retained placenta and manual removal*. This is our only hope.

Washing my hands under a bucket with a tap welded to the side, putting on sterile gloves from our box, I take a deep breath. The MSF obstetric guidelines are open on the right page beside me.

Nyabol's face has paled, her eyes seem more vacant. They shift towards William, who has silently taken a step backwards after I explained to him what I'm planning to do. Eventually, he says something to her. I hope it's accurate, and I pray she understands. It's so hard not speaking Nuer.

The pre-dawn air is like warm soup and thick with insects. From time to time we hear the reedy cries of the baby whose mother is dying.

While William explains, time seems to stretch out almost unbearably, but at last Nyabol clicks the back of her tongue and hitches up her long skirt, showing rows of coloured beads around her belly. She looks at me for the first time, a look of trust, and submission that both humbles and frightens me. She's given me consent.

I'm crouching beside her, headtorch on, jaw clenched. When Nyabol lets out a groan, a new wave of blood runs like thick lava. With my left hand I feel her belly, then clean away the clots in her sparse pubic hair. With my gloved right hand, I reach into her vagina, past the end of the umbilical cord tied with a piece of string, tentatively at first and holding my breath.

'I believe in you, Anna.'

James's voice coming out of the dark startles me. He's holding the baby in his arms, the husband is on his knees in prayer to Jesus.

Deep breath. I don't want to hurt her. *Come on, Anna, get the placenta out. We're running out of time*. Scared, determined, I push up into the vagina, towards the open cervix. The placenta, rubbery but soft, has the texture of raw liver. I hold my breath…

Then… plop! Seconds later, the placenta slips out, just like that. I have no idea if it was the nipple thing, or the medication, or my manoeuvre (which I didn't even finish), or just plain luck. But there it is, lying in the dirt. It just fell out and was complete, and almost immediately, like a tap turning off, her uterus muscles are tight and the bleeding stops. Just like that.

Relief and shock. But mainly relief. I can breathe again.

'Sha loi de tele long,' says Nyabol.

A gentle and respectful thank you (I don't know how to write the Nuer, so I've written it phonetically). She looks at me with awesome strength, even musters a small smile. It's in this moment I see how many women are heroes.

Don't thank me, I think. *You deserve so much better.*

James slaps me on the back, a joyful comrade. He's setting up the inpatient tukul, where Nyabol will get rehydrated, IV antibiotics and maybe a greenlight to Leer if she needs a blood transfusion.

'The baby's gonna be fine. She's a beaut.' James beams as the baby starts to nuzzle at Nyabol's breast.

But once the relief has passed, my stomach is still so tight I think I might throw up. I yearn for a hot shower, rather than washing off the blood up my arm from a cold bucket-tap trickle. What this night has shown me is the knife-edge I live on now. My terror, my incompetence.

Seeing me struggling, James says, 'I felt like you do too, you know, always wishing some obstetrician would swoop in and help us out, but I don't see them lining up to be here, do you? We do our best, that's all we can do.'

He smiles, but it doesn't soothe me.

That's not enough.

CHAPTER FOUR

Following a run of dry days, the ground grew firmer, and the MSF plane came again, delivering medical supplies and letters from family and friends. I loved receiving a new pack of knickers from my mum, a star-gazing map from my grandparents, or a trashy magazine and sweets from my friends, which I took off to my tent like a hungry dog and devoured alone, joyful and a little appalled by my pettiness at not sharing. James and I were still tense.

Letters from Jack, which I pounced on, now brought both happiness and a new confusion. He apologised repeatedly for the 'mundane news', though it sounded exotic to me, making me ache for the peaceful life I used to live, while worrying if the person who'd lived it was gone forever.

Writing home, I automatically censored myself. It was easier to tell him about the large green snake that had fallen at my feet while I was examining a patient and had turned out to be harmless, or to joke about James, than to tell him about the dead baby, the stiffness of my ever-clenched jaw, or that I'd started to grind my teeth in my sleep.

This sense of separation from home might have drawn me closer to James, who seemed to have no censorship button whatsoever, but it didn't. During those first few weeks, I drew in on myself, became as sullen and inarticulate as a teenager. I longed to eat meals alone in my tent, but the words wouldn't come out of my mouth to suggest this.

James kept trying to talk openly with me. Sometimes he'd slip a Buddhist quote under the tent flap. *The whole secret of existence is to have no fear*, said one, but I *was* frightened, and, at this point in my life, completely Buddha-proof.

Our differences reached boiling point one hot afternoon when an aircraft was spotted in the overcast sky. Excitement tinged with anxiety rippled through the clinic: we weren't expecting another MSF delivery and hadn't called for a greenlight – Nyabol was already in Leer receiving a blood transfusion. Occasionally, aid drops by other organisations took us by surprise, but as this aircraft grew closer, it didn't make the sound of the usual cargo plane. It was the 'putt putt putt' of a helicopter, and now it was circling in the grey sky above us.

Nervous chatter grew on the ground. James looked like a kid who'd just heard the Mr Whippy tune.

'It's not a helicopter gunship,' Queth said, making my heart beat fast, as that hadn't crossed my mind.

'Come on!' James urges, 'let's check it out!'

I'm immediately scared. We have no idea who this is, or what the helicopter carries, but a few minutes later, I'm being swept along by an excited crowd on the runway. We've gone further away from the clinic than we ever have before, towards the town centre of Tam. When the rotor blades slow down, my hair slaps my cheek and James jogs ahead, bursting with adventure.

Helicopter doors open and off steps a South Sudanese politician. His fat belly strains below his tailored suit, a gold tooth winks in the sun, in grotesque contrast to the hundreds of skinny people surging towards him for their glimpse of fame, or maybe just happy that someone with power has remembered them.

James is revelling in the unfolding drama, for him the perfect release after silent evenings in the compound. Strutting across the runway, the politician is shaking hands, grandstanding, as the crowd streams forward, uncontrollably. Then, when I look up, James is gone, but what I see in front of me are six or seven men, all in dark glasses and all armed with big guns.

Panicking, I start to run back to our base. All my security briefings emphasised the importance of MSF employees being politically impartial and never associated with weapons. Running faster and faster, I then stop. *I've lost my bearings.* The scattering of tukuls on the horizon suddenly look exactly the same in both directions of the runway. Hearing my own breath rasping, I want to cry. Stuck in a roaring crowd, I can't ask for help because I don't speak their language.

Stephen appears from nowhere. He takes me by the elbow and guides me back to the quiet end of the runway, where I can easily see the Waiting

Tree. We weren't far away after all. I try to give him a grateful look, but he's already jogging back towards the crowd to find James.

I'm furious with James. He'd thought it a great game to find the action, but I'd been so scared – scared I'd get hurt or lost, scared I could lose my job.

An hour or so later, James comes back to the compound, giving me a look of, *What the hell is wrong with you, big baby?* and I finally flip.

I had no practice in anger. For years with Jack it had been a point of pride with me that we'd never even had a row. But now everything inside me exploded.

'Fuck you!' I yell. 'I was *scared*, James. We shouldn't have been there. We risked this whole project.'

James, still flushed with excitement, takes off his Stetson and rubs his head. His blue eyes stare at me but, unusually, he says nothing.

*

At supper, I take my bean stew to my tent, wash up in silence and ignore him. Inside, I write to Jack, '*This place is hell. I'm coming home. I'm not cut out for it.*'

Taking off my boots, I lie on my mat and have a big silent cry, shoulders jerking, snot bubbling from my nose. James is tossing and turning on his roll mat in the tent next to me, his physical proximity is torture.

At 2.00 a.m. he clears his throat and breaks the silence.

'Anna.' His voice is raw and earnest. 'I fucked up today. You were right and I am so, so sorry. Let's start this project again tomorrow, properly, hey?'

Lying in the dark, I'm dumbfounded. Having braced myself for a lecture on manning up, instead this moment seems like a refining fire, it burns away so much confusion. It also shows me something I hadn't seen before – that I can't leave now, that it's too late for me to cut and run and leave these incredible people to their suffering. *This is where I want to be.* It was later I saw too that this was when my amazing friendship with James began – one based on mutual respect and brutal honesty.

Screwing up the letter I'd written to Jack, I take out my MSF maternity and obstetrics textbooks. Sitting cross-legged on the hard ground, by the light of my headtorch, I start to make some notes in the margins.

I am not going home.

CHAPTER FIVE

To know I could speak truthfully and the world wouldn't fall apart felt amazing.

Now I could tell James to stop talking when I needed to think, or dictate play when a situation demanded it, and the more I spoke honestly like this, the less uncomfortable it felt. Shouting had been cathartic and brought James and me closer, and I reminisced sadly on the times in my life when shouting might have been so much better than polite silence.

Part of me wished Jack had shouted 'I don't want you to go,' or my parents had yelled 'We're scared you'll get harmed.' I knew their silence was an act of love, respecting how I'd chosen to live my life, but it had enabled me to ignore the fear and hurt they might feel. Wistfulness swelled sadly inside me. I wished it had been a two-way conversation, realising how much I had kept from them over the years. 'Without the truth, we have nothing,' James would often say.

Our new nicknames for each other were a good barometer of our moods. 'Kent' was a subtle hint that I was so focused on what was in front of me, I was missing the bigger picture. When he was feeling affectionate, I was 'Anna Banana' or 'Swamp Mama', and for more poetic moments as the sun set I was 'English Rose'.

He was 'Papa Whisky' when he passed wind, which he did exuberantly most mornings; 'Matron' when annoying me; 'Juliet', an affectionate shortening of 'Juliet India', his VHF radio name; or sometimes 'Captain Diego', because when James wasn't working overseas, he lived on a boat in Mexico.

When we weren't too exhausted, we'd lie in the dark and talk to each other through the walls of our separate tents, some of the richest, deepest, conversations of my life. There was something of the confessional about it, for there is nowhere darker than South Sudan at night, where there were no electric lights for hundreds of miles, and here we were, small dots of humanity surrounded by space and silence. We lay under a star-studded sky that didn't give a toss about our human frailties, yet close to a warm human body who did.

James was a superb listener: never judgemental, or malicious, and never trying to fix unsolvable problems. His lodestar was simply to tell the truth.

Quite early on in these tent-à-tents, James said, 'You could smile more, Anna. You hardly ever do in the clinic.'

This remark shocked me and filled me with nostalgia for the relentlessly cheerful nurse I used to be. But he was right. Burdened by this new job, I'd forgotten how to smile. When I tried, I felt rusty, my jaw clenched, my cheeks puffy. I was out of practice.

James gave me a moment to absorb this.

'Here's the thing, Kent. As hard as this place is, we get to fly out, and the people we see don't. These are their moments of comparative peace when they've been through hell. They've been shot at, bombed, lost loved ones, seen their villages burnt to the ground, their babies have died, their kids have been kidnapped. So everyone you meet needs your smiles, even more so than they would at home. I'm not trying to tell you what to do, Anna Banana, just saying what helps me.'

One night, after the click of both our torches going out, I felt I knew him well enough to ask, 'Why don't you ever talk about your mum?'

The silence stretched so long, I thought he'd fallen asleep. He shifted in his bed.

'My childhood was a train wreck,' he said at last.

Long pause…

'My mom was a heroin addict. I was born addicted.' His voice so low I could hardly hear him.

'What did that do to you?' I asked, trying not to sound too shocked or sorry – I'd never heard him sound so sad.

'The docs didn't know that much about its effects on babies then, but I guess I didn't sleep much; I was jerky, couldn't soothe, a nightmare baby probably.'

'What about your dad?'

Another long pause…

'Him…ugh…he was an addict too.'

More silence.

'I found out, when I was sixteen, he'd been incestuous with my thirteen-year-old sister, who was deaf and vulnerable. Hated him for a long time, told him I'd kill him if I ever saw him again, which fortunately I never did – sure you want to…?'

'…if it's OK. I don't want…'

'It's OK. My dad was also a vicious drunk. When I was four years old, my parents sent me to live with my alcoholic grandmother in California, and then my step-grandfather, a Sicilian, stepped in. He was a good man, kinda gruff but compassionate. He believed work was the measure of a man, so when I was seven, I worked in his liquor store, or collected wood for him up the mountains. I hated him for this sometimes – couldn't play with other kids – but it might have saved my life; he gave me a work ethic.'

I stared at my tent walls with no idea of what to say.

'Did you go to school?'

'Yeah, but I quit at fifteen to drink and do drugs and ride motorcycles. Got married at seventeen, just like my dad, had a daughter at nineteen, divorced at twenty-three. I was a full-blown alcoholic during my young adult life. Still there, Kent?'

'Yeah.'

'I somehow got myself through college, though I was drunk and totally screwed up, then I travelled the world to avoid the draft for the Vietnam War. I ended up working on a farm in Israel during the Yom Kippur War. Came back, married again, had two kids.

'That's when I did a first aid course – I was trying to be a good father.' His voice suddenly eager and warm again, like he normally sounded.

'Went back to university, took a BS in nursing degree; my specialty was intensive care. I just loved it, I was really good at it.' I closed my eyes, trying not to cry.

'So you stopped drinking.'

'Hell, no! I was a full-blown alcoholic all the time I was working in intensive care. I was so bad in the end I thought I'd lose my kids, my career and my sanity, and for a while I did.

'I quit drinking when I was forty-two and haven't drunk, or taken a prescription drug, since then. I became a Zen Buddhist; life was grand. Don't sound sad about it, I've never regretted who I am. Buddha says: "The pure white lotus grows only from muddy waters, yet remains untainted." Not saying I'm a pure white lotus.'

Nylon rustled as he adjusted his sleeping bag, a snort of laughter at his own little joke.

'But when I became a nurse I knew absolutely it was for me, and that's a really lucky thing, because I've loved every day of my forty years since then — even the bad days, and how many people can say that? I was so grateful to my new life, I vowed that as soon as I'd put my daughters through college, I'd do two years of voluntary work, so here I am.'

He did up the zip of his sleeping bag, his voice trailing away.

'I'm tired, Swamp Mama… Sleep now… I've still got that big car accident to tell you about…another time.'

*

Lying there in the dark, hearing James honest and raw about his life after my mild interrogation, it hit me that I hadn't opened up to him in the same way. Still new to this self-awareness and accountability, did I even understand my own complexities yet? What I did know is that James inspired me, I wanted to be more like him; comfortable in my own skin, with my own choices. I had so much more to learn.

I thought about his faded tattoos; how I'd once thought him a knob for having so many. I got it now: that dagger plunged in the badly drawn skull on his right arm, the snake coiled and hissing around his left arm, the two Buddhist symbols that sat on his shoulders — they felt poignant now, not crude and ridiculous, but road maps of a life that must have felt like ten.

I was starting to love him. There was nothing sexual about it, though sex between co-workers in the field is a well-known occupational hazard. Hardly a surprising one, with men and women living in pairs, far from their families, in remote and dangerous places. Had we slept together, few eyebrows would've been raised. We were miles away from prying eyes, and most of the national staff assumed we were married anyway – in their world, men and women almost never worked together like this.

But James had told me early on that celibacy was part of his Buddhist practice, and I wasn't exactly his type anyway. The feeling was mutual, and it was a relief not to fancy James in that way. Plus I was determined to stay faithful to Jack, and this felt like the easiest thing in the world since arriving in Tam, because overnight my sex drive had disappeared. I didn't think about sex, I didn't masturbate. Nothing.

The only way I could explain this to myself was that in Tam my body was in a constant state of alert, either living with, or anticipating, emergencies, and this seemed to short-circuit the sex drive. It's like you wouldn't think about sex if you were running from a blazing inferno or had just had a car crash. Eventually, I would learn the hard way that it wasn't that simple, and as with all coping strategies, sex used by aid workers could be a complicated form of escapism. But for now, the only thing I missed was Jack hugging me.

My periods stopping felt like no big deal. If anything, a relief. Using tampons in such heat with limited sanitation wasn't hygienic, and sanitary towels would've felt hot and yucky. Of course, the women I treated didn't have the luxury of choice – just a few old rags which they washed over and over again and tied around their waist with string, knickers being a sign of wealth here.

Much more worrying, and I wasn't even ready to talk about this in my diary, was my new screwed-up way of thinking about sex. Because here was the truth: when I thought about vaginas now, I pictured them as bomb sites – bloodied and torn, part of the life/death zone, never as sources of joy and satisfaction, and I wondered if I might never have carefree, happy sex again.

I was bone tired too after one month of constant work and interrupted nights. On Sundays, our one day off, when the national staff went to church in a large local tukul, or spent the day with their families, James and I still saw emergencies, and used any extra time to do our cleaning, planning and ordering. We had no alcohol in our food supplies, as James didn't drink, so no chance for me to unwind that way, and I didn't know any other methods to lose that sense of fizzing urgency in my brain. Bit by bit, the stress began to build.

If I sound like I was aware of riding for an eventual fall, I wasn't. Like the frog in that old story, placed in cool water that slowly, slowly gets hotter and hotter, I was adapting until the inevitable happens.

Instead, I convinced myself I was adjusting well to the non-stop adrenaline. What distress I felt was hard to put my finger on, except I knew that when I saw patients in the UK, there was the sense that I mostly left them feeling happier, better, and that gave me some sense of satisfaction. Here, I might patch up the immediate problem, but what next? That young woman with the retained placenta might step on a landmine on her way home. She might have malaria by now or be slowly starving to death with her other children and the baby we saved. As soon as she left the clinic, I had no way to protect her.

*

James and I were seeing over 1,000 patients a month now, dividing our time between two projects – one in Tam, the other in Koch, a small village a couple of hours' flight away. In both these rural clinics with similar set-ups, we faced the same difficult choices.

On one fairly typical day in Koch we'd successfully greenlighted a boy with a spear injury to his arm so severe it would, without surgery in Leer, have been amputated – or killed him; we'd dealt with multiple cases of malaria, dispensed the three-day tablet regime of drugs called AS/AQ, and handed out endless supplies of mosquito nets. But there were also the cases we couldn't help: an old man with a massive goitre dangling under his chin; a woman with a large laceration to her foot we couldn't stitch because our needles couldn't puncture her skin, which had been toughened by a life of walking without shoes; an older woman in agony with chronic back pain from scoliosis.

James, who saw these perceived failures beginning to boil inside me, tried to teach me how to absorb them without going mad. One night after supper, we were sitting on the metal seats outside the tents, thinking about what dried soup packet to open that night. I was telling him about some problem in the clinic, when he put his hand on my arm. Above our heads, a flock of geese was flying so close that we could hear the sound of each wing beating.

'Let's both take a deep breath,' he said, 'and think about what's in front of us.'

Together we watched the geese absorb the colours of a blood-red sunset before they disappeared like black specks of burnt paper in the vast empty space around us.

I stopped opening the packet. I stopped grumbling as this awesome sight brought a few moments of internal peace – my first steps into mindfulness.

And so it was that I gave up rolling my eyes, or making paper darts of the Buddhist quotes James sometimes poked through my tent flap. Instead, I read them, thought about them, and occasionally stuck some in my diary. Despite the mountain of anxiety bubbling away in me like a dormant volcano, other parts of me were softening and starting to see how James's Buddhist beliefs sustained him. Kept him healthy and strong, regardless of the trauma around him, which in turn enabled him to keep helping others. *Can I open my mind to think in new ways and be more at peace with myself?* James had warned me: when you first come face-to-face with the truth behind your own motivations and actions, you might feel a lot worse before you feel better, but maybe, just maybe, it was worth a try.

CHAPTER SIX

'Delta Charlie.'

On the following evening, a short call on the sat-phone brought bad news. Leer Hospital was dangerously short-staffed, as the Kenyan midwife and American doctor both needed R & R. Our orders were to up sticks and leave Tam the next day to fly to Leer.

This was a shock. A sad one. Medical supplies were to be quickly ordered and dropped, but with Tam being so close to the border of northern Sudan, there was always a risk of local fighting breaking out again. If this happened, we'd find it difficult to get back. Our awesome, but still-learning, staff would have to grit their teeth, man the clinics and do night shifts on their own. They would understandably worry about the next payroll until we returned, and what injuries any fighting might bring in this isolated region. Stephen's long and heartfelt Sudanese farewell was upsetting, and Mary, our clinic cleaner, was in tears. 'You will come back. You must come back.'

The only good bit of news was that Nyamac, a young woman with one of the biggest breast abscesses I'd ever seen, would now get the treatment she needed, as she would be greenlit on the same flight. (When they eventually operated on her in Leer, over a litre of snot-green pus poured out of the grapefruit-sized abscess.) While frantic arrangements were made for her and her one-month-old baby, she sat quiet and uncomplaining, regal almost, though she must have been in agony.

'What does her name mean?' I asked Stephen.

'*Nya* is a woman's name,' he said, 'and *mac* means bullet.' He gave a sad smile. 'It's a common name in South Sudan for women born in conflict.'

*

Dust exploded beneath the wheels of the plane that came to collect us. Then a miraculous thing happened: my friend Anita walked down the steps. I'd dreamed of meeting her here.

Anita is part English, part Hawaiian, a stunning, smart woman with a razor-sharp wit, who I'd met studying in London. After we'd passed our exams on tropical diseases, she'd easily drunk me under the table. I'd been longing to see her since hearing a few months back that she was also working as a nurse for MSF in South Sudan.

We embraced in a joyful hug, linked arms, skipped away and squatted on the dry mud in the middle of the runway, a clear sign that we wanted to talk out of earshot. You had to be this blatant, otherwise the chance to chat would be missed for another few weeks.

While we were talking, five skinny kids appeared, pointing and giggling at our light skin. They were heading to an outdoor school, held sporadically under the biggest tree on the other side of Tam, the plastic chairs carried on their heads making them look like miniature sputniks.

'Where are we now?' Anita asked, a question we'd repeat for years to come. She laughed, showing her perfect teeth and lit a cigarette.

'Tell me quickly how you're doing,' she said, 'we don't have much time.'

I let it all out: the patients we'd seen, the decisions we'd made, my constant fear of not being good enough, early fears about James.

Anita nodded intensely, taking a long drag, her face in shadow underneath her cupped hand.

'Anna,' she said when I stopped, 'everyone feels like this for the first three months. That's why MSF insists on the nine-month mission. You spend the first block just finding your feet. Sorry to be blunt, but how many deaths have you had at the clinic?'

'Only one.' I described the baby in the storm, who was dead on arrival. She gave a deep sigh.

'Horrible, but only one fatality means you two are making the right choices.' I felt a huge surge of relief when she said this because Anita is an awesome nurse, I trusted her.

'And you?' I touched her arm.

She took a deep drag and blew out a hot blast of smoky air.

'Well, I lost all my toenails on a five-day trek to a distant outreach clinic. We had to wade through swamps – I thought I had renal failure.'

'God! Will your nails grow back?'

'Maybe.' I checked out her gnarly and nail-less toes poking out of worn Havaiana flip-flops.

'A South Sudan pedicure,' she laughed, brushing off any chance of pity.

'Anything else?'

Silence. A long one.

'Yeah… No.' I saw her face working, a crack in her voice. 'We lost a four-year old girl last night. She had measles, then a pneumonia that didn't respond to any medications…'

'Measles is a truly miserable way to die.'

Another moment of silence.

'It's shit.' She stubbed out her cigarette forcefully on the ground, put the butt in a pocket of her khakis, lit another and took a deep drag.

'Living the dream, right?' She exhaled the smoke firmly, in a that's-enough-of-that way, but her eyes showed hurt, bewilderment.

Anita quickly turned the conversation back to me. 'You might want to start thinking about what you want to achieve here – you'll be shocked how fast these nine months will go.'

My brain stirred. I hadn't even thought of it in that way. Just getting through the patient caseload each day felt more than I could handle; the thought of leaving a legacy was a new one.

The kids stopped goggling at us; they put the chairs back on their heads and disappeared into the heatwaves over the runway. James ran up to Anita on his rickety knees and gave her a big bear hug.

'Looking after her, Captain?' Anita gave him a quizzical look, punching him on the shoulder.

James said, 'Anna's the best nurse partner I could've asked for.'

I couldn't help myself glowing when he said that. He was my partner; this was my tribe.

*

Touchdown Leer: mud, dust, whirring engines, a sweaty goodbye hug with Anita, James whisked away to work in the hospital outpatient department (OPD). I'm assigned to work with Dr Simon while I get to grips with this new hospital, our base for the next week.

Simon is, in his own words, 'a fat, wonky-eyed Welsh weirdo', though I certainly wouldn't be so unkind. He's mid-forties, about my height, 5 ft 8 in, wears shorts, and sports his baseball hat backwards like an American schoolboy. He's incredibly well spoken, which is such a contrast to his neck festooned with coloured beads – collected from years of emergency medical aid work across the globe. Eccentric, but brilliant – was I starting to notice a theme here? Fiercely dedicated to patient care when in the hospital, I'd also learn Simon was the king of innuendo when back at the Leer living compound (I'll never look at a papaya in the same way again).

Leer Hospital alone sees over 4,000 patients a month. Simon's in charge of mentoring and supporting the international team, plus assessing the medical needs of all the medical projects throughout the country. It's a crazily difficult plate-spinning task, and the daft jokes are his pressure valve. Now, as I follow his surfer-boy flowery shirt around the hospital, frantically making notes, his demeanour is affable, smiling. He wants to hear all about me and has already nicknamed my boyfriend Jack 'Beardy Boy'.

Leer Hospital's main building is a large, brutally utilitarian, U-shaped brick block, the bottom of which is painted turquoise. When I ask about the bullet holes in the walls, Simon explains, in a carefully neutral tone, that the hospital has been bombed, burnt and attacked from the ground and air many times. Leer is the centre of an oil-producing area, and strategically important for the military.

Inside the courtyard, there's an 'under the trees' ward during the dry season, where patients lie on mattresses on the ground, erecting mosquito nets around them with twigs.

Simon shows me where I'll be working: the delivery room and maternity ward, a general ward, a surgical ward, a fully functioning theatre and registration area. Outside the maternity ward, Simon stops and looks at me with some urgency,

'We're absolutely desperate for midwives here,' he says, and reminds me that there's no Sudanese government training of midwives. Those who assisted at births were often well-meaning, but mostly untrained attendants who possibly harmed as much as they helped. The traditional birth attendants (TBAs) in South Sudan, who at one point would have held knowledge and skills passed down through generations, were displaced as war hit, and those skills were often lost. Simon grimly reminds me that the World Health Organisation estimates that South Sudan has one of the worst records for maternal death in the world, if not *the* worst.

'Have you thought about midwifery? I've heard you're pretty good,' he continues.

It feels like I'm being strapped into a car with no brakes, and I haven't even taken the test yet.

'Can I… Could I…?' is all I manage to stammer. 'I have…'

'…so much to learn? We all feel that,' he says, 'but think about it.'

'I have,' I say.

*

Pregnant women, dressed in a kaleidoscope of bright materials and with various sizes of bump, queue patiently outside the bare brick walls of the antenatal clinic, under the shade of a tin roof. Depending on how many women attend, they may be here for several hours, in stoic, proud silence. There's another queue outside the OPD where James works now, sometimes seeing up to 250 patients a day.

'Are you OK?' Simon stops. We're standing outside one of the two large khaki tents to the left of the antenatal clinic.

'This is where we treat severely malnourished children.' He gives me a swift glance.

'OK?' he says again, all traces of jokey boyo Welshness gone.

He pulls aside the canvas flap; the light inside the tent is dim. When I walk in and my eyes focus, I see that each one of the twenty beds holds a starving baby or small child. It's a scene from hell.

Hot, heavy air moves slowly around the inside of the tent, stinky-sweet with the smell of milky diarrhoea and therapeutic milk powder. Simon washes his square hands as we approach a tiny boy in the middle of a big metal-frame bed – no specialist cots or cribs here. There are also no sheets in the hospital, no pillows – patients cover the mattresses with their own material, which their caretakers (mostly their mum or auntie) wash and hang on a long line to dry. They bring their own plate and cup for meals.

This boy's skin is as wrinkled and loose as an old woman's. His large hopeless-looking eyes flick briefly towards us; there's a feeding tube up his nose.

Simon puts his hand on the toddler's head and moves it very gently backwards and forwards over the tufts of brown hair that remain. The boy cries feebly as he squirts yellow diarrhoea onto the black plastic mattress, and his mother rushes with a soapy cloth to wipe it away.

'He's called Bol. You can tell quite a bit from palpating the fontanelle,' says Simon. The fontanelle is the soft spot children are born with at the top of their head.

'This little guy's is sunken, which shows dehydration and malnutrition.'

He says the Sudanese nurses will give Bol oral rehydration solution and therapeutic food – either milk or medical biscuits – and antibiotics, if necessary. Lessons will be given to Bol's mother on handwashing (a skill sometimes lost to the war), plus a mosquito net and soap to take home. If little Bol responds well, he might need admitting for only a few days. After that, he'll be discharged with therapeutic food to take home.

Simon touches Bol's cheek in gentle farewell, washes his hands, as he does between each patient, and we move on to the next bed. In it, a girl of about three lies panting for breath and staring at the ceiling, her young mother asleep beside her on the bed.

'This girl is also malnourished and her raised and swollen fontanelle suggests meningitis or another infection.' He touches her hand and moves to another bed, where a child with a painfully distended abdomen and skinny limbs is suffering from a different and complicated type of malnutrition called kwashiorkor. Lack of nutrients has turned his hair tufts a copper colour.

Emotionally, I'm right back on my comfy sofa as a child, watching other children starving from a guilty distance. But in reality I'm here, trying to help, but not knowing where to start, as malnutrition is so much more complex than simply feeding people. These children didn't have enough food, yet the world has more than enough supplies for everyone. It becomes clear that food insecurity is inherently a political problem.

Simon gives me a sideways look as we leave the tent, his face has aged under the jaunty baseball cap.

'Shit, right? And you'll never get used to it.'

*

Our next stop is three isolation rooms used for cholera patients, which have grey cement walls and floors that can be easily disinfected with chlorine. Far to the left of the hospital perimeter, steam rises from the huge metal pot that hangs over a wood fire, cooking the patients' dinner.

'That's the TB area.' Simon points to a fenced-off village of tukuls that houses whole families for treatment, which can take over six months.

'And there's the quiet ward.' He points towards a tent standing on its own, far off to the right. I'm about to ask why it's called that, when he says in Arabic, 'Yalla' – come with me.

A horrifying sound is coming from the tent.

'Eeeeeeeeee!'

The squeal comes again.

'Eeeeeeeee!' like the awful sound of a newborn puppy whose tail's been stamped on.

We race across the scrub and into a tent where a stricken-looking mother holds a seven-day old baby in her arms.

'The baby's called Mary.' Simon speaks quietly, wiping sweat from under his cap.

All the bones of Mary's body are outlined through her paper-thin and broken skin. She's writhing in pain, her back arches as if possessed, her facial muscles pulled back, revealing her gums. Her eyes are sunken and wide like a skeleton's, her eyebrows drawn up in folds of loose skin towards her forehead. I don't have the words to describe the horror of this moment.

Michael, a Sudanese nurse, leans over Mary, trying to make her and her distraught mother more comfortable on the bare metal bed.

This sixteen-year-old girl is silent as she holds the writhing, shrieking baby in her arms, her expression vacant, as if the horror is too much and she's left the world.

Baby Mary, Simon explains in a whisper, kneeling beside her on the mud, has neonatal tetanus. Her horrendous grin-like grimace has a medical name: *risus sardonicus*.

'The best we can do now is give muscle-relaxing medication.'

Feeling otherwise helpless, I kneel next to Michael and help draw up the medications. Every time there's any stimulation – a sound, a touch, the light – Mary's whole body jerks in painful spasms and her spine bends backwards.

It's called the Quiet Ward so that staff can tiptoe in silently to nurse dying patients.

'She's so thin,' I say pointlessly, wishing we were surrounded by incubators and bleeping machines.

'Mary can't breastfeed,' Simon says, 'or even bear to be cuddled.'

'Eeeeeeee,' Mary screams painfully again, as she passes mucous diarrhoea.

'How does this happen?'

A bead of sweat drips from the end of Simon's nose. Mary, he explains, was born in a village two days' walk from Leer. Her umbilical cord was cut with a piece of glass and tied with a reed because that's all the untrained birth attendant had. For a couple of days, she'd appeared healthy, but the tetanus infection (from bacteria spores that live in soil throughout the world) probably passed through the umbilical cord and into her brain before she'd reached hospital. Antibiotics had been given for the infected umbilical stump, but it was too late to stop the tetanus.

He leans over her. 'Poor love,' he says.

Simon washes his hands and helps Michael to deliver a small dose of diazepam through a cannula taped to the baby's head. This gives baby Mary a short grace period, when she can lie in her mother's arms and be soothed. Silence falls inside the small tent ward.

Once upon a time – back through the looking glass and a world away now – I'd sat in a cool mahogany library in London and written a thesis on neonatal tetanus. I'd learnt that the infection, which still claims the lives of 50,000 children a year, is completely preventable. If Mary's mum had received a simple tetanus vaccination, Mary wouldn't be here, screaming in agony. Even in pregnancy, it's not too late for the woman to be vaccinated. But now the reality of doing nothing is shrieking and writhing in front of me. I want to cry but I mustn't, my tears are an indulgence here. They help no one.

This baby was born in South Sudan, where vaccination is a hit-and-miss affair; some children were given the injections, and some missed out. In the absence of a government-led, national approach, it depended on where you lived and if any aid organisations could get to you in the war. Our only small comfort is the line of women in Leer Hospital, waiting for their vaccination in the antenatal clinic.

'So…?' My voice trails off. I don't want to finish the sentence.

'Tetanus gives a painful death. There is no chance of survival.'

Simon swallows and mops his head, disposing of the empty syringe.

'All we can do is try to ease it for her.'

CHAPTER SEVEN

In two days, I'll fly home to the UK for my first R & R, one of two planned holidays in a nine-month mission. I'll see Jack again. During my ten-day break, we'll go to our friend's wedding in a smart hotel in Yorkshire. I must buy a dress. I must discover lipstick again. It's an under-exaggeration to say I'm feeling apprehensive about all of the above; basically, about being anywhere but here.

My life in South Sudan has become all-consuming; patient care takes up most of my waking thoughts, and I'm already planning the next teaching project in Tam. Anita's words have taken hold inside me: what can I realistically achieve here? Mary's torturous, short life has shown me that vaccinations and clean delivery kits might (in the regrettable absence of trained midwives) go some way towards stopping the next baby getting tetanus. With hard work, it could be achievable in Tam, and by now, I'm so tunnel-visioned that a short holiday just when I'm getting into my stride feels almost like an inconvenience.

And then, one day before my flight out of South Sudan is due, the plane is cancelled. Ridiculous amounts of rain have started to fall again, and the runway is simply too dangerous. Now I know I can't leave, my emotions flip-flop and I feel trapped, longing for home.

Leer Hospital is only a short drive from the living compound, but heavy downpours have turned the road into a sticky red bog, almost impassable, even in a 4 x 4. To know that most of our patients will struggle to get to us makes everything feel worse.

On the night I should've left, we're bumping slowly through mud on our way back to the living quarters. It's a pitch-black night, eight of us are crammed in the back of the 4 x 4, our wet shoulders knocking together as wheels hit rock and mudbanks.

Today, for the first time, I saw the death of a pregnant woman, and something inside me feels smaller now, maybe a diminishing sense of hope. Eve, the woman, was at the point of giving birth, but she'd come to us too late. The footpath was a torrent, and she'd contracted cholera from drinking contaminated water. By the time she reached us, she'd passed so much milky, liquid diarrhoea, litres upon litres, her heart had stopped from acute dehydration and there was no way we could start it again, no intensive care to send her to. Eve's dead baby was still inside a warm belly, sloshing from side to side as we rolled Eve onto her back on the cement floor of the cholera treatment room. It's possible that the baby had died a couple of days before, when the placenta had stopped working due to such fluid loss; there was certainly no foetal heart sound by the time she was brought to us. But here in South Sudan there are no post-mortems, no death certificate, no headlines in national news.

With scraps of cloth tied around our mouths, and our eyes streaming from the chlorine vapours that we'd accidentally made too concentrated, James, Simon and the rest of the team-rallied to make Eve's body safe for burial. Cholera-infected body fluids are highly contagious, even after death, so we washed her with as much thoroughness and dignity as we could before stuffing chlorine-soaked material into each infective orifice and wrapping her. The rain was pummelling down outside. Five other dead bodies joined her as the night-time grew. They lay illuminated like mummies by the light of our headtorches. All of them could have survived if they'd reached us sooner.

The scene was so horrific, I'm trying hard to block the memory of it as we bump back to the living compound, focusing on the outreach team that has already been sent to 'track and trace' the contaminated water source and prevent further transmission. It's then, randomly, that James starts to recite (from memory) a scene between George and Lennie from John Steinbeck's novel *Of Mice and Men*: 'Guys like us, that work on ranches, are the loneliest guys in the world. They got no family. They don't belong no place… With us it ain't like that. We got a future. We got someone to talk to who gives a damn about us.'

The rain is still pelting down. My stethoscope sticks to my wet T-shirt. We listen as if our life depends on it.

When we reach the compound, Simon, who's on call tonight, showers first. I'd planned to go with him to learn the ropes of the hospital at night, but my body feels drained: not only was Eve my first maternal mortality, but baby Mary died a horrible death this morning. When I heard, I wanted to curl up on my bed and howl. At times, this place feels like hell.

I've barely touched my plate of rice and stew when the on-call walkie-talkie springs into life: 'Cccchhhhhhhttt', the sound of static that makes all our stomachs flip with nerves, followed by, 'Expat compound to IPD.'

My chest tightens. *What now?* The Sudanese voice continues: 'Pregnant woman. Baby not coming out.'

Simon, pale and tired, leaps up and looks at me.

'The driver's at the gate,' he says, like he wants me to come but doesn't want to pressure me.

'I'm coming,' I hear my voice say. I need all the midwifery experience I can get for the patients we *can* save.

*

Our 4 x 4 grinds back through treacly brown mud towards the hospital. When we arrive, headtorches on and wet to the skin, Simon and I rush straight into the maternity ward. It's crammed with women – new mothers, aunties, friends, babies – all gathered around four beds covered in ghostly mosquito nets, patients sheltering underneath. Two patients are also nursed on mattresses on the grey cement floor because the ward has run out of space. A ceiling fan, powered by a generator, moves hot air around like tepid water.

A woman is panting behind the flimsy curtain of the tiny delivery room at the end of the ward. When I draw the curtain back, I see a girl of about seventeen, legs akimbo on an old-fashioned delivery bed, grimacing her way through strong contractions. Her feet are bare, legs splashed with mud up to her knees.

Machar, a young male nurse, stands next to the girl, looking frightened and clutching the walkie-talkie in his hand. Nyawan, the girl, has been in labour for three days in her village with no midwife, and now she's had to walk through storms and mud to get to the clinic while continuing to have contractions.

When Nyawan grunts, I'm shocked to see the woman beside her, who I think is her mother, give her a hard smack on the leg. We're light years away here from a birthing pool and whale music. I'm left appalled with my mouth open.

It's Simon who mutters that this awful hitting is sometimes traditional here. As labour is so dangerous, birth partners want women to use all their energy for pushing, not shouting. It's a valid fear in a country where more young women die in childbirth than go to secondary school. Eve was testament to that risk, though of course we didn't for a moment condone the smacks. My own desire to be a midwife is sparked again – there are hundreds of thousands of other girls and women across this country just as vulnerable as Nyawan.

Another wallop on the thigh, a groan, a crack of thunder outside. When lightning comes, the single light in the ceiling flickers and dims, forcing us to work by the light of our head-torches. Simon, calm, reassuring, picks up a Pinard stethoscope – a simple trumpet-like piece of equipment that's used as a listening horn. When the contractions seem to have slowed and tailed off, he holds the Pinard against Nyawan's belly, his face three inches away from her body.

'Good foetal heart rate.'

He shows me how to listen, my cheek so close to Nyawan's abdomen I feel the warmth coming off her skin.

After a vaginal examination, Simon looks worried. Nyawan, he says, is fully dilated, she should be birthing now. But the labour seems to have slowed, the baby's head still high in the pelvis, and without contractions it could be dangerous to use forceps to aid delivery.

The older woman stops smacking, frowns at Machar and shoos him away. In South Sudan, it's unusual for a man to attend a birth. Simon, she doesn't seem to mind about, maybe because he's a kawai (foreigner). Machar runs round to the other side of the shuttered window to stand in the rain and shout through translations.

Lights flicker again, thunder booms. Nyawan lies back panting and crying, her eyes darting around, petrified. It's clear she's come to the end of her strength, unable to push or create any expulsive energy to get the baby out.

Simon says, 'The baby may die if it doesn't come out soon. She's fully dilated, the placenta may try to separate from the uterus, and then there'll be no oxygen for the baby.'

He uses the walkie-talkie to call Camilla, the team's Italian surgeon back at the living compound, and ask for assistance, as we might need an emergency caesarean section. Headlights flash through the delivery room window as the 4 x 4 roars off to fetch her, and there's shouting outside in Nuer to scramble the national staff operating theatre team.

Simon's assessing the woman's belly to see what direction the baby's lying in.

'Do a blood glucose test,' he says.

'OK.' Finally, a job I could easily do, second nature from my work in ED.

'It's 2.6 mmol.'

Anything below 4.0 mmol indicates dangerously low blood sugar, especially in labour, but Nyawan's lack of food, long-term malnutrition, days of labour with no fluids and long walk in the rain has left nothing in reserve. I get a tray ready to put in an IV line, all the equipment basically the same as I'm used to at home, but none of the frills. Lack of plastic wings on the cannula makes it hard to hold, no cannula dressing either, just zinc medical tape. But it's working, and almost as soon as we connect the dextrose infusion, Nyawan's contractions begin again in earnest – this baby is coming.

'Get new gloves on,' Simon instructs. 'I'm here to help you.'

Legs akimbo, still on her back, Nyawan's vagina seems to open involuntarily as a black head of hair pushes itself forward and squeezes its way down the birth canal.

All the mother's muscles are working now in miraculous synchronicity to bring this baby into the world. Anus flares open, body contorting, a tiny head fills the space of the stretched vagina, labia now lost in the pull of the skin, warm amniotic waters gushing out over my poised hands and up my arms. I'm holding my breath. In the next push, the head is born, face down at first then turning sideways with restitution. Simon shows me how to gently check for a cord around the neck. When I see the cord is clear, I feel I haven't taken a breath for an eternity.

Nyawan lets out an enormous, bellowing grunt, her final push.

And suddenly, a limp pale body is handed to me. A boy. Blueish with a sparse covering of creamy vernix, half the size of any newborn I've ever seen. Simon is beside me, kind, reassuring, knowing the next time I have to do this, I might be back in Tam with no back-up.

'You can do this, Anna, you know what you're doing.'

Taking a deep breath, I somehow remember my training. *Wrap and vigorously dry the baby. Take the stethoscope, listen for heart rate and breaths while you observe for signs of life.*

But this boy is pale and floppy. His eyes are still closed. He looks dead.

My knees are wobbling as I pick up a tiny baby-sized bag and mask, putting the mask over the baby's nose and mouth as he lies between his mother's legs. Simon puts gentle pressure on the bag to inflate the baby's lungs. *Careful! Not too hard.* Only a small amount of pressure is needed.

After the longest few moments of my life, I hear some kind of a cough. Yes! And when the blue baby has a slight hint of pinky-brown, relief rushes up through me.

'*Waaaaaaaaaa!*' the baby screams, the best sound in the whole world, filling my soul with joy.

We wait until the umbilical cord has stopped pumping blood before we clamp and cut it, knowing this tiny baby needs all the blood it can get. Looking back later over my time in South Sudan, I'll realise I never once saw a baby born over 2.5 kg (about 5.5 lb), which is the cut-off for a *normal* birth weight in the UK.

'*Waaaaaaaa!*' the baby keeps crying. I cry, I laugh. I'm so elated I want to punch the air.

'Not over yet, Anna. The placenta's not out.'

An older woman arrives to take the baby next door. I want the mum to hold him skin-to-skin, or to breastfeed him, but I can't argue with this group of determined women and their traditions. I don't even speak their language. With consent, I inject Nyawan's thigh with oxytocin, the drug that stimulates uterine contractions, and within a few minutes, and after one more contraction, out plops the placenta, glistening and complete, with barely any more bleeding.

'A complete birth,' Simon beams at me. 'Now we can celebrate.'

We stand down the theatre team and hug awkwardly, trying not to touch each other's T-shirt with bloodied gloves.

The women next door are shouting their joy too, holding their highest possible screams for as long as they can, ending with a ululating 'la' on the last note. They flood into the room, laughing and rubbing us on the head with their saliva as a traditional thank you. In three days' time, at the runway, they'll give me a belly teek carefully threaded with delicate red, white and black beads. As they tie it around my waist and use a match flame to seal the ends, I silently vow never to take it off. Nyawan will wave as she walks home across that runway, her baby held aloft in a woven reed basket.

Meanwhile, they hand me the baby to hold.

'Moses,' says one of the women, her wide smile showing off a mouth of missing teeth, and Simon offers to take my photo. Nyawan agrees to this, and it's a picture I'll hold dear for years to come, my first delivery, of baby Moses in the storm.

*

An hour later, Simon and I stride back into the dining room of the living compound, exhausted but feeling so connected.

Femzi, the Kenyan team logistician says, 'I feel like dancing!' and loads some exotic music into the CD player. I've never heard it before, but I love it: lingala, the rumba music from Congo that you can't help but dance to. Simon whispers that he'll do the rest of the on-call that night, and I should stay and enjoy myself, so I quickly shower and change. When I get back, those first sips of Kenyan Tusker beer slip down my throat like pure nectar.

Dancing feels so good! I'm ecstatic about the baby and my head is full of exciting new music – 'This Is Time for Africa', then a French singer, Manu Chao with the beats of 'Bongo Bong'. While I'm dancing, I even laugh out loud. After two small cans of lager, I'm wildly free. *I can't remember ever feeling this happy.*

James catches my eye, beams at me and puts both thumbs up.

*

Around two in the morning the rain stops, and we drag our mattresses outside into the compound courtyard. We link arms and lie on our backs, watching stars dazzle against a black sky. I'm still buzzing from the birth, full of marvel at the universe. Simon rests his head on my shoulder as James and I sip cups of Kenyan tea. There's no sense of loneliness. This group feels like my people: we are all in this together. We all understand the crazy, awful pendulum swing in emotion between the deaths of Eve and Mary, but also the contrasting 'up' of the live birth of Moses, which makes the babies that do survive seem even more of a miracle.

Forty-eight hours later, I'm scribbling in my diary: *Just heard that the runway is cleared, and I can leave tomorrow. Don't be frightened.*

CHAPTER EIGHT

At Schiphol Airport in Amsterdam I change planes, and the thought that I'm now only a couple of hours from home gives me a tightly buckled-up feeling in the pit of my stomach. I won't have time when I get there to buy a dress for Sue's summer wedding, so I head to an airport boutique crammed with gaudy dresses, jewellery and belts, a place where the handbags on sale would cover a year's salary for our staff in Tam. There are no mirrors at all in Tam, no windows either to sneak a look in, so it's a shock to see how scrawny I look in the changing-room mirror, how hollowed out and sad. My legs are hairy, my farmer's tan looks agricultural in this scented place, as do the red, white and black teek beads around my belly that those joyful ululating women gave me. Now I have fluttering feelings of anxiety up my neck. In some ways, not being able to see or judge how I've looked for the last three months has been liberating.

Endless delays on a hot plane going nowhere at Nairobi airport have left me smelling fusty. I should've washed on the plane, not stood at the door of the toilet, gaping at its incredible luxury: hot and cold running water! flushing loo! free soap and hand cream! I should've dived in and enjoyed myself, but instead I peed like a fugitive and scuttled back to my seat, cramming on the headphones, which have been pretty much stapled to my head ever since the plane took off.

I've been listening, on repeat, to Gorillaz' 'Feel Good Inc.', trying to bludgeon myself into a holiday mood: *Sha la la … feeling good!* For a while it works, and the song's tumbling rhythms, plus several glasses of red wine, have blasted me back. In these brief, beautiful moments of amnesia, I can forget hugging James goodbye, how the women on the runway shrank to the size of matchstick toys outside their tukuls, how a whole world of unsolvable misery and hope had disappeared.

'Thanks!' I signalled to the flight attendant for more wine.

Sha la la … feeling good!

Back in the airport shop, handing over close to £60 for a dress I don't like much, I have the dizzying thought that this is the rough equivalent of Queth's weekly wages, despite MSF always paying fair wages for the context. I sternly remind myself, *You're going home to a wedding. To dance! To drink champagne and have fun.* I don't want to be that Tarot card figure, black gown, sickle, wagging her bony finger at the guests. Last time I'd heard 'Feel Good Inc.' was in Leer, when we'd danced like kids at an illegal rave after the birth of Moses. Don't think about Leer! Stop feeling ashamed about the women giving birth right now. Think about lying in Jack's arms again, about sprawling on Mum's sofa, her lasagne melting in the oven, the long bath, eating a fresh chicken and lettuce sandwich … Oh, my God, a chicken and lettuce sandwich!

A week or so ago, during a what-I-plan-to-do-on-my-holidays type discussion with James, who's in Mombasa right now on his own break, I'd cracked him up describing the chicken sandwich I was going to eat at the Malt Cross Café in Nottingham. I'd groaned orgasmically taking that first – no no! no! no! stop it! – bite into the tender whiteness of the bread, the plump buttery chicken, the crisp lettuce, the creamy squirt of mayo.

'You're totally nuts,' he'd said, giving me a mock blow around the head. But to me the sandwich represented all the food I couldn't enjoy in South Sudan – fresh bread and salad included.

'I sure hope it's as good as you think it's gonna be.'

*

Walking down the long white corridor towards the arrivals sign, I make a conscious effort not to look hunched from the weight of my backpack. My flip-flops making a light, pointless flapping sound.

When the door opens, I see Jack before he sees me. He looks so handsome, so clean-looking, so healthy, standing there. He's wearing beautifully pressed jeans. His beard is trimmed. He's holding a bright bunch of flowers, and when he sees me, his face lights up.

My heart flutters with hope and happiness. I'm also fearful and half-broken. When we move in for a kiss, a large part of me is yearning for time to stand still and for me to be the girl I was again. But the awkwardness is a shock. Who puts their head which way for a hug? How dry are my lips after too much red wine? Have I even looked at my encroaching facial hair?

Later, I won't be able to remember what we talk about in the car back to our immaculate apartment, only that inside the locked door, the air smells of lavender polish and bleach, the conversation feels stilted, and I'm putting a muddy backpack down on a pale vacuumed carpet. Jack, leading me into the kitchen, shows me the fridge full of lovely cheeses, cold meat and smoked salmon. His welcome back is flawless, but I'm panicking at how numb I feel; it's as if I'm speaking to him from behind a pane of glass.

He dashes about making coffee, taking my backpack into the bedroom, putting ice in my glass of water. We chat about the flight, his work, and when conversation peters out, he says he'll run that bath I've been dreaming of.

Inside the bathroom, I lock the door and add a reckless slug of Radox to the water. The bubbles smell so sweet and look so enticing, so with my 'Feel Good Inc.' reel still on a loop inside my head, I smile as I step in, expecting to immerse myself for hours.

Heaven! I sink until the water comes up to my chin. *Better than I imagined even.*

But after a few minutes, I leap out, uncomfortably hot and restless. My wet footprints on the floor remind me of my chlorine footprints in the cholera treatment room, of Eve's wrapped pregnant body in the corner. Staring at myself in the mirror, the dark circles under my eyes, the ugly tan, the next step should be to slip into something pretty and fall into bed with Jack, but I can't and I don't know why. Tracing the edge of my belly teek, I'm relieved it's still there. It's the only thing that feels real right now.

My memory of the rest of that evening is hazy, but I do remember sitting on the edge of the sofa feeling as numb as Styrofoam, watching TV while Jack cooks dinner. Flicking through the channels, I see people selling houses, cooking, competing for cash. I'm desperate for it not to feel glary and gross, but it does. Did I use to watch this and enjoy it? *Feeling good!* The six o'clock news feels surreal too: I had no idea that Gordon Brown was the new prime minister, that there was a potential banking crisis or that a girl called Maddie McCann had recently been abducted.

When Jack and I fall asleep holding each other, the closeness and the duvet feel hot and heavy after months of not needing even a sheet. I feel the absence of my grab bag medical kit, like a child without their bedtime teddy. Was Jack awake? Was he hurt when I'd turned away from him? I have no idea. Although I'd caught him looking warily at the beads around my belly, he didn't say anything.

*

Jack's working the next day, so I wander on my own around Nottingham, glad for time alone to break the circuit. I knew it had been a confusing, disappointing evening for him, but he'd been so gracious about it. Now, walking through streets damp with warm August drizzle, I have the vague idea of buying him a present, and also hair removal items, which I hope will make me feel desirable again.

Stopping at the entrance to a huge supermarket, my feet refuse to go any further, paralysed by the impossible number of decisions in front of me – the shampoos, the hair dyes, all that food – so I leave without buying anything. By now, it's starting to rain properly, big fat drops, but I'm sweating again. Wrapping my plastic mac around me, I sit on a wall in Market Square, breathing deeply, trying to use the mindfulness techniques I'd picked up from James. It's then I see a woman take one bite of her Greggs sausage roll and throw the rest in the bin, and that pretty much finishes me off. Shock and rage fizz through my body, giving me a strange homesickness for the chest where James and I kept our pitiful food supplies, but where nothing was wasted.

Thoughts of James make me think of the chicken and lettuce sandwich I'd fantasised about. Right! Hungry after no breakfast, and less than a hundred yards from the Malt Cross Café where I'd first eaten it, it would be something satisfying to do. Inside the beautiful warm fug and the familiar murmurs of the coffee shop, I sit down. My cappuccino arrives in a vast bowl with a leaf decoration on the foam, and moments later the sandwich is put in front of me. I sink my teeth into it and all those anticipated sensations come flooding back: the pillowy lightness of the fresh white bread, the creamy chicken filling, the crunch of lettuce, but this time, when I've finished and am looking at the few remaining crumbs, I feel nothing.

Putting my head in my hands, I'm glad no one's there to see how absurdly upset and disappointed I feel. How stupid, how lonely. I give myself an angry pep talk: *you have seven days of holiday left, you must find a way to relax, or at the very least impersonate someone who's relaxed.* I mustn't freak out the people who love me. I still have the wedding, then a family party to look forward to. Granny would find a way to make me smile, Grandpa too with his thoughtful questions about South Sudan. If they could make it through the war together, I can make it through this.

*

Two days later, shaved, plucked, lipsticked and in my new green and brown dress, I'm sitting in the back row at Sue's wedding. She looks beautiful as she walks down the aisle, elegant train unfurling behind her, diamantés sparkling around the delicate neckline. Jack, in a perfectly fitting suit, sits a few feet away from me, facing the guests. His guitar lies across his knees, ready to play once the Registry Book is signed. His Adam's apple bobs as he swallows his nerves. When he sees me looking at him, he winks, a wink that says, *One day this will be us.*

*

Ancestral portraits adorn the walls of the stately home in Yorkshire where the wedding and reception are held. The fresh flowers and gilded ceilings leave me staring like I'm at the Sistine Chapel. Sue's new friends are young and upwardly mobile; the car park's crammed with expensive cars. My chair has a pristine white covering that I'm trying not to mark with my sweaty hands. The green and brown dress I chose too quickly at Schiphol Airport is too tight, and my freshly shaved legs feel gangly.

Sitting in this room with its antiques, its gorgeous pictures, its rich mixture of fabrics, perfumes, hairspray, make-up and shining shoes, I want to be grateful for such hospitality, to celebrate my friends, to tell the bleak Tarot figure to stay the fuck away. But every single emotion, good and bad, is packed into a tight ball in my stomach, which I don't know what to do with.

Jack and I hold hands after one glass of champagne and that feels good. When someone asks me about South Sudan, his grip tightens, and I wonder if he's protecting me or signalling *keep it light*?

'Don't you worry about getting sick yourself?' asks one woman in lilac.

'I hear you're living in a tent. How ghastly!' from a handsome, young, cologne-smelling lawyer.

I smile politely and tell a snake story because that feels safe, not too vagina-ish. Jack's shoulders relax a little.

But I feel the betrayal: South Sudan consumes most of my thoughts, and I *want* to talk about Nyachoul, or Nyabol, or baby Moses. Or tell a funny anecdote about James. I just wouldn't know where to start to do them justice. One thing I do know – the bubbles are making me feel warmer and calmer; I like the feeling of Jack's hand in mine. We've had sex once, but I'd suddenly wanted it over, so faked an orgasm, then felt bad all over again. We haven't talked about it. Instead we focus our conversations on where we might go on our next break – Zanzibar? Paris? – we've skipped over the big stuff.

Jack hasn't asked me any questions about my patients yet, though they're all I think about. When he moves towards me at night now, I tell him I'm exhausted, which is true, that I just want to sleep and have cuddles, which is true too. But I hate seeing the hurt in his eyes when I roll away from him, my belly teek like a force field between us.

My goals for the holiday are now simple, yet selfish: to eat well, to sleep lots, to rally my energy for the next stint in the field. In the dark, when I can't sleep, I draw intricate spider diagrams over my notebook, obsessed with ideas of how we can deliver safe-birth kits in Tam.

'More champagne?'

'Yes, lovely, thank you!'

The young lawyer gives Jack an affectionate punch on the arm. 'Pretty great of you to let her go away like this.'

Two more glasses of champagne on and I visit the loo, where I overhear a conversation between two women topping up their lipstick in front of the mirror.

'Doesn't she look amazing!'

'Yes, sooooo thin, and I'm sooooo jealous. She dropped three sizes to get into that wedding dress.'

They laugh. I think of baby Mary.

Three glasses of champagne. We're sitting at the dinner table listening to the end of the speeches. Jack, on his fourth glass and reaching for the red wine, is drinking much more than usual. When the food arrives — smoked salmon, fillet of beef, rich gravy, tray after tray of side dishes — the heavy-set guy with the too-small suit to my right leans in with a blast of alcohol and the air of someone about to make an earth-shaking announcement.

'I can't *believe*,' he says scornfully, 'they chose the square crockery and not the round!'

Later, when he asks what I do, and I briefly explain I'm a nurse overseas, I feel Jack's arm around my shoulder again.

'So what's the worst thing you've ever seen?' His eyes are bulging in excitement.

I hate him in this moment, this arsehole in the luxury suit, the Audi TT keyring purposely left out for all to see. Flashing back to the woman on the plane leaking faeces from her vagina, I think, *do you really want to hear? Does her suffering amuse you?* without a word coming from my mouth. I miss James, who would've handled this brilliantly with an eloquent put-down. Or Anita, who would have sent me a knowing wink from across the table.

'Well, she's seen a lot of snakes,' Jack comes to the rescue. 'Yesterday, when I squeezed the air freshener, she jumped in the air and yelled!'

Everyone laughs. I smile and look at the floor. I must find more things to make light of.

Too many glasses of bubbly later and I'm dancing alone on a packed dance floor. The band is playing Van Morrison's 'Have I told you lately that I love you?' – and its lyrics make me crumble after so much champagne and so little Jack. Upstairs, the beautiful bedroom and the four-poster bed he's promised lie empty; he's fallen asleep in a chair. Much as I want to be that girl tonight, I'm guiltily relieved.

When the music stops, my face is wet.

It's a relief to sleep alone; I finally admit to myself. Because I've reached, without knowing it, a point of no return. I'd thought I could go to South Sudan, do my bit and come home satisfied. If I'd known myself better, I might have said some of this to Jack, or even broken up with him. I do know it's not fair to leave him in limbo. He's of marriageable age, talented, handsome... There are scores of women who would snap him up. Plus, I can't understand why he's sticking with me, except that like him I'm still full of hope that maybe we can work this thing out, and love will win in the end.

CHAPTER NINE

On the plane back to Leer, I sit next to Valerie, a thirty-year-old Canadian nurse based in Leer Hospital. There's a purity and sweetness in Valerie's smile that makes me think of a young evangelical, fresh from college, eager to tell you how swell the world is. Her hair is scraped back in a ponytail, her eyes a cloudless blue.

Valerie smiles kindly as I tell her the highlights of my R & R: my young nieces running upstairs to give me toys they wanted to donate to the kids we worked with; the bags of knitted hats my mum and her friends had made for the tiny babies we delivered; Dad slipping a twenty-dollar bill in my wallet to spend at one of the many airports I'd change at to get from the UK back to Lokichoggio. Valerie looks tired; she's been part of a team dealing with a massive measles outbreak, putting in long, gruelling shifts, but she doesn't complain.

'Isn't this just lovely?' She looks out of a dust-smeared window at the miles of dry mud below. No mention of the tumbling cargo of the dilapidated aid plane, the odour of the hot leather seats, or the flies clinging to our ankles. Valerie's strong, she looks for the beauty in things.

I'm following her gaze when I feel a tap on my shoulder – Jaan, the pilot. He's left Elijah, his co-pilot, at the controls. Jaan's wearing a khaki shirt with pilot epaulettes and combat trousers. He's looking straight at me with mischievous green eyes.

'You girls want to come sit in the cockpit? Great views from there.' His South African accent is charming.

Valerie, who doesn't notice the innuendo, is unsure. 'Well, I don't…'

Immediately I jump up. *This sounds fun.* After my reunion with Jack, I'm craving some kind of release. We wobble down the aisle as the plane thunders on, into the cockpit which smells of fuel and male sweat. I blink in the midday sun, at the rudimentary gauges and switches on a large black control panel.

From here, you can see everything: those village elders gathered in a circle for a meeting, old men, mostly wearing oversized shirts and trousers, a cowboy hat or two. And down there, cattle being herded by young boys with sticks, women staring up at us shielding their eyes from the sun.

And around them, mile upon mile of the pock-marked beige and red earth, unfenced, unstable, some of it planted with landmines.

Jaan is standing so close to me I can feel his breath on my neck.

'Wanna fly it?'

'The plane!'

'Yep, why not?' The way he says this is sexy. No big deal, the shrug implies.

And because I stupidly want to impress him with how cool I am, and because I'm back in the what-the-hell, Wild West thinking of South Sudan, I say, 'OK,' and meet his eyes.

He reaches a tanned and muscular arm over me, points to an empty chair that faces the control panel.

'You sit here. Hold this control stick, keep the plane at the right altitude,' he points at a circular gauge and I have to keep the horizontal line straight.

I take the stick. When I move it gingerly to the right, and then to the left, the plane moves.

'Oh, my God! Oh, my God! I'm flyiiiiiing!' I shout a few seconds later.

'Whoa!' Valerie's shriek in my ear surprises me. I glance to my left expecting to see co-pilot Elijah sitting there, but it's Valerie at the controls, looking a little queasy. Elijah, who's standing behind her, looks uneasily at Jaan, but stays silent. We keep the plane flying for a couple of minutes, not daring to move a millimetre. It feels a long time since I had such fun.

'Time's up, girls.'

Jaan eases me out of my seat and takes over again. He has a reckless, bad-boy smile, his confidence intoxicating. When he holds my gaze again for a few extra seconds, my heart races. And then I feel so sad and awful, thinking of Jack, standing in his dressing gown in Nottingham that last morning. That broken jigsaw feeling again. Those mismatched pieces of me.

*

'Kent!'

Back in Leer, an hour later, James enfolds me in a great big bear hug. He's wearing a new pair of bright blue tinted glasses and looks tanned and energetic after his own R & R in Mombasa.

'Great to see you, gal.'

'You too,' I grin up to him. Feels like home.

We go straight into the meeting room at the Leer living compound, where Reshma, the Canadian project coordinator (PC), faces us across the table. Reshma, a childhood cancer survivor, is as tough as old boots. She's also smart, beautiful, calm in an emergency, kind, and widely respected as a great strategist.

Her MSF T-shirt is, as usual, spotless, her trousers pressed. Her thick glossy hair from East African and Indian heritage is tied back neatly. For Reshma, humanitarian aid was a life-long commitment, and being well dressed a way of not losing herself.

'Bad news, I'm sorry to say.' Reshma never wastes words. 'We have no expat midwife now in Leer. Maggie went on her R & R and didn't come back.'

James gives me a look, stroking his handlebar moustache. He was the first person to warn me that international staff come and go here, sometimes on the same day, saying no way – too crazy, too hard. Others would try to tough it out, but hit a sudden wall overnight and leave on the next plane possible. We'd joke with morbid humour that people left the projects because of a medevac (illness), shagevac (needing to get laid, then return), or crackevac (breakdown). I don't judge any of them. Maybe we all end up in those places eventually.

Reshma doesn't gossip about why Maggie left, instead she's staring at me.

'We've advertised, but there's no midwife here now.'

I stare back, my stomach dropping. Taking sips of water, I think *I can't be this person*, but with no one else here, what can I say?

'And you won't like this,' Reshma drops the next bombshell quickly, 'but outreach is suspended in both Tam and Koch for the time being. There are reported soldier movements north of Bentiu, it's unstable.

We'll need reports from other MSF teams in that region before you can go back.'

'Ah, hell! Fuck! Shit!' James takes off his Stetson and scratches his head as though his brain hurts. James was always placid until he wasn't, and I share his sense of crushing disappointment. Stephen, Queth and the other national staff are desperate for us to come back to Tam. They're due another shipment of medications, their payroll, they're keen for more study. All my carefully drawn spider diagrams mock me now.

But it's a done deal: James and I must stay in Leer for at least the next week, where the hospital is full to overflowing. I'm to help Valerie and Camilla, the Italian surgeon. Dr Simon, Reshma adds in the same matter-of-fact voice, has gone to work in the Pieri project.

So another security blanket gets yanked off, and before I have time to think about it properly, my body has registered I'm back at the brink again: that feeling in my gut of being out of control and massively out of my depth.

*

Next day, Valerie and I are put in charge of the antenatal clinic, the maternity ward, the inpatient ward and the post-surgical ward. With all inpatient beds full, the hospital is splitting at the seams, and many patients lie on mattresses on the ground. Working with us are four male Sudanese nurses and Sunduk, an extremely competent local doctor, who trained in the north of Sudan before joining MSF.

Today my heart sinks as more and more patients are carried across the central courtyard. Camilla, the surgeon, all waving arms and curly brown hair, is shouting at everyone in earshot. She's extremely skilled, with over twenty years of aid work and war surgery to her credit, but I'm intimidated by her. One look through the spectacles perched on the end of her nose, and I'm struggling to find the next word. While Camilla deals with ridiculous caseloads in theatre with her national staff team, Valerie and I must act as her gatekeepers and decide who's admitted and who must go home. Turning people away is horrible. In the UK, I've never had to make these kinds of life-or-death choices, and I know I'll never get used to it. For instance, I must watch one teenage mother, discharged after childbirth, put a four-day-old baby in a reed basket on top of her head. Fragile, brave, she turns and smiles at me before her ten-mile walk home alone across a landscape strewn with landmines.

In this place, where everything is so chaotic and we have to make awful choices, I know I will go crazy if I fully respond, so bit by bit, I start to block out the things I can't control, and focus only on the things I can.

*

That night Valerie confides to me something that scares her. The Sudanese nurses she teaches here are hardworking and willing, but often struggle with basic drug calculations, as wars have destroyed even the most basic education for so many.

Valerie, who's exceptionally patient and kind, is at pains to point out that these men aren't stupid, they simply lost out on the privileges of education. The trick is to repeat the same messages over and over, as future lives depend on it. One day, MSF may be gone, and these nurses will be the only ones left to give health care.

Back in the empty kitchen, boiling a kettle for tea, I watch a trail of tiny ants march across a splintered shelf that holds jars of Marmite, Kenyan jam, the sweet, sad, familiar things people stuff in their backpacks to remind them of home. A blinding sun falls through windows that aren't windows, just rusty glassless frames, and a giant beetle buzzes through the mesh. Valerie seems to know what her legacy will be here, but what do I want to achieve? For women to give birth safely in South Sudan, they would all need, at the bare minimum, regular antenatal checks, and a birth unit with trained midwives. But this was a lifetime's work and I had only six months left.

We'll soon be able to dispense birth kits – gloves, a new razor blade for cutting the cord, cord ties and soap – I'd ordered stock to be delivered with the next shipment to Tam. I know this is better than nothing as a clean birth kit might have saved baby Mary, but it seems such a drop in the ocean of women's needs here.

We do our best, that's all we can do. James's words ring between my ears.

CHAPTER TEN

Just a few days later, something so extraordinary happens it will stay with me for the rest of my life. I'm in Leer operating theatre, checking the blood pressure of a recently amputated patient, and Valerie is in the ward next door. Camilla's at the sink, washing her hands with her usual ferocity, getting ready for the next patient, when...

'Anna! Valerie! Quick!' a frantic voice comes through the window. It's Michael, a Sudanese nurse. Valerie and I race after him through the lines of patients, along the veranda and into the small, dark maternity ward now crowded with a group of tall women all wearing brilliantly coloured material tied over one shoulder. They cluster with an air of concern around a young Nuer woman, who I guess to be about sixteen years old. Her name is Grace. With her long thin neck and large scared eyes, she looks like a skinny kid, but she has the most enormous pregnant belly I've ever seen – especially rare in South Sudan, where gestational bumps are usually small. This girl's bursting belly is so enormous she can barely move.

The three of us heave Grace through a small doorway into the delivery room, where Simon and I previously delivered baby Moses, before the women shout at Michael to leave. Almost immediately, the contractions come with such force over Grace's body that her toes curl and fists clench. Valerie and I look at each other with fear and bemusement – so many limbs are moving inside her extraordinary belly it looks like a bag of snakes.

Michael bobs up again outside the delivery room and starts to translate in a low mutter through a rusted window covered with a frayed cotton sheet.

Grandma, aunties and friends are shifting and murmuring. They can feel electricity in the air. When Valerie, after a preliminary feel of the girl's abdomen, says, 'Twins!' a charge of excitement shoots through the room. Amniotic fluid dribbles down Grace's legs as she tries not to groan with her next contraction.

Valerie and I exchange sideways glances, trying to look supercool and competent so that the women relax, but neither of us have done this before. We know from our notebooks that, even in the UK, a twin delivery can quickly become an emergency if, say, the first baby is lying sideways, or a limb is delivered before a head. Often, in fully resourced hospitals, mothers of twins choose a planned caesarean section.

We ask Michael to call Camilla, but he murmurs through the window that she can't come – she's scrubbed and halfway through an emergency operation.

Valerie takes what sounds like a yogic exhalation. My skin prickles. *It's us, then.*

We know enough to recognise our first job is to figure out if a vaginal birth is possible – but that's not easy without an ultrasound scan, or a trained maternity team, and with two babies packed into such a small space.

Grace's face is wet with sweat now, eyes rolling, contractions coming fast and hard. Then, *crack!* A female relative gives her leg a hard smack.

'Stop!' I say, before I can hold my tongue, and the women stare at me, muttering to each other in Nuer. I'm back into the dry-mouthed, swooning terror of midwifery on the wing. Focusing back to the birth, there's no safe way to slow down this labour – the babies are coming and we must do our best.

'Two birthing kits,' Valerie yells through the flyscreen as we pull on our gloves. Michael runs to the man who sterilises surgical equipment in an autoclave above a woodfire behind the hospital.

One auntie, who's stopped smacking, stays as a caretaker, the others leave – there's no room in here for all of us. I put in an IV line. That's fine, do that well, used to it. Valerie gets out emergency drugs and antibiotics in case the waters have been gone for some time.

OK. Calm down.

Grace, who's so far been quiet, lets out a deep grunt. Putting the Pinard stethoscope on her abdomen, I'm hoping to hear the first baby's heart rate. *One, two three, or is that my own heartbeat ringing in my ear?* and then *Thank God!* I can hear one baby's heart rate, it sounds like an adult beat, only faster and fainter.

I'm straining so hard to hear for a second baby on a different section of abdomen, but it's difficult. Grace's body is twisting in labour and picking up on two different heartbeats for two different babies is like trying to tune into two competing, but ghostly, radio stations.

Valerie says, 'We need to do a vaginal exam to assess cervical dilation.'

Too late! With another stifled groan, Grace bears down, her vagina widens spontaneously and it's happening so fast and I can already see a small head pushing forward determinedly at the perineum.

Oh, God! It's scary, but also amazing. This very small head with no hair, is covered in a thick creamy vernix, a sign of prematurity.

'Aghhhhhhh!' Grace lets her cry out for the first time.

Valerie stands like a wicketkeeper between the girl's legs, holding a clean cotton sheet from a delivery kit handed to us through the window.

When the baby arrives quickly with the next push, Valerie catches it like a pro.

'It's a boy!' she yells, her smile one of pure delight. This baby is tiny, bluish, but crying. I'm still frightened, but so focused and alive, nothing exists but this moment.

I'm trying to delay clamping and cutting the cord, when one of the aunties dashes in, scoops up the tiny boy, puts him to her mouth, sucks out any sputum from his nose and mouth, spitting it on to the floor beside me. Honestly, I want to gag; it's a local practice I won't ever get used to, but in a world with rare medical assistance, it works as a basic resuscitation manoeuvre. We clamp and cut the cord.

Now swaddled by the auntie, the boy is quickly whisked away next door into the arms of a delighted older lady I assume is Grandma.

'No! No! Skin-to-skin,' I shout through the window to Michael, so he can instruct them to put the tiny baby directly onto their skin. There are no incubators in this hospital for prem babies – I don't think there are any other quality neonatal facilities in the whole of South Sudan. Only the new supply of knitted baby hats my mum and her friends donated, and the life-saving warmth of being next to skin. 'Kangaroo care' it's often called, and is life-saving here.

But Nuer women have their own customs, and they bundle up the baby. They don't have to listen to us, and I can't talk directly to them.

'Tell them he needs to feed in the next hour,' Valerie shouts over her shoulder to Michael. This tiny boy is at risk of both heat loss and low blood sugar unless he has breast milk promptly. It's his only chance; formula milk in South Sudan, where the water could be contaminated, is simply too dangerous.

Back on the table, the labour continues with force, but thankfully very little bleeding.

'Oh, my God!' Valerie's staring between the mother's legs, her eyes wide. 'What's that?'

Two bulging purple sacks start to deliver. My first thought is that it's a deformity as only the previous week a baby was born with gastroschisis (its bowel outside the body) and sadly died. A baby that most likely would've survived with surgery in the UK.

Grace is still pushing, and with the next grunt, a tiny scrotum appears, then buttocks. The legs are wrapped around the baby's ears – a frank breech position. With the next final expulsive push, another tiny boy shoots into my waiting, trembling hands. He's blue and startled – *rub him vigorously with a clean sheet to stimulate him* – an imaginary Dr Simon is next to me, giving me resus instructions. Within a minute, the baby starts to cough and snort, with his legs still in a frog-like position due to the way he'd been lying inside.

When this second baby cries, tears brim in my wide, shocked eyes. What incredible joy to deliver two premature boys, weak and only 1 kg each, but alive in spite of all the odds against them. Moments later, when he's taken through to be wrapped and cooed over by the women next door, I hear shrieks of happiness and loud shrill ululating calls, and I want to yell too.

But instead, I watch Valerie's smile die. She's giving Grace's abdomen a final feel, before injecting the oxytocin and ergometrine that helps the placenta deliver.

'Something's wrong,' she says. 'Get Camilla.'

Her face is white. I feel confused, sick. Why? Grace's tummy is half the size it was before. The traditional X-shaped scars are back in place, the belly teek loose. And then I follow her stare and put my hand over Grace's uterus. Something is moving in there. Something alive.

'There's another one,' I yell.

'Get a delivery kit, get a delivery kit!'

My hands are shaking. I have enough textbook knowledge to know that in the UK, triplets are almost never delivered vaginally, the risks of one child dying, or of a limb obstructing the delivery, are simply too high.

The women next door pick up on our change of tone; they're screaming now too.

Calm down, Anna! Concentrate, take a breath. Grace's child-like hands are bunched into fists so tight that her nails are digging into her palms, her eyes are squished. *She needs you to think.*

A few seconds later, she bears down again with such effort that her bowels open. And just as I'm wiping away the faeces, a third head appears, and a baby girl is born with one final push into both Valerie and my hands.

The baby girl is quickly dried with a golden sarong an auntie unties from her shoulder – we have no new sterile towel. She's unbelievably small and so fragile. Later we'll weigh her and find she's only 900 g, less than a bag of sugar. But now she's screaming loudly as if to announce her own arrival. We cut the cord, and when she's raced next door, the aunties and Grandma explode into an all-singing, all-ululating dance of celebration.

'Oh…my…goodness!' Valerie and I gawp at each other in disbelief.

'Any more in there?' we laugh, as I give the injection of ergometrine and Valerie feels back to her tummy.

Camilla runs into the room, pushes past us and puts her hands onto Grace's belly.

'Give another injection of ergometrine,' she barks, 'Start the IV. Get the misoprostol ready.'

The placenta delivers, but has broken into pieces. Immediately Camilla puts a gloved hand deep into the girl's vagina. When she pulls out other broken pieces, they look like lumps of liver. Blood starts to pour from the girl like a crimson river.

A PPH (postpartum haemorrhage) like this could easily escalate and kill Grace. I'm frantically giving more drugs, but they're not working.

'No tone in her uterus, there's tissue left inside' Camilla says bluntly, her face wet with sweat. Grace collapses before our eyes on the birth table and I have no more drugs I can use.

'I'll prepare for surgery. Do this.'

Camilla gives me a sterile glove, bunches up her right hand like a boxer and shows me how to push my right hand deep into Grace's vagina, while my left hand simultaneously pushes hard on her abdomen from the outside. I squeeze the uterus between my two hands, a manoeuvre called bimanual compression, only to be used in very dire circumstances. It's something all UK midwives are trained in, but thankfully few ever have to use.

'Do until I say stop!' Camilla commands.

Grace is carried to theatre on a stretcher made of sticks. Thin legs sticking out, me shuffling alongside, my fist in her vagina, arm painful from cramp, but desperate not to let go. Valerie throws a bright purple and green sarong over her for dignity.

Grace, who I've known for just under an hour, is at the brink of death. Her face is waxy, her eyes unfocused. Michael is squeezing IV fluids into her; he's shouting to family members saying they'll all need to be tested for blood donation. Person-to-person blood transfusions are our only hope out here.

Door frames slamming, people shouting, *deep breath*, Grace's unconscious arm flops off the stretcher. When Camilla quickly injects her with ketamine, the girl's eyes roll back in her head. Ketamine, used in the UK to tranquillise horses, and illegally as a club drug, may sound like an odd choice of anaesthetic, but it's our only option here. Enough of a dose will knock her unconscious for surgery, but she'll still be able to breathe for herself. Put simply, the complex ventilation equipment that's standard in UK theatres is just not available here.

I'm not needed in theatre. Camilla has her excellent national staff team, one of whom is armed with a swat, squashing the flies that happily followed us in. Camilla's bundled her wild hair under a sun-bleached green theatre hat, she's inserting the knife, telling me to leave.

Back in the maternity ward, Grace's sister, who has her own baby, is expressing drops of her breast milk into three babies waiting mouths. This potentially runs the risk of a blood-borne virus being transmitted through breastmilk, though rates of infection are low here and we'll later screen her to find she's thankfully negative. But in the circumstance, it's probably the best way of keeping these babies alive – the usual rock and a hard place of choices.

When I walk into the room, an auntie I'd shouted at earlier for smacking smiles and points at the girl baby.

'Nyakawai,' she says, lifting the baby up like a chalice. Like gold. She can't stop smiling. Nor can Grandma, who has a big toothless grin and who touches me tenderly on the top of my head, saying sweet-sounding words I can't understand.

'Nyakawai means "foreign woman",' Michael says.

They've named the baby girl after Valerie and me, and at last proper tears pour down my face, tears of relief and disbelief that these babies are so bright and alert.

Tears of fear too – if Grace dies, these babies will probably die too. In South Sudan in 2007, some 1,500 women died in childbirth per 100,000 live births, a figure that compares starkly to maternity care in the UK, where, in the same year, there were ten deaths per 100,000 births.

That is the clear difference made by access to maternity care and absence of war.

*

An hour later, a drowsy Grace is stretchered back to the maternity ward with a large plaster covering the lower section of her abdomen. She looks like a sleeping child, but at sixteen she's just had a complete hysterectomy, because without this operation she would almost certainly have bled to death. She will never bear children again.

Camilla explains that the triplet placentas had grown vessels through the wall of the uterus and actually into Grace's own blood supply and organs (a condition known in medical textbooks as placenta percreta). Again, in the UK, this abnormal placenta would have been detected on a routine ultrasound scan, though a hysterectomy might still have been the eventual outcome.

Grace stayed with us for the next ten days. After a blood transfusion, I saw her first tentative smile as she successfully rotated the woolly-hatted triplets between herself and her sister for breastfeeds. Then I watched her walk home with a basket of babies balanced on her head. She was wearing the same purple and green sarong that we'd flung over her in a moment of extremity, now washed and dried, and tied smartly over her shoulder.

As I write this, I yearn to know what Grace's life was like in South Sudan as a girl/woman no longer able to bear children. Baby Nyakawai would be thirteen now, if she survived, which is unlikely, but I force myself to believe that she did.

*

Driving back to the compound two hours later, I'm feeling euphoric and, in truth, a little heroic. My emotions are higher and deeper than anything I've ever felt before: *this is what I came here for!* For these brief moments, ecstasy masks the pain I feel from witnessing suffering that I can't help, and I understand why people can grow addicted to this work. The high coming out of the deepest lows is incomparable. *I can't wait to tell the team what happened.*

Steaming pots of stew and ugali, a maize porridge, are being put on the dining table when I walk in. Normally this brings a babble of chatter from the team, but there's an odd feeling in the air I can't work out. Reshma hardly looks at me; she eats and exits quickly to take a sat-phone call from the head of mission in Loki. James shrugs his shoulders at me in an 'I dunno' way, rolling his eyes. After eating silently, we all drift back to our tukuls, where I lie, exhausted and confused, on my squeaky metal bed, staring at mud walls that flicker in candlelight. *Have I done something wrong?* Overstepped the mark during the triplets' birth?

*

When, on the next day, Reshma calls Valerie and me into her office, my chest tightens. Something dreadful has definitely happened.

Reshma's expression is thunderous and we stand in front of her desk like schoolgirls.

'What happened on your flight here?' she says in a very quiet voice.

A moment's silence as our brains search.

Shit!

Valerie's sweet, sincere face looks as if it's been slapped. When her knees go, she sits down heavily on the chair I was going for and ends up perched on my knee. It might have been funny if I hadn't felt like throwing up.

'Is it true that you flew the plane without a pilot?' Reshma couldn't look more aghast.

'Is it?' Reshma glares at us. We nod.

Reshma's glossy ponytail shakes with indignation. Her tirade is short but deadly. Had it escaped our notice that nurses were not pilots? What we'd done was monumentally stupid on so many levels; we'd jeopardised the reputation of MSF and our entire project. We could have killed ourselves and the other passengers (thankfully no patients) on this packed flight. She'd also been in contact with the management in Loki.

'They're talking about terminating your contracts.'

When she says this, I feel like I'm punched in the stomach, though I know she's just doing her job. All the hard work, all the work still to do, and we could lose it all.

'You'll know tomorrow,' she says. 'Go back to work now.'

We nod like schoolgirls and back out of the room.

CHAPTER ELEVEN

During the twenty-four hours it takes to learn our fate, I can't eat or think properly, and my excuses go round on a loop in my head: everyone's boundaries are skewed in this chaotic place, so why not fly the damn plane? Flying was the first fun thing I'd done for months, and I was actually quite good at it; flying was nothing like as hard as managing an acutely unwell baby.

None of these flimsy defences stick. Mostly, I hate myself for being stupid, knowing I made an awful mistake. A public firing would be humiliating, and I really don't want to go home with my tail between my legs. *And then what?*

James, who loves the idea of me being the naughty one for once, says I need to take a 'chill pill'. If I leave, he'll leave with me. We'll commandeer a boat, sail up the Nile and fuck 'em. But I don't want to leave, not now. On the good days, I've started to imagine a career in this type of work – future missions. *This could be my life now.* I'm not sure yet how Jack fits into that idea, or marriage and children, but I do know the elation of saving those triplets gives me an incomparable high, an existence full of meaning, a reason to be here, and I want to hold on to that feeling. All of that will be lost if I get fired now.

Valerie walks around, a shadow of herself, burying her feelings in work.

When Reshma finally calls us into her office, her dark brown eyes narrow as she reminds us that MSF takes its security rules with the utmost seriousness. There's a long pause and we both hold our breath.

'You've been lucky,' she says at last. 'You've fallen through a tiny loophole: MSF's security policy didn't specifically ban nurses from flying the aid plane. It does now.'

I start to breathe again, making a vow to be more serious from now on and concentrate only on work. Reshma goes on to say the head of mission in Loki decided we can keep our jobs, but we'll be under special measures for the next month and report to Reshma daily.

On the following day, every member of MSF staff got an email headed, *Nurses are not Pilots*, which James found hilarious. Jaan, the hot South African pilot, also has his knuckles wrapped by his employers – sort of: he was back in the air the next day. Needs must. Pilots weren't lining up to fly into conflict zones. Neither, I guess, were nurses who were not yet midwives. When Reshma finishes her lecture, Valerie's sent back to the wards.

'Anna, you stay behind,' Reshma says in a quiet voice.

When the door closes, there's a long and fraught silence. Reshma looks as efficient and immaculate as ever, but I can see she hates having to be the 'parent', and I regret putting her in this position. She lines up her pens and clears her throat.

'I've heard rumours about you and the pilot, Anna.' Her frank stare makes me blush like a teenager. 'And I want you to watch him. Yes, I get it – comfort is hard to find here – but he's like that with all the young female staff.' She stops lining up her pens, looks straight at me. 'You do know he has a wife at home?'

I didn't know, and the truth makes my stomach lurch as I start to stammer, 'Good…thank you! I know… I mean nothing happened.'

*

Two weeks later, at the start of September, James and I finally get back to Tam. We're carrying pay packets, medicines, large supplies of mosquito nets and – what I'm most pleased about – the new birth kits. James has also bought a massive pack of toothbrushes as gifts, after he'd seen Stephen using a fraying twig, plus some reading glasses – there are no opticians here. My backpack's stuffed with bright knitted baby hats and donated toys for the poorly children that come to us. It's a joyful reunion: patients lining up on the runway, tears and dances.

Queth, hugging James ecstatically, says, 'You're so fat!' James laughs graciously at the compliment but is secretly mortified. 'Gettin' saggy in my old age,' he whispers to me, after discovering he's twice the weight of Queth. And so we start running.

Running when the temperature is over 45°C, and when you're about to work (or have just finished) a twelve-hour shift, sounds mad. We're both seriously bad at it. James's knees are so arthritic he can hardly rise from his sleeping mat some mornings. At school, I came 75th out of 77 in one cross-country run, only narrowly beating two asthmatics in the bottom placings. But we don't care. Running gets me out of the panic in my head. Running stops me feeling like a caged animal when living in a compound that's roughly 14 x 12 ft.

When I'd crossed paths with Anita, on the runway on our way here, she told me she'd been running too. 'It's like your brain can make sense of your racing heart and chest tightness when you're running – it's exercise, not anxiety.' I was going to miss her now she was on her way home to the UK at the end of her mission. We'd promised to meet up there as soon as we could.

James and I are given permission to run along the half-mile, landmine-free, mud runway. We look an odd pair in our combat trousers and T-shirts. Pad, pad, pad, past herded cattle, past kids with chairs on their heads, past locals pointing and laughing – further evidence that foreign people are very, very, strange.

*

When the pilot-with-a-wife flies us up to Tam, I don't talk to him. I don't talk to him the next time he flies in either. By the third time he lands in our project, he's genuinely the last thing on my mind. Having been awake for forty-eight hours, I'm so tired my mind is slipping its moorings.

John is the reason, the eight-year-old boy who'd turned up under the Waiting Tree. He has huge brown eyes and a sweet face contorted in agony. Two days ago, he was playing in the town tree with his friends when he fell, snapping his femur, which now sticks through his thigh like a splintered branch: a compound fracture. We're almost certain his pelvis is fractured too, a life-threatening injury, even in the most advanced medical facility.

For the past two days, he's been lying in the inpatient tukul writhing, shrieking, pleading, the whites of his eyes showing as he begs for help. We're trying desperately to greenlight him out for surgery, but it rained again this week and the runway is wet and unlandable. Desperate, we've made a cardboard brace around his hips and leg. James, who's since built a log cabin from scratch, is a brilliant improviser, and the brace has gone a small way to reduce John's pain by restricting movement. He's been given antibiotics and as much IV morphine as we can spare, but the blank expression in his mother's eyes show she's already mourning.

Zzzzzzip! After checking on John, I close my tent, no running today. Click! Headtorch off, then James, three feet from me, zips and clicks too. It's boiling hot inside the tent, but I'm fully dressed on top of a cotton sheet, boots beside me, headtorch around my neck – always ready. Only my breath moves in this stifling space. But sleep doesn't come, and when it does, it's not restful, more like being on the twitchy borderlines of sleep and waiting. Our big decision now is how much morphine we can spare for John before supplies run out, and that feels evil when the sweet child is dying in front of us.

'Don't worry, Anna,' James says suddenly out of the darkness. 'He's gunna make it. I'm sure of it.' His deep Californian drawl feels like home.

I know he knows this may not be true. Two nights ago, it rained so hard that it sounded like a pressure hose being trained on the straw roof of the tukul where John's slipping in and out of consciousness. Our tents sag like swollen jellyfish. With the runway still wet, we're basically marooned.

At first I think I'm hallucinating when, on the next day, I hear the distant groan of aircraft propellers. Mud sticks to our feet like thick red porridge as we trudge, confused, to the runway. But wait! There it is again – closer and closer. Above us, a small dual-propeller plane is circling, not our usual big aid plane, and is dropping through the nicotine-coloured sky, scattering birds as it falls. Its wheels touch down, then it slithers and slides through the mud like a drunk trying to avoid a pratfall.

When it comes to an abrupt halt, Jaan jumps out, smiling, not even breaking a sweat from the crazy-dangerous landing. Against all advice, he's come alone to rescue the boy. When he runs towards me, I hug him, crying with relief and gratitude. Anything else that has gone on before between us is forgotten, as I'm relieved that he *is* a pilot that takes risks.

Dashing back, we carefully start to lift John, who's semi-conscious but wakes to scream when he's moved. Within minutes, he's whisked off with his mum in the small plane. Before the plane rises, she shoots one last desperate look back at us – she knows surgery is the only chance of saving her son's life. I wish I could hug her, or connect to her in some way, but I can't. Ten minutes later, the plane is a speck in the sky, then gone.

*

It might work, I write in my diary later that night. *Shit doesn't always have to happen. Hope can thrive.*

When John dies two days later, I'm sucked into the darkest mood yet. Thinking of the mother, I worry about her flying back on her own – she's never been in a plane before, or even out of this town. John's dying shrieks ring in my ears. In a country ravaged by war, this child had simply been playing. He was innocent. They all were.

*

You can't predict where and how the cracks begin to form, especially when you're in the thick of things and there are yet more patients waiting with such incredible patience and dignity under the Waiting Tree. Cracks form so stealthily. You think you're fine, you think you're getting better at coping with the pressures of the job, and in some ways you are, but it was only years later, when I read a book on trauma called *The Body Keeps the Score* that I understood what was shifting inside me; what parts were closing down.

'After trauma,' the author Bessel van der Kolk writes, 'the world becomes sharply divided between those who know, and those who don't. People who have not shared the traumatic experience cannot be trusted. … Sadly, this often includes spouses and children and co-workers.'

James and I mourn John, but I don't mention the boy's death in my letters home or how it made me feel – too sad, too dark. Had I done so, a scornful voice in my head would probably have said, *this is not your drama, it's his, and the mother who'd behaved with such quiet courage.*

Also, I was conscious that if my letters home became misery memoirs, my parents, my friends, might say, *well, just come home, then*. That was the luxury I had.

So I write perky, reassuring letters, thanking everyone for the baby hats and the gifts, telling a funny story. In return, they send sweets and magazines, packets of Marks & Spencer knickers, accounts of weddings and parties and family meals.

Sometimes I gobble up the letters, especially the exciting news that my own sister is now expecting twins, knowing that this pregnancy is safe back home. 'God is very bountiful,' Queth had said when he heard, his bright teeth flashing in a wide smile. Jack has sent a brochure of the hotel in Zanzibar where we'll spend my next R & R together in a couple of months' time; it has large mahogany beds, a swimming pool and cocktail bar. Having been in South Sudan for nearly six months now, I know I'll need the break, but sometimes guiltily admit to myself that I wish I could go with James instead – it would feel so much more normal.

That's because the space between me and home is growing, and sometimes it simply feels too large. A dear friend in Edinburgh writes to complain that her in-laws have offered to pay for landscaping *only half* of their enormous new garden. Although I do love hearing this news, and I want to stay connected to friends, home increasingly feels like a planet or two away. A world where kids don't die from falling out of a tree.

My rock in *this* world is James. We work well together, and on good days take pride in it. Our average caseload of 1,000 patients a month rises and falls, depending on the rains, but by some miracle, we've still had only two more deaths in the clinic: a baby with anaphylaxis after a snake bite, and a boy with complications from cerebral malaria. And now, of course, John.

Whatever's happening inside me, and regardless of the teeth grinding, the lack of periods, outwardly I'm calmer now in emergencies. I know more. When births come to us, I don't always have to scrabble frantically through MSF's obstetric guidelines. Writing in my diary helps, but I also rehearse the protocols every night, like mental worry beads, as a way of relaxing before going to sleep. Years later I'll still do this, unconsciously. They're engraved on my heart and mind.

I'm getting through.

*

When the rains stop, Jaan and Elijah fly in about once a month with medical supplies. It's Jaan who hands me the hessian sack full of letters and sweets. One day he quietly slips a handwritten note into my back pocket, along with a packet of Smarties.

'I can't help thinking about you,' written in a neat, schoolboyish hand. He's gone as quickly as he came, an urgent patient loaded onboard, leaving me winded and a bit giddy. The next time, he brings a bottle of Amarula, an African liqueur made from the fruit of the marula tree. It doesn't feel like cheating, as I have no intention of kissing him. Plus, now Reshma's opened my eyes to him being a well-known flirt, it feels somehow safe to enjoy these moments because they don't mean anything.

Even so, his smile, this sense of still being a desirable woman, is something and I start to feel excited when I hear the rumble of a plane arriving. It gives me something to look forward to.

CHAPTER TWELVE

I'm not proud of this, looking back it seems stupid, but once, when I was working in the ED in Nottingham, I walked around for two weeks on a broken ankle. A fractured talus, to be specific. One day, I actually hobbled down the corridor towards the X-ray department, pushing the wheelchair of a patient who turned out only to have a sprain. It was a doctor friend, who saw me with my foot up in the staff room, who said I should get it checked, the bruises looked wrong. When the X-ray confirmed I actually had a fracture, he said I must have a high pain threshold, and maybe I have. But a less flattering explanation might be I'm slow to notice when things go wrong, which may go some way to explain why it was such a shock to spin out of control and feel surrounded by darkness just before my next R & R two months later.

Zanzibar itself was perfect: a room with a dark mahogany bed and red velvet curtains that parted to reveal a sapphire-coloured sea; a power-shower with proper hot water, sweet-smelling soaps and lotions; spice markets; bubbling chatter in narrow alleyways; dhow fishing boats gliding through blood-red sunsets; Jack, wet from the shower, beautiful with his tousled hair and skin turning brown. It was me that was all wrong.

We meet at Dar es Salaam airport in Tanzania. He seems excited, nervous, his first time in Africa. I'm nervous too. At one time I'd felt like a seasoned traveller, and in 2005 I'd climbed to the summit of Mount Kilimanjaro with a friend before travelling alone to Zambia for a short hospital work experience. Now, standing in this foreign airport on holiday makes me feel unexpectedly exposed and missing the strict MSF security rules. We hug. I remember that much. I'm pleased to see him, but the rest of that first day is a blur to me, even my diary talks only of Tam.

Our pattern for the week is set the next day, as I walk out of our hotel to the beach, leave a small pile of beach towel and sun cream, then step into the beautiful warm waters. Hours are spent either floating alone and amoeba-like on my back, or swimming long distances to get my body moving again. Being immersed in water is my first sense of true release for months. I want to be in the water all day.

Jack sits on the beach, under a palm tree, reading a book. A history of the island, I think, though I can't exactly recall. From time to time, we wave at each other. One day, we go into the hills on a spice trail, to see how cloves are grown. Jack's suggestion, and my heart aches for him. He's doing everything right, but I'm not even trying to talk to him about this stuff going on in my head any more. At night I go into the bathroom and look in the mirror, hoping to recognise my face. Out of the water, I'm overwhelmed, and silent. The worst travel companion ever.

On our last evening, we're eating a seafood platter and drinking white wine at a restaurant overlooking the harbour. A dhow is sliding across the horizon as he says quietly, 'When are you coming home?'

And I feel the hurt in my gut, as I'm the one who makes him look so wary.

I take a larger than usual sip of wine. Most nights we're getting through at least a bottle, which after teetotal-Tam is a lot. The wine helps fill our silence around not having any sex, but also numbs the dreams that my antimalarials make so vivid. In one recurring nightmare, the boy John pleads with me to help him; in another I see Eve's body opening its eyes while still wrapped like a mummy; in others I'm running and running towards a faceless emergency in which I'm never the heroine.

'I don't know yet.'

Knowing he's too kind to push me, knowing I've extended my assignment in South Sudan but haven't had the guts to tell him yet.

He takes my hand and squeezes it, still with that look on his face as if trying to read my thoughts, and suddenly I'm so sick of myself: my prevarication, my pain-in-the-arse moods, when he's trying so hard. Our lack of sex must hurt, when once it had all seemed so right. *We used to have such fun together.*

He pours another inch of wine. 'Don't look so sad, Anna,' he says. 'Tell me a funny story.'

My voice falters and I can't tell him the story I want to tell him. The one that might save us. The one that explains why I've been spinning out of control, and feel so angry at him, which is unfair because this really isn't his fault; except it was, partly.

It had happened a week ago, when I was working in Leer before my flight out. We'd had a ridiculously busy day at the hospital, and unusually, desperately, I'd phoned Jack on the sat-phone after it was over, because I needed a rope to cling to.

On that day, queues of patients needing admission had stretched from IPD all the way to outpatients, hundreds of them. I was tired, freaked out too from the black mamba snake that had slithered past my foot as I crouched to assess a child in the 'ward under the trees'.

Maybe I should've taken the day off, but there was no one else to cover me, and the patients kept coming.

'Another child with diarrhoea,' I'd said to Peter, a diligent Sudanese nurse working with me at the triage, before instructing him to record the child's temperature, heart rate and respirations on the patient card.

'Send for stool sample and admit to the children's tent.' We handed out soap and a mosquito net to the mother, then the nurses would check on them every four hours.

The next child had malaria. And the next pneumonia. The list went on, making us feel like we were firefighting a blaze with only a sprinkler. This felt like a frontline.

'Next please.'

The next child was Mariam, just two or three years old, with a slightly sunken fontanelle and diarrhoea. Although she was mildly dehydrated, her observations were normal and there wasn't a fever or rash. She was alert, able to eat and breastfeed.

'OK, find her somewhere in the ward under the trees, check on her every two hours and tell mum to let us know if anything changes. I'll try and check on them all before we go back later,' I'd said, before calling the next patient in a still long queue,

That night, exhausted, I'd collapsed onto my squeaky bed, but as I closed my eyes, a wave of dread washed over me – like I'd forgotten something.

'Cccchhhhhhhttt…'

The on-call walkie-talkie, clutched in my hand, woke me with loud static.

'Anna! Come to IPD. Baby Mariam. Very sick.'

My memory of the next bit plays out in my head like a silent film, one I've since replayed maybe a thousand times, often painfully pretending the outcome is different. But the silent scene moves too fast: I'm scrambling out of my mosquito net, jumping into the awaiting 4 x 4, the solemn guard opening the gate. Screaming at the driver to go faster, I'm thrown across the passenger seat as we hit mound after mound of mud hard as rock. Running alone to the IPD, headtorch on to avoid stamping on the endless number of sick and dying patients being nursed on the floor. There's a light on in the IPD surrounded by a thousand flying insects. Mariam lies under it, collapsed across her mother's legs. Her fontanelle looks deep in the feeble night light, mouth gaping open, eyes sunken back. Peter, the nurse, is trying desperately to insert an IV. He tries her arms, legs, head. He's our best at this, but her veins have totally shut down. She's stopped breathing. I'm shouting for the intraosseous (IO) kit we keep for emergencies. Now I'm pumping on her tiny breastbone to give CPR – we don't have a defibrillator out here. Our only hope is to rehydrate her, correct electrolyte imbalance with IV, keep her heart going.

The next bit plays out in my mind in painful slow motion: I'm shouting instructions, how many breaths, how many chest compressions for an infant. Peter is back with the IO, a massive needle, which in dire emergency we must stick right through the bone and into the bone marrow to administer IV meds. *It's our only hope.* Choosing the proximal tibia (the front of her lower leg), it's a procedure I'd been taught on a trauma course a couple of years before, and it goes through her bone more easily than I anticipated. She didn't feel it, she's unconscious, but it's in and it's too late.

I keep doing chest compressions until Peter says, 'It is time to stop.'

And then the mother's wail. She crouches over Mariam, dead beneath her. The same cry I'd heard outside the Nottingham ED when a kid was killed by a hit-and-run driver.

Next come my questions: *why didn't I review her before I went to bed? Why didn't the mum tell us she wasn't breastfeeding any more?* When I close my eyes, Mariam will always be there. Flopped in her mother's arms, being carried back to the family tukul for burial, her dad asking politely to borrow a spade.

When I got back to the living compound, I felt dreadful asking James to finish my on-call, but hand him the walkie-talkie. He'd offered some words of comfort that I don't remember. Did I shower? Have some water? I don't know, but I do know I tried to call Jack. Needing a lifeline back home as I was scared and mentally spinning out of control. I think he answered, but said he was in a meeting. Of course, I can't blame him, how was he to know? He was busy. *We were planets away.*

My next memory is of lying on my bed. It was out in the courtyard – dry season was starting and the Leer tukuls were too hot to sleep in now. Under my mosquito net I was staring up at the stars, feeling unbearable grief and completely responsible for the death. Wanting to disappear, to run away, but there was nowhere to go. Then it got really wacky, as in the next moment I was watching myself up among the stars, I was made of stars in a bizarre art nouveau version of myself, touching the stars. Each movement of my arms left a twinkling spray of stardust. I wasn't asleep or awake, but had entered another world, born of stress, where I couldn't feel anything. There in the stars I watched myself move until I finally fell asleep.

*

More wine. The Zanzibar night growing dark between the red velvet curtains. Sea lapping outside. Jack takes my hand and asks again for a funny story, so I snap myself back to the conversation. Trying to bury the memory of the debrief that followed the death of Mariam, how the team assured me it wasn't my fault that she'd died. How little comfort that gave me. But I know now that every aid worker has a patient they carry in their conscience.

Let me think. Ah, yes, I do have a funny story: a new, true snake story.

'Two weeks ago, I was in the bucket shower in Tam when: BANG! BANG! BANG!'

Saying this too loudly, the kissing couple at the next table jump and look at us.

'Gunshots! Loud gunshots! Really close by.'

My ears were pounding as I grabbed my towel from the stick fence, trying to cover myself as I crawled through the mud to James's tent. *Get to the ground, cover your head*, just as we had been shown on my MSF preparation course.

'James!' I'd called, but he was still having a lunchtime snooze. 'Gunshots!'

'Is that a frog?' he asked drowsily.

'Gunshots!' I'd hissed again.

Jack hasn't smiled yet; maybe this wasn't such a good story after all.

I censor the next bit, how, half-naked, I'd crawled into James's tent, put my muddied, towelled body next to him. BANG! Another shot fired.

'Shit,' James had said, grabbing his glasses, 'what the fuck?'

Hearts galloping, the few seconds we lay together waiting for the next shot felt like an eternity. Then suddenly we heard Stephen laughing, calling to us and telling us not to worry.

Jack's expression shows he isn't finding this story anything like as funny as I do. My voice is faltering, like a bad comedian.

'The man in the next tukul had found a red cobra while he was fixing his roof! We saw it!' I pause while the waiter fills our glasses. 'It was a dark red cobra missing its head, over a metre long and thick as a Coke can. The proud slayer was standing over it with an AK-47 slung over his shoulder.' I wish I could stop now.

'So how dangerous is a red cobra?' Jack's expression is guarded, like I'm another wild animal.

'It's venomous, known for its ability to permanently disfigure people.'

'Wow!' I see distance in Jack's eyes; he doesn't want to visit this planet I'm from.

But I still think I can make him laugh.

James, who tried to find love in all sentient beings, looked at this headless snake on a pole and said, 'Poor thing – probably only wanted to find some shelter.' And then, 'Actually, screw that, I'm glad it's dead.'

'Ha!' Neither of us can think of a thing to say next. When the pudding menu comes, we both study it like an exam paper. It's only nine o'clock. *Is it too early to go to bed?* When we lock eyes suddenly, I know I should either tell him, or leave him. I can't do this for much longer and I suddenly feel like I'm spinning out of control again as pressure builds in my chest and my heart rate soars. And this was the missed moment. The moment when I should have said, *ask me now and I'll tell you*.

Because the next bit of the story would confuse him more. After the snake was killed, James and I went back to look at it again, half-eaten by a vulture. Both admitting how terrified we'd felt as the shots rang out, but then standing in a silence as we looked over a horizon of tukuls.

'But look at all we have here,' James had said.

I'd followed his gaze over the fence and across the runway, where children were playing with kites made from sticks and old plastic bags. The sun was setting, making the earth glow all around us, and in that moment I felt we had all we needed.

CHAPTER THIRTEEN

When I got back to Tam, I poured my heart out to James. Telling him what a horrible and unsatisfying girlfriend I'd become and how I was still angry because Jack hadn't responded about baby Mariam on the night I'd tried to call him. I knew how unfair that was.

'Did you even try and explain any of that?' James asked. He was fixing the hinge on our supply chest at the time. 'Or did that jolly old British stiff upper lip come into play?'

Wiping his screwdriver, he carefully put it back in its cover.

'I tried, but neither of us are very good at that sort of thing,' I said, drawing patterns in the mud with a twig. It strikes me that in South Sudan I am desperate for women to open up to me about their lives, yet I'm struggling to do that with someone I'm in a relationship with, who speaks the same langauge as me. Concerned, James gazed at me for a while.

'You're getting better, you're talking to me.' He gave a little huffing laugh, stroking his handlebar moustache. 'And I've had some pretty shit holidays like that myself,' he said. 'Trying to be the person I once was when that person is gone. It's one of the toughest things about this job.'

He sat back on his heels. 'But listen, because this is important: in a couple of months you'll be going home, and you have to know this. You didn't kill baby Mariam; it was *everyone* in the world's fault. A million events that we had no control over led up to her death. We have to—'

I cut him off mid-sentence: 'Do our best? I don't agree with you, James. It's not always enough to just *do our best*. That wouldn't be acceptable in the UK, so it's not here. If I'd done more for Mariam, maybe…'

James picked up his toolkit. 'Go down that route,' he said quietly, 'and you'll drive yourself crazy. When we bear witness to these important lives, that has meaning too, *especially* for the ones we can't save.'

More silence.

'But bearing witness hurts,' my voice cracking as I say it. There's so much I still can't tell him.

*

After nine months here, as I get to the end of my mission, I'm really frustrated that most of the women I treat are still such a mystery to me. Knowing so little about their hopes, their marriages, their lives. It's strange to know so little when I meet them at moments of such intensity, such intimacy. We're told that local villages have large tukuls where women and children live together, and another tukul for the men and cattle, but I don't know if this is the case for everyone, or where the pregnancies are conceived. One small victory is that all pregnant women coming through our clinic now get a birth kit with basic essentials, but I don't know if they're being used for their intended purposes.

MSF's no socialising rule, plus the many communication barriers, make it hard to go deeper, though I yearn to. What I do see and marvel at is their astonishing stoicism, their beauty – even the poorest come to our clinic dressed with panache. Women like Angela, who turns up at the clinic each morning, regal and smiling, her slender neck unbowed by the gallons of heavy water she carries on her head. She's a wonder to me.

And actually, I don't get it: on paper, the story of women in South Sudan in 2007 is one of almost complete powerlessness. Forced and child marriage is common here – 46 per cent of women with no education marry before their eighteenth birthday. We recently treated a thirteen-year-old with gonorrhoea, and another horrendous day in Leer caring for two sisters raped by their uncle.

Polygamy is reported as common, but only in the form of a man being allowed to have multiple wives, and not the other way round. Often, it seems, men are encouraged by their leaders to have as many children as they can, despite South Sudan having one of the highest infant mortality rates in the world.

These women run households, but have little decision-making power, and close to zero opportunities outside the home, thanks to the wars and lack of education. Elizabeth, another clinic cleaner, arrived at work more than once with a black eye, but refused to tell me what was happening. If it is domestic violence, there's no support system to refer her to, no rehab for her alcoholic husband, no safe house. It's a bleak irony that staying in an abusive marriage may be Elizabeth's safest option.

But one curious thing I've noticed is that although most women here appear docile and accepting of their lot, a certain kind of pseudo-seizure is strangely accepted as normal. We've seen it a few times in all the medical projects; the woman collapsing to the floor, moaning and writhing, eyes rolling wildly for no discernible medical reason. Although these 'seizures' are essentially being acted, whether the woman is aware of that or not, it's an extremely sad and disturbing sight – like watching the pressure cooker finally explode. The event gets labelled as 'fitting', which buys her forty-eight hours of rest in our inpatient tukul with no questions asked from the husband. Other women come to sit by her side in quiet prayer, mopping her brow and spoon-feeding her food, until she eventually stands up and starts walking home. We're all left hurting as we bear witness to this, but can offer only brief respite.

*

When Nyawik arrives at dusk with her husband Riak, she's a snapshot of the price you pay for being powerless.

Riak looks about twenty years older than her, a scowling man, with prominent scar marks on his cheeks. Our clinic's closed when they arrive, the chairs under the Waiting Tree folded and James has just begun to chop onions for our lentil soup. We direct Nyawik to the outpatient tukul, help her into the rusty old dentist's chair, the one I find so useful now. She's breathing fast but at least she's conscious and alert.

Stephen, our exceptional CHW, does the usual basic assessment with a cluster of mosquitoes buzzing around his light, and talks me through his findings. My trust in him is now a given, and his in me. I no longer feel shy or tentative when I teach him, and I constantly learn from him in return. Taking his head away from the Pinard stethoscope being held against the woman's abdomen, he states accurately:

'Thirty-six weeks pregnant. Swollen ankles, very high blood pressure, headache and blurred vision.' Then adds, 'Good baby movements and heart rate. No bleeding. I suggest severe pre-eclampsia.' He smiles gently at Nyawik.

'Sounds right.' I try not to sound as worried as I feel. Severe pre-eclampsia is an emergency, with several possible awful outcomes including stillbirth, seizures and death. The only cure is birth.

Anger and futility boil silently inside me. Had this woman had access to a midwife in pregnancy, the eclampsia could've been picked up earlier with routine blood pressure and urine checks. Now it's life-threatening, but I don't have time to dwell on this, so I push those feelings deep inside. Instead, we work fast, we're slick. Leer is called for a greenlight medevac as Nyawik needs IV drugs we don't have, and possibly an emergency caesarean section.

'Your wife is very ill. She needs help fast.' I look directly at Riak, while Stephen translates my words. Riak nods silently and asks no questions, seeming to understand all the information, but how the hell do I know? He doesn't talk to Nyawik.

When it becomes clear there's no chance of a flight to Leer until the next morning, I try to reassure myself; the baby's still moving, there's no sign of premature labour and Nyawik's blood pressure is responding well to the medications we do have. But the situation is a ticking time bomb. Full eclampsia is so unpredictable, so dangerous, but I have no idea whether Nyawik and Riak understand this or not.

*

'So how's your family, Kent?' James asks in a conversational voice later that night, after our slow jog. I know, at least I think I know, why he's doing this. We talk at night for fun, for relief, but tonight to stay awake and do hourly checks on Nyawik. Yawning, I start to tell him something mundane, but this time he wants more.

'Tell me some real stuff about your family,' he says at last. 'Were your parents heroin addicts too?'

Chuckling, I think of Dad at his train enthusiasts' meetings, of Mum, gardening and pouring tea for her knitting circle. The warmth and the gentleness.

'What? Of course not! I had a very normal childhood, and I mean that as a compliment.'

'Then why are you here, Anna Banana? What are *you* atoning for?'

Reeling out the tried and tested, I tell him about being shocked as a child by TV footage of starvation in Ethiopia, how I'd wanted to help, somehow.

'Yeah, yeah, I know all that.' He sounds unusually impatient. 'Everyone's moved by news of starving kids, right? They stuff a dollar bill in the charity box, they don't risk losing their leg on a landmine out here.

'Tell me why you're *really* here.' There's a long, long silence.

I feel the old breathlessness of secrets locked in my chest. *You don't have to say.*

Instead, I say another true thing, but not *the* thing. How, during my training, I'd loved emergency work the best, inspired by the smart and dynamic nurses. How we'd seen the worst injuries – shootings, stabbings, car crashes, sexual assault. How being able to help in those awful moments felt like a kind of privilege. Did that make sense? It also left nothing to be so scared about.

'Sure.' I hear the nylon swish of him changing places in his tent.

'What were you scared of before then?' he asks with unusual delicacy.

'...'

Words seem to stick in my throat. There are things I want to say, but I'm scared to talk, scared that if I open up the box locked inside my heart for the last seven years, all the rest of the mess and guilt will come tumbling out uncontrollably.

'My brother's girlfriend was murdered.'

When the sentence blurts out, I think someone else might have said it. 'She was on a train heading home, a student, but a serial killer was on the same train. I think he raped her too, or maybe tried. They found her body on the railway track – he'd thrown her off.'

'Oh, fuck! Are you OK with this?'

'I don't know. I've never really said it before.' My voice sounds strangled.

The truth was that it had never felt like my story to tell. I didn't know my brother's girlfriend very well, and he, private in his grief, had never spoken to me about it. It was incredibly scary for me to be so close to such a violent crime, but I didn't want or feel I should get attention for it, so I became silent, like it was a secret.

And here's the thing: I'd been shocked by kids starving on TV because it meant awful things could happen in the world. But when someone close to your family is murdered, it means the threat is at the door. Realisation hit that awful things can happen to those I love, *and to me*. Although it felt dreadfully confusing, selfish even, to think of myself in the wake of someone else's death.

'Where were you then?'

'I was eighteen years old.' I can feel my throat tighten, just as it had when I got the news. 'I had just started living in university halls, a first-year nursing student, surrounded by strangers, but wanting to make new friends.'

'Oh, boy.'

'For a few days it was on the national TV news every night.' I remembered her face appearing on the screen in the common room while I chatted to a new friend, the newsreader stating how she was a missing person. How I'd carried on nodding with a frozen smile as the story unfolded and it became clear it was a murder investigation. My eyes flicking to and from the screen, not knowing what to say, before making my excuses to leave as a re-enactment of her body being thrown from the train came on. I'd only been at uni for two weeks; who could I trust with something so personal?

'What did it do to you?'

'I guess it made me hyper-alert, scared of pretty much everything – going out to clubs, taking a taxi. All the things you're expected to do as a fresher at uni. Even walking across campus alone felt impossible. For a while I even considered carrying a rock in my bag, though God knows what I thought I'd do with it.'

'Oh, fuck's sake, Anna. Did they catch the guy?'

'Eventually. He'd murdered two other women; they found the body of one of them in his cellar. Killed himself while in custody.'

Staring at the circle of canvas my torch lights up, I'm remembering how tiring it was feeling scared all the time. How, after a while, I couldn't stand it, and later drinking, partying, sex became ways to escape the fear, or at least pushed it far, far down. These escapes seemed to numb the sense of vulnerability, though this was an illusion – in the end it made everything feel worse.

'I worked hard at my studies too – really hard – anything to stop feeling anxious.'

That was when I started to choose the most extreme clinical areas. Weirdly wanting to see the worst scenarios because I wanted to believe there was always something that could be done to make it a tiny bit better. Even if it was giving bad news to relatives, if you could do it in a way that absolved them of any unnecessary burden, it made the world seem slightly less scary for me.

'Did you ever speak to your brother about it?'

'No. Not really. I didn't know how to. I still haven't.'

'Aw, Christ.'

And suddenly I'm holding back tears as it dawns on me why James had used the word 'atonement'. I'm wishing I had said or done something helpful to my brother in his time of grief. And understanding too, for the first time, why helping vulnerable women feels so important to me, and had become my specialist interest both clinically, and emotionally. *I hadn't been able to help her.*

And maybe too my work was guided by how *I* would want to be treated if the worst-case scenario happened to me. I still held that sense of vulnerability simply because I was a woman.

'Did you ever talk about it to anyone?' he asks, bemused.

'No, not really.'

With some sense of epiphany, I realise that after the murder of my brother's girlfriend, my default had become *not* to talk about traumatic events. In my former emergency department, we'd witness dreadful injuries, see awful crimes, and yet to Jack I'd just deflect it with a two-line story, then go out drinking and dancing. If I could bury these painful feelings, I thought they would somehow disappear. But James has dug up the box and opened the lid on this, just as he had with my first expressions of anger.

There was so much to think about when life broke in. Stephen's voice, shrill in the quiet night air, called:

'Anna! James! Come quick, please. Emergency!'

*

When we reach the space between the clinic tukuls, an odd and disturbing scene is unfolding. Nyawik stands in a dim circle of light, frozen like a theatre actor before the curtains come up. Her husband glowers down at her like an angered Zeus. Holding up my kerosene lamp, I expect to see a birth emergency, but there's no blood on her legs. She's not showing signs of pain. If anything, she looks slightly better than she did an hour ago, except her shoulders are stooped, she's staring at the floor as if in disgrace. Riak starts to push her from behind. His silhouette in the half-light is large and oppressive.

Something's very, very wrong here. Stephen has his hands up in submission, as if Riak is holding him at gunpoint, though there are no weapons here. With his eyes trained on Riak, Stephen says slowly, carefully to James and me:

'The husband is going to take Nyawik home to a traditional doctor. He does not want her to fly to Leer.'

Processing this, my brain starts to fizz. As calmly as I can humanly manage, I ask Stephen to explain again to the husband that Nyawik and the baby will probably die without medical help. The anger I've learnt to express will not help here.

Shouting loudly over me, the husband blocks my words; he doesn't want to hear anything I have to say. When James repeats the same warning; the man momentarily appears to listen. Outraged, I want to scream in the face of misogyny, but hold my tongue.

'He does not want to fly with this wife,' Stephen says, his head bowed, 'He has another wife and children in his village. He will not leave them.'

Tentatively, I suggest Nyawik could take her sister with her instead of him? Or the whole family could travel together, or even her alone? Or, at the very least, we could keep her admitted in our Tam clinic to keep her blood pressure down, to keep the baby safe. Tactfully, Stephen tries to get the message across, but Riak won't listen. He puts his head down like a bull about to charge, frowns and shakes his head. James tries a new angle: with the right medications, it's still possible to deliver a healthy baby, maybe it would be a boy. But Riak is looking at Nyawik with disgust, like she's the worst investment he's ever made. She hangs her head in shame.

In a last desperate plea, I bow my head and with a look of submission, try to reach Nyawik to hold her hand, to plead with her to stay in the clinic even if her husband leaves. Refusing to meet my eyes, she is the first to walk away. Her husband follows, pushing her from behind. A few moments later, they're swallowed by darkness.

After they leave, my knees give way.

'What can we do?' I'm squatting in the mud. 'Call the police? Arrest him? Send staff to her tukul?'

Stephen looks stricken, but shakes his head. Apparently, the man is a tribal leader, he allegedly has armed workers, he's untouchable. If we try to pursue them, it could be dangerous for us and the clinic.

This is so screwed up. I know we can't risk the hundreds of people each month we do save, but we came so close to saving her. Traditional 'witch doctors' probably won't help either; all the good ones – who knew the land and its healing herbs – have been lost in the years of fighting. Unless she's very lucky, her fate rests now in the hands of the con artists, pedalling fake hope and expired medicine vials they have no training in using.

James, in a rare moment of rage, throws his Stetson into the mud.

'Goddam bastard fucking men!'

Stephen looks haunted. His eyes seem to sink into his head. This isn't the first time he's witnessed such scenes; it wouldn't be the last. We saw men leading their women away time and again in South Sudan.

'Agh!' I shout with venomous hate into the dark. Hate towards Riak and his pig-headedness. Hate for his lethal disrespect for women. Hate for the man who murdered my brother's girlfriend.

'I'm sorry,' I silently mouth. *Another woman I couldn't save.*

Nyawik, whose name means 'gift'.

CHAPTER FOURTEEN

I am preparing for my end of mission in Tam. It's an unofficial MSF rule that you stay in the field for less than a year in your first project, but leaving hurts. Realistically, I know I can't lead the rest of my life in a conflict zone – that I'm tired to my core and my antimalarial-fuelled dreams are more disturbing than ever. I still have no periods – I don't for the next year. But there are other health issues too: the thorn I've had in my ankle since I arrived is full of pus, even though I thought I'd got it all out ten months ago; the unattractive skin fungus on my chest that looks like athlete's foot. I don't think of these things as a problem, just part of life here.

Tam has become the bad boyfriend you know you have to leave. Tam is the end of a long hospital shift when you feel guilty about leaving a patient who needs you. Tam is people I love, the closest friends of my life. Tam is the miniature world where I feel safer now than in the big world outside.

But it's difficult to survive this kind of work without being obsessive, and handing over is hard. Before my replacement arrives, my internal dukes are up. She'd better not dare criticise our dentist's chair, with its sprouting foam and rusty joints, or our string IVs, or forget to order the paediatric version of paracetamol, as it's so hard to grind the adult tablets down and weigh out the right amount. Or question our shortcuts, our compromises. I'm ridiculously petty when I think James had better not like her more than me.

Her name is Lindy, twenty-five years old, a well-qualified nurse from Toronto with four years' experience. When I see her name on paper, I imagine a prom-queen type with an insincere smile. But Lindy – big hair, big smile – is bouncy and sweet, and hard not to like. 'Hi, hi, hi,' she says as she gets off the plane, walking towards us with her arms out, in her pristine white MSF T-shirt. It's mine that's now covered in mud-dust and ripped at the collar. Now she's real, I'm surprised by how relieved I feel.

James is staying on for a few more months. He's as buoyant as the day I met him, which is probably why he seems exempt from the one-year rule. Regardless of the craziness and the terror, he meditates for at least one hour every day.

'You must meditate for an hour every day,' he would tell me, 'unless you're really busy, then do it for two. Ha!'

Now, when I hear 'om' sounds emanating from his tent, it's a reassuringly sturdy sound, like the hum of a good generator, or running water, not a worryingly flaky, New Agey sound. I can see it keeps him sane, grounded.

Equanimity. Sometimes, with the air of a man inhaling a particularly fine wine, he says this word as horrific events unfold around us. It's his talisman, his worry bead, his way of settling himself for the fray. Sounds ridiculous? I thought so too, until I totally lost my inner balance and said it to myself in the mirror. I still do when I need to.

It's James who looks at me over our last bean stew together. I've grown sad about things left undone. In particular, I'm frustrated that we haven't managed to set up a full vaccination programme in Tam, as we still don't have the ability to keep stored vaccines refrigerated out here, and this feels like a massive failure. James tells me I must make peace with the limitations and take home some memories of good things done here.

'All pregnant women here now get a birth kit. Not only that, you've been responsible for the care of thousands of people, and your teaching will continue beyond your time here. We've saved lives, lots of lives... You've also grown as a person before my eyes... You know yourself more now.'

He stops suddenly, gives me a look from those piercingly blue eyes.

'I couldn't have wished for a better partner,' he says, 'now shut the fuck up and peel that onion.'

*

Just today, James showed his diagnostic brain was as sharp as ever when a man called Majak came to the clinic. Four other men carried him on a stretcher knocked together from sticks, with a sarong tied between them. There was a buzz about him, as if he was important, though he looked terrible, naked except for some material tied around his middle, his belly massively distended, sweat dripping from his skinny face. Stephen and I helped him into the dentist's chair. When I felt his forehead, the seven tribal lines carved into the skin burned like hot craters. After multiple tests, and much discussion and deliberation between Stephen and me, it was James who swooped in:

'Pretty sure that's kala azar.'

Kala azar, or visceral leishmaniasis as its officially known, is a disease spread by sandfly bites. After malaria, it's the second biggest parasitic killer, and almost always fatal without treatment, but it's widely ignored because it's expensive and complicated to treat. James got on the phone to arrange a greenlight to Leer, and Majak will fly out on the same plane with me tomorrow. In Leer, a blood test will confirm the diagnosis, and he'll start the month-long treatment of IV AmBisome, and probably make a full recovery.

Bags of fresh clothes and sheets for Majak's medevac had arrived minutes later; water came in dried-out gourds, parcels of food and flatbreads wrapped in material. This speed and efficiency was wonderful to see, but made me feel crushed to think of Nyawik, who was denied any health care at all. It was so unfair.

*

On my very last evening, Stephen brings a big Nile perch to roast on an open fire. I have no idea how he sourced it, but it's fresh and tender, expertly prepared by Mary our clinic cleaner. It might sound small, but it's a massive gift when you have limited money. With the sun setting on a scorching, bone-dry day, sparks from the fire reach up into a sky the colour of a blood orange. When it grows dark and millions of stars are out, James drains his can of Coke (another treat) and entertains Lindy with a story of a tall, blonde Swedish woman he met in Israel in the 1970s.

'She walks right up to me and asks me to cover her naked body with fruit and lick it off her. Sure, I said.' He mimes his nonchalant shrug, his debonair smile. 'Years later, when Facebook starts, we make contact again. I have these lovely memories of her, and she's still dreaming 'bout me giving her pleasure, except now, when she turns up, she is morbidly obese.' Long silence. 'It cost me a lot in fruit.' The punchline expertly timed.

Lindy's deep, proper belly laugh is such a relief to me. I'd been scared she'd turn around and fly off at the sight of Tam. I'm not so sure how much Queth understands the anecdote, or if he just likes to see us having fun, but his horizontal teeth are out and he slaps his long, gangly legs.

I'm laughing too, but the sight of Stephen raking over the dying coals, of Mary covering the fish bones in dust, gives me an ache inside as if I'm handing over one of the most precious gifts of my life. I must never forget their patience, their dignity, how little they expected and got from the universe.

'What's next, Kent?' James looks at me fondly over the embers after the rest of the staff have wandered back to their tukuls.

'I don't know,' I say with a big sigh. Everything in my life to date had been pointed to coming here, so I honestly hadn't given much thought to what would come next. Marriage and babies had been the vague idea, but now *I don't know*.

'I've been thinking about training as a midwife...' Those words hang in the air as the fire goes out and we're left surrounded in total blackness.

'I think you should,' says James softly.

*

When the plane comes on my last day, Majak is loaded aboard for his greenlight, and more friends gather, Mary and Angela's ululating high-pitched notes mingling with the sounds of the engine roar. When they hug me, I cry. Tears of thanks. Of love.

A romantic end to Tam, right? Except seconds before the plane takes off, Stephen comes running after me.

'Anna! Anna! Wait! One more question.'

'Of course.' I'm expecting a last clinical query: an antibiotic regime maybe?

'We've all been asking! Please tell us! Are you a boy or a girl?'

He's serious. After ten months in Tam, Stephen and the rest of the crew have absolutely no clue of my sex or gender.

'I'm a *nyakawai* [white or foreign woman],' I say, trying to keep the hurt out of my voice.

'Ah! OK. Great news!' and he joyously runs off.

I can laugh now looking back. I'd ticked none of their 'female' boxes. First, I can't be a woman working in a foreign country with a single man. My long hair gives no clue either, as all the Sudanese women I've met have naturally short hair. I have a little moustache hair and some underarm hair, while all the women here seem to be naturally free of body hair. I'm pretty flat chested, whereas many women in South Sudan have big breasts, and I wear combat trousers most of the time. There was so much I didn't understand about Tam, but in return, so much was misunderstood about me.

So yes, funny looking back, but at the time it's a further knock to my self-esteem, because my body isn't behaving like a natural woman, so maybe he's right?

I almost don't tell Jaan, who's in the cockpit. When I do, he nearly falls off his chair laughing. Beneath us the vast stretch of flat soil is running out.

'I think you're beautiful,' he says, and I glow a little, I can't help it.

'And I bet you could do with a beer.' He glances at me as the Waiting Tree, and all it held, disappears over the horizon. 'So let's take you home.'

CHAPTER FIFTEEN

Nothing has changed in my childhood bedroom. On the bedside table is the mushroom light I won when I was four, as a clown in a fancy-dress competition. Mr Ted, my bear, is on the same chair. The curtains I chose aged five are the same hectic pink and orange flowered ones, though faded now. On the top shelf, my sixth form friends and I, giddy with relief after A level results, are frozen in time, clutching each other and making silly faces for the camera.

Mum's making me fish pie for supper – my favourite. Through the floorboards, I hear the whirr and thump of her food processor, the clink and clank of pans, the low hum of Radio 4, once the most soothing sound in the world to me, except I feel like I'm spinning out of control again and I don't want my parents to know – I don't want to worry them.

When I broke up with Jack I'd only been in the UK for a week, so came back to my childhood home in Shropshire to try and work out what the hell I'm going to do next.

Outside, the garden has a sleeping look about it, with the plants cut back, the bushes shrouded and the misty Welsh hills beyond. It's March 2008 and hasn't stopped raining for three days. This afternoon, although the ground is hard and cold, I've been out in the garden digging as if to save my life. Amy Winehouse is blasting in my headphones, her lyrics of 'Back to Black' perfectly describing the turmoil I feel about having to say goodbye to Tam, but unable to truly let go.

Digging is my attempt to stop my thoughts circling obsessively around the trail of wreckage I left behind in South Sudan. Baby Mariam, Eve and Nyawik were my crosses to bear. I could've saved them, and I didn't – I'll never stop blaming myself for that. I see Mariam's fragile ribcage in my dreams; trying to get the big needle in, the sound her mother made when it was clear she wasn't going to make it.

Passing my mum on the stairs as I head back to bed, she gives me a troubled look. Since I got home, I've been as inarticulate and quiet as when I was a puberty-angst teenager. Watching me digging, running, sleeping, I can see my parents have no idea how to bridge this gap. They're scared I'll either bite their heads off or become even more sullen. It's embarrassing to be acting like this: to jump from being in a position of such responsibility to this morose woman-child lying on her bed all day, especially when I'd been so stubborn about wanting to join MSF. Going to South Sudan, leaving Jack, *these were my choices*, I remind myself angrily, *so get a grip and shut up*.

'Glass of wine, Sausage?' Dad calls up the stairs as evening sets in.

'In a bit, Dad, thanks.'

I stretch out my toes. *I must get up soon.* Sleeping on a soft bed has been difficult, the covers feel so heavy. Mum's stopped the food processor. The shipping forecast. *The Archers*.

'I could bring one up if you like?'

'In a bit, Dad. I'll come down.'

But I can't. I've more crazy thinking to do. About Jack, about the complete mess I'd made of leaving Africa.

*

On my last night in Loki, Kenya, there was a lively farewell party for me at Trackmark. The usual scene: red and white checked tablecloths, cold Tusker beer, whisky with extra ice, shared confidences – bleak, funny, heartbreaking – Afrobeats music, dancing, freedom. Extreme emotions, both happy and sad, a sense I was leaving what felt like the richest experience of my life in ways I couldn't begin to explain. Scared too, of going home, of not knowing what was to come. My life goal had been working with MSF, and now that was over.

Jaan was there, we'd danced, flirted, I'd grown to love and depend on him as a friend. A kind friend – a source of chocolate, bacon sandwiches, gossip – a vital link with Loki and the outside world, someone I admired for his bravery. But at the end of the night, I'd suddenly felt his breath on my neck, his attempt to kiss me and I froze. That wasn't what it had meant to me at all!

'But I thought you wanted…' His voice had trailed off as we'd looked at each other, shocked that we'd got this so wrong. He looked like I'd just slapped him – confused, hurt, embarrassed even.

'Fuck,' I'd muttered, before scrambling drunkenly back to my bunk in the MSF compound, like a complete idiot. Next day, exhausted and without a word to Jaan, I'd flown from Kenya, leaving the tatters of our friendship behind. I felt horrible about it as we hadn't been in touch since, and it was a shock to be the one handling everything so badly, when normally I was so in control.

*

The fish pie smells good. I wish I was hungry, but I've come home to England with a belly worn out from a previous giardia infection, a type of diarrhoeal disease. It's no big deal, pretty much everyone gets it from time to time in South Sudan, and there James used to nurse me through my groans of abdominal pains by reading poetry or Steinbeck through the thin tent walls.

Mum knocks tentatively on my door. She sits on the end of my colourful bed. Her eyes scan my face, looking for signs of her stubborn but happy daughter.

'Are you OK? Can you talk about it?' she asks gently, clearly concerned. But because I don't understand my anxiety, or my silence, when I open my mouth, no words come out. And if they did, what would they be? A spew of sadness, or regret, or fear, or self-loathing? That would frighten her, and me. My world has been divided into those who I think would understand and those who would not.

'I'll just keep dinner warm until you're ready to come down,' she says as she leaves the room. Rolling on to my side, I think about my MSF debrief in Amsterdam.

*

The operational manager who interviewed me was kindly and listened well, but it felt like a trip to the headmistress, and I was too tired to think or talk coherently. Also, with my stomach gurgling like an ancient boiler, I was terrified of not making it to the toilet in time. Life outside South Sudan – the shops, traffic, pubs – was overwhelming, overstimulating, like coming out of a long, strict lockdown.

At the debrief, I could've talked about the immense number of things we had achieved in Tam, but the dead baby followed me to every floor and into every room. Nodding and smiling like a mechanical dog, I could no longer remember any of the successful patient stories. I could only vaguely discuss the recent troop movements and disease outbreaks across the projects, all things that could've helped them plan for the future.

Next stop was the psychologist. All staff who've been in the field are given the chance to talk to one on their way back home through the looking glass.

Mine wears a bow tie, rainbow braces, a beautifully cut suit. He smiles a lot and offers me a mint humbug from his glass jar.

'How are you coping?' He leans back in his chair and looks at me intently.

'It's a lot to take on board.' I do more dog nodding, not daring to speak the truth about how anxious I feel, telling myself it's normal. Plus, I might want to work for MSF again, so I don't want to look crazy.

'I think I'm OK.' I'm chirpy, I'm good at this act. 'Thank you, bit tired maybe.'

'Bit colder here than there,' he says before I leave. He looks at my flip-flops – I'd given most of my clothes to the team in Tam when I left. 'You'll need some shoes.'

'I know. Thank you.'

He slides a slip of paper to me with the psychosocial unit email address on it: 'In case you need us.'

After saying goodbye, I don't hear from them again. Looking back, there was further support I could've accessed, a 24-hour mental health helpline, for example, but I didn't think I needed it. I felt these support systems were for people worse off than me, plus I didn't want to burden the system – essentially my suffering was solely due to my own failures, and I had to bear that responsibility.

Snow was falling as I walked along the canal-side streets. It melted on my uncovered toes. Young people were spilling out of warmly lit cafés, laughing, smoking weed, or sitting framed in restaurant windows, jabbing at mobile phones. I got drunk with other MSF-ers at the pub near the office, and after three pints of Amstel, I finally felt a bit calmer as we shared stories and black humour from our time in the field. Everyone felt it, the tribe sticking together, but this was not the place to talk about my angst, my fears. I had no right – said the same old voice in my head – what was my suffering compared to a colleague who had just finished their twelfth mission? Or just got back from an intense mission in Syria?

Sitting beside us, at a separate table, I saw a young man wrap his coat tenderly around the woman he was kissing. Their dog was sitting beside them. I turned my back on them and ordered another beer.

*

'Thanks, Mum, it looks lovely.'

I'm sitting between my parents at supper. Dad pours us all a glass of chilled white wine; I take a small amount of fish pie and a helping of peas. They've both put so much effort into the meal, wanting to look after me. On the mantelpiece are pictures of my nieces, happy and smiling, an ultrasound picture of my sister's twins tucked into the corner.

Looking around the softly lit room, I feel an idiot for thinking I could do humanitarian aid work and come back feeling fulfilled, even a little heroic, ready for marriage, for children. The memory that I once imagined getting an MSF tattoo and proudly regaling stories from the field shamed me now. In reality, I feel broken into pieces, but also loathe this feeling because, looking at this table – the food, the lamps, the house, the green fields around us – we're so obviously the lucky ones.

'It's really delicious.' I want to be her healthy child again, the one who would once have wolfed down the pie.

I know I must tell my parents soon what happened between Jack and me, but the thought makes me shrivel inside. They'd got to know him quite well through dinners, afternoons in the garden, family occasions. Of course, they'd loved him, he was perfect really. All gone now.

When I'd finally stepped off the plane at East Midlands Airport, what happened was this. Jack was there smiling. He'd hugged me tight before grabbing my backpack and heading for the car, full of plans for the week ahead. *Starting our lives together.* The part of me that wasn't totally shut down, exhausted and overwhelmed, even that part, couldn't respond properly.

We drove home. Inside, he'd started to cook a delicious meal that I felt too nauseous and guilty to eat, so wandered aimlessly from room to room, through the flat I'd once loved. The white walls, the carefully chosen art, comfortable sofas, the eBay grand piano he'd stayed up all night to bid on for me, had become strange, mocking objects.

Over the next few days, I couldn't sleep more than a few snatched moments. My mind came alive as soon as I lay down, or if I slept, I'd wake drenched in sweat. By day, my eyes were heavy with weariness, I couldn't concentrate. There was so much I needed to say to Jack, but I couldn't. Irrationally, unfairly, I'd hoped to tell him about Jaan, to offload some of the guilt and get his absolution. Or at least to tell him about the patients that visited me every time I closed my eyes, but the words didn't come.

On the fourth night, he asked a friend of his over, maybe to relieve the tension. In the year I'd been away, Facebook had soared in popularity, so when I walked into the sitting room I stood at the door watching them type and send messages to each other in silence. In that moment, with the dark room, the flickering screens, the bent heads, I felt like an alien in a place of unbearable loneliness. Although it wasn't fair, I'd longed for James, for tent talks, for wild dancing and frog choruses, for stories, for the beating of geese wings, the sun on my face.

When I told Jack I was going out to meet a friend for a drink at The Jam Cafe, he looked relieved, but for every beer my friend ordered, I downed several shots of vodka. Desperate to unlock the words stuck in my throat, stupidly hoping this would help with the talk Jack and I so desperately needed. My memory ends with a greasy pizza on the way home.

It was Jack who found me at one in the morning, cradling a vomit-smeared toilet bowl. Stumbling into bed, it got worse when I woke after an hour with a warm patch growing underneath me. I'd wet myself. It was then, in slurred words, swearing and weeping, I'd told him I couldn't be with him any more. Mortified does not cover it. I felt dirty and ashamed.

He was kind and cleaned me up, helped me back into clean, fresh sheets, eyes lingering wearily on the teek tied around my belly. Being tucked in felt so sweet and innocent, I couldn't remember the last time I'd felt that. But in the harsh morning light, as he put on his work suit, his hurt and bewildered look told a different story. I'd become a complete stranger – unreliable, unrecognisable – from the bright-eyed girl who'd kissed him goodbye nearly a year before as she set off on her intrepid adventure.

'It's over, isn't it?'

He said it simply and sadly. When I nodded without speaking, he stood up and left the room.

Five hours later, my backpack was in the boot of a hire car. I'd packed everything of mine from the flat, phoned my parents, told them I was coming home. Jack was at work and didn't know. *I'm so sorry,* said the note I left on top of the piano. It was cruel, and I knew it, but I had nothing else to give.

My parents have said I can stay as long as I need to. Lucky, that. I try to remind myself that in South Sudan, if I'd left a man, I might be homeless, starving, beaten, worthless forever, but I can't make this help me today. On the A50, I push my Gnarls Barkley CD into the player again, having listened to 'Crazy' eight times in a row already. As soon as the track ends, I play it again and again in a frenzy, the lyrics about remembering and losing my mind touching a raw nerve. I'm pushing it back in again when I suddenly get the cold sweats, the stitched feeling in my bowels. The day that couldn't get much worse suddenly has, because I'm not going to make it to the next service station. I'm about to shit in a hire car.

Skidding over to the frozen, grassy verge, I luckily find a bush, and use my own knickers to wipe away my alcohol-smelling diarrhoea. Driving off, I'm singing and crying at the same time, knowing I've hit rock bottom. Am I crazy? Possibly.

CHAPTER SIXTEEN

By June of 2008, apart from bad dreams, a poor digestive system and no periods, I'm doing a pretty good imitation of a normal 27-year-old single girl and feel ready to work again.

It's a summer of seven weddings, when half the girls in my A-level photo, whom I have known and loved for most of my life, are getting married. Knowing this will not happen to me any time soon, I dutifully buy presents and throw confetti, but then reliably seem to be the most drunk at the reception. My libido remains stubbornly absent and I have no boyfriend. In my worst moments, part of me feels I deserve this lonely life, that I'm poisonous, like a black hole that could hurt anyone who got too close. *I don't know what I want anymore.* Although I try not to feel lonely, I miss the close bonds with MSF friends now scattered all over the world.

One big excitement of this summer is a new flatshare, and on a sunny morning I move everything I own into Mum's Ford Fiesta. Kissing Dad goodbye, two hours later I arrive at my new digs, a lovely three-storey Georgian property: 23 Lace Street, Nottingham. Putting my bare mattress on the floor, Dad's Dansette record player on the lone chest of drawers, I stand at the window looking out at the small garden behind the house.

My new flatmates, both nurses, have furnished the house with lovely things they've accumulated over the past few years. They don't seem to mind that I have nothing to add. Jenny, petite, ginger-haired, sassy, has a killer wit that allows no bullshit. Hannah, who lives on the top floor, is mother earth, an ITU specialist nurse with a huge heart, the sort of rare person who gives you their full attention and compassion when they speak to you.

When I tell them about my awful break-up with Jack, tactfully missing out the bit about shitting myself on the side of the road, Hannah hugs me and says I should stop kicking myself about the note on the piano. When I tell them about Jaan, Jen lifts the mood by laughing, 'To be fair, I'd have probably shagged him.'

We all like to party, so when we're off duty, the Dansette is on full blast, nights normally ending with me insisting on Gnarls Barkley or Amy Winehouse. Singing heart-breaking lyrics while drunk feels strangely healing. We have a glorious motley crew who are always there too. My new tribe, who seem to accept me as I am, bad singing and all.

Another typical Lace Street scene is Jen, Hannah and me all crammed into the tiny bathroom, one chin-deep in a bubbly bath, one sitting on the closed toilet lid, one cross-legged on the bathmat. Glass of wine or herbal tea in hand. Talking, laughing, crying, sharing – whatever was needed, and in some ways, I wish it could last forever. Nothing's off limits, and thanks in part to James's disinhibition training, I'm much more open now. But there are limits: South Sudan is just the name of another country to them. I can tell them a story of a patient here, or of James there, but I've found these intense stories all too easily monopolise the conversation. If I talk about the death of a child, it's hard for chat to return. Although a five-minute story of South Sudan feels comfortable, fifteen minutes maybe, if I'm still talking after forty-five minutes, there's no longer a balance. I feel like the bore who's trying to describe a horror film that the other person hasn't seen, and it just doesn't work, so I learn to stick to the topics we share.

Sometimes I wish I could forget about MSF altogether, but a flame has been lit, and in the quiet of my small room I pendulate between wanting to stay with these friends in the UK and going back to MSF. Deep down, if I do go back, I know I'll need to learn more, *to make up for what I couldn't do last time*.

Reflecting on this, I know humanitarian aid work has sometimes been described as an addiction. Almost a malfunction state in which having experienced the high-octane adrenaline of working in dangerous places, your body learns to crave the intensity, and makes everyday life, by comparison, seem a tame affair. I get it; I've felt it; I've heard foreign correspondents admit to this too. But the other part is, once you've seen the suffering, it's hard to walk away. The weight still feels too heavy as I sit in a comfortable chair watching the latest disaster unfold on TV, when I know I could be doing something to help.

Neither explanation really satisfies; both are partly true. All I know for sure is that on the sunny morning when the buff-coloured envelope falls on the mat to say I've been accepted on a midwifery degree course at the University of Nottingham, I dance around the kitchen like an idiot. This *is* what I want now.

*

Flipping between two different worlds of maternity care is not easy. Somehow, I'll have to learn to make peace with the huge inequalities women face and the kind of care they can expect. Although my midwifery course is amazing, when we get to the birthing emergencies theory part, I learn to keep my mouth shut, and dutifully write down that mothers expecting twins or triplets often choose a caesarean section. To this day, I've never met a UK midwife who's seen a vaginal triplet birth, so to say what I've seen and done would make me that most hateful of creatures: the class smarty-pants. Or worse, a fantasist, or even a cowboy who loved taking risks, which is the opposite of how I felt. I'm still clinging to normal, still on a tightrope.

Sometimes this makes student days lonely. By showing only half of myself, I don't quite fit in with the rest of the class. But I study the hardest I have ever studied in my life, knowing one day I might be alone and needing these skills.

*

It was thrilling for me during this year of learning to be given work experience in Ethiopia with one of my heroines, the obstetrician Dr Catherine Hamlin, who with her husband, Reginald, started the now world-famous Hamlin Fistula Hospital in Addis Ababa. There I saw first hand the effective treatment of obstetric vaginal fistulas, and how to take care of women emotionally afterwards. This new knowledge felt like some form of atonement for that woman on the plane in South Sudan, whose wrecked and reeking body had so horrified me on my first day.

But there were new horrors too, such as female genital mutilation (FGM), where young girls had their genitalia cut – some completely removed – and the remaining tissue sometimes sewn together to remove their vaginal entrance. It's an abhorrent act, sometimes done by women themselves, which only ever increased the health risks, especially in pregnancy, often causing infection and death. Thankfully, the Hamlin Hospital was able to offer emergency obstetric care, but was also a leading voice in getting FGM internationally recognised and subsequently outlawed.

One afternoon I drank tea from a porcelain cup and ate macaroons with the elegant and unflappable Dr Hamlin, who was then eighty-six and still working hard. She told me with quiet passion that vaginal fistulas would never be eradicated without women having access to a trained midwife.

'A midwife can identify the problem early; their work can be the difference between life and death.'

I felt proud to be joining this profession.

*

Not long after this, I'm back in a UK hospital, assisting an amazing and highly experienced midwife called Amy, who teaches me another valuable lesson.

On this particular cold winter's night, sparkling fairy lights twinkle through the warm scented steam of the hospital's birthing pool room. Cello music, Arvo Pärt's *Spiegel im Spiegel*, rises and falls from discreetly placed speakers. I open my mouth to offer the usual words of comfort to the woman, Jane, who's groaning in the birthing pool, when Amy gives me a cautionary frown.

Motioning for me to squat cross-legged on the floor beside her, Amy shows me Jane's birth plan, which runs to several pages of instructions about our role here tonight: we are not to mention pain, not to speak unless Jane calls for us, and to hide ourselves as much as possible.

The labour is long. Jane's husband looks tired and nervous.

Around three in the morning, I can't help raising a sceptical eye at all this, but Amy brings me round. She tells me this woman's last birth was traumatic. Jane had been given the full-on bells and whistles modern obstetric experience: induced labour, epidural, episiotomy and forceps delivery, and felt completely out of control. Her son had been born healthy, but Jane had been left unable to sleep, and anxiety from this had carried into her current pregnancy.

'So our job is to support her,' Amy whispers to me, a slight Jamaican lilt in her voice. 'To be a midwife means to be *with woman,* I don't care if that means a planned caesarean or a birth alone in the woods, as long as the woman feels informed, listened to and respected.' Then, after a pause, 'It is *her* body after all, these are *her* choices to make.'

Of course it's absolutely right that Jane has the birth options she wants, and anything we can do to reduce her anxiety and adrenaline actually makes her more likely to have a safe delivery. But would Jane still want no intervention if this labour became obstructed? Maybe the forceps delivery actually saved her baby's life last time, so surely it was worth it? Women I'd met overseas experienced such horrors when denied access to obstetric care, and without forceps, babies died and women were left with birth injuries, such as an obstetric fistula. *But that's not Jane's fault,* I remind myself.

A few hours later, a beautiful baby girl was handed to a laughing and relieved mother by a happy father. Something I wasn't used to, something I would have to get used to and learn from, if only I could stop myself remembering.

So much of my new role as a student midwife in the UK has been joyous, magical even, and witnessing the healthy arrival of a new life was often profound. Of course, birth emergencies still happen in the UK, but when I experience these now on my clinical placements, it's such a relief to be able to pull the red emergency call button, and in rushes a team of midwives, obstetricians and anaesthetists. All the people I wish had been with me in Tam.

But as much as I'm loving the work, when I try too hard to block out the worst memories of South Sudan, they creep back into my dreams. Waking in a cold sweat, I'm left with a vision of baby Mariam, her eyes rolling back, and me trying and failing to get the IV in. Sometimes it's a birth under a full moon, with an unstoppable flood of bright red blood pouring into the mud under the Waiting Tree. Dreams that startle me awake, panting and wondering where I am. In moments like these I try to channel James's 'Equanimity', and sometimes it works, but sometimes I fall off a cliff.

Waking in the night, when I'm drenched in sweat, it's like full bathtubs have been upended over me. So much so, that my GP sent me for TB tests (knowing I'd worked with TB-positive patients in South Sudan). It's a relief when they come back negative. It's also been eighteen months since I had my last period, and despite blood tests and scans of every orifice, all my consultant concludes is that I still have a high level of blood cortisol (a stress hormone), which they think is the cause. Maybe that's also the culprit for my still absent libido, but I was too embarrassed to ask.

During these moments of stress, my fingers find the teek still discreetly tied around my belly, and as I run my thumb over the dainty beads, my fizzing brain calms a little. My memory expands to remember the joyous women celebrating the birth of baby Moses, and how we'd saved the life of both him and his mother. My own suffering, my own loneliness, was a fair price to pay for the lives we'd saved. And now here I am, training to be a midwife so that next time *I can make it better*.

CHAPTER SEVENTEEN

In January 2010, Haiti was ravaged by a catastrophic earthquake that ultimately claimed the lives of about a quarter of a million people. I went there for six weeks in November of that year, as a member of MSF's 'E' (emergency) team. Haiti was, by then, in the midst of a major cholera epidemic, and we set up a hospital on the outskirts of its capital, Port-au-Prince.

It was the most harrowing of times – the city and its infrastructure collapsed, slums were full of sick and dying people, streets were ruled by gangs – but the arrival of a live baby in the midst of such devastation felt like a miracle. These mobile, emergency hospitals felt like MSF at its clinical best – efficient, professional, innovative – and tired as I was when I got home, I felt proud to have been part of the emergency effort.

My old fire for aid work was reignited: *maybe this could be my life now?* Somehow the idea felt perfect – to be based mainly in the UK, but do occasional E-team missions for short emergency responses after natural disasters. This was actually how I'd imagined aid work would be before I'd joined MSF.

But I had new dilemma too: as I was feeling stronger again, I had spent time rekindling my friendships and had the sense of deepening roots in the UK. I had a new qualification and a good job as a midwife. I'd loved living with my new flatmates, partying and sharing. So why, when I woke in the middle of the night, was I drawn like a magnet to the MSF staff vacancy page? I'd sit for hours, my face bathed in blue light, reading with fear and fascination of the jobs I could apply for in over seventy countries – Ethiopia, Bosnia, Congo, the list was endless. Each one an essential, life-saving project for the people there, and I was better qualified now. *Could I hack another long overseas tour?*

It was unsettling, trying to balance on this see-saw between staying home and going away again, especially when my flatmates Jenny and Hannah found their own partners and planned to move into new homes with them. For me, there was still a deep sense that something was missing. So it felt fortuitous when James wrote, out of the blue, to ask if I'd like to visit for a holiday on his boat, which was in Mexico, near Cancun, where the Gulf of Mexico meets the Caribbean Sea. He'd asked Anita along too, so I immediately said yes, knowing how much fun we'd have, and how we could talk in the old uncensored way. Maybe they could help me make some sense of my deep need to return to the field and leave my other life behind.

'My boat's nothing fancy,' James warned, 'she's tethered to a rickety pontoon on the Isla Mujeres, which means the Island of Women – so pretty much the perfect place to meet up with my two best friends.'

Four weeks later, I flew there with Anita.

*

'Captain Diego!' Anita squeals when she first sees James, a nickname given to him by his Mexican neighbours. We drop our backpacks on the pontoon slats and pelt towards him. He's standing on the deck, topless, tanned, his veneered teeth winking in the sunlight. Opening his arms to embrace us, our deep hug ends in laughter.

'You made it!' he says when we finally let go. 'You actually made it.' We take a moment to let this sink in because it feels like some kind of miracle. Over two years had passed since I'd left Tam.

James was in Haiti after the earthquake too, though our time there didn't overlap. Anita's done another year in South Sudan, followed by a gruelling year in the Democratic Republic of Congo.

'So, ladies, welcome to your new home aboard the good ship *Serenity*.' He gives a florid head-waiter wave towards his boat. 'I hope you'll be very happy here.'

In truth, *Serenity*, a forty-year-old, 32-foot downeaster sloop, is a bit like her owner: battered but beautiful. It looks nothing like the stupendously expensive shiny white American boats moored in the posh marina next door. But James loves this thing, and spends hours sanding her, polishing her teak decks, her brass fittings, restoring her to charm and seaworthiness. The pontoon, shared with Cuban and Mexican neighbours and fishermen, is shabby and friendly. It could easily be the setting for a John Steinbeck novel – probably no coincidence, given that he is a favourite author of James's.

Mrs Tiggy-Winkle is back, as James eagerly shows us around below deck, to the galley with all its hidden storage spaces and where everything is immaculately tidy. On a shelf above the sink there's a small shrine with a jade Buddha, incense and paper flowers. When he opens the cupboards underneath, Anita and I laugh to see half the storage taken up with *shisha* paraphernalia – coals, tobacco-free *shisha* mix, two different pipes. James laughs, a little sheepish.

'Yeah, I know – still a few steps from nirvana.'

Next he shows us his small cabin and the humble bathroom inches away from our beds: the sink, the toilet that flushes the 'black water' out into the ocean, just like most ships do. No one's embarrassed; it's posh compared to Tam.

We're shown our own makeshift beds on the side of the gangway, when Anita takes my hand and says in mock bemusement, 'So where are we now?' Something we often say when we meet again. It's a joke, sort of, but also a moment of knowing how weird and dislocating these leaps between extremes can feel. She'd been in Congo that year and seen human suffering en masse. Now we're sitting under a cloudless blue sky in Mexico with nothing more demanding on the agenda than whether to go sailing that day, or sit in the sun and talk.

That night, we sit on deck and watch a huge orange sun flop like a collapsed jelly over the horizon. The rigging hitting the mast sounds like wind chimes. James cracks open the cool box, hands Anita and me a cold beer. He fires up his *shisha* pipe, raises his diet cola in my direction and says, 'I would like to propose a toast to Midwife Kent.'

I hadn't seen him since I'd graduated at the end of March 2010 with a first-class degree with honours that I still couldn't quite believe. 'To Midwife Kent. And,' he adds, blowing out smoke, 'not that I wanna brag

or nothing, but I'm pretty sure one of the first things I said to you in Tam
was that you'd make a great one! Ha!'

We all chink bottles and smile at each other, me feeling lighter
and more at peace than I have in such a long time. *My tribe reunited.*
Dislocation gone.

*

There are so many things I want to talk to James about on this holiday.
Like how he manages to bounce back so quickly after overseas projects,
or how he can he be so sure of his life's path. But first he wants to
tease me.

'So tell me, Anna Banana, what was the deal with you and that pilot?'
He winks at Anita.

'Oh God, James, no, I humiliated myself.'

Anita, who's lying beside me on the deck, shoots me a sympathetic
look. I'd confessed all on our flight to Cancun.

'Well... I made a mess of everything.' When I told him about that last
night in Loki, I felt bad all over again about breaking Jaan's heart.

'Ah, he's a big boy, Kent. I think he got over it.' James's blue eyes are
twinkling. 'And besides, we all loved that runway gossip.'

I hit him on the arm. 'You knew! You made me 'fess up for nothing!
But seriously, James, you haven't heard the worst bit yet...'

And I told them about Jack, my shitting on the side of the road, all the
shameful scenes that I'd tried to block out. Secrets that a few years ago
I'd have taken to my grave.

'Come on, Kent!' James takes a deep toke on his *shisha* and exhales
apple-scented smoke into the air. 'Some of the best people I know have
crapped their pants.' His blue eyes fix mine. 'Hell, it happened a few
times in Tam, don't you remember?'

Who could forget! Those days when he couldn't get out of his tent
quick enough because of his wobbly knees. How we'd hated going
to the drop latrine, with the maggot-infested moving heap below.
I remembered too, groaning in my tent when my belly boiled with
dysentery and how James had soothed me by reading *Of Mice and Men*
through the thin tent walls.

'It's just crap, Anna. We all do it. Every day on a good day!'

Oh, how I loved this man, this bringer of lightness. *Maybe I did just need to talk about it after all.*

Anita and I look at each other, smiling and shrugging. We say in unison, 'It's *just* crap.'

Later, when they asked about Jack, I told them how I'd met him again at a party last month, with the beautiful smiling girl on his arm who was to become his wife. He'd looked so pleased to be with her, so complete. I add, partly as a joke, 'You know how when you leave someone, that awful part of you half hopes they never quite recover? I honestly didn't feel like that. He deserved her. And to be happy.'

It's dark on the pontoon now, just a scattering of lights on the shore, the cicadas chirping an evening tune. Anita and I are wrapped in bright scarves made of Congolese material; the stars are amazing.

'He made the right choice,' I add philosophically.

I can feel James's quick glance at me, smoothing down his handlebar moustache.

'Do you really feel that now?'

'Feel what?'

'That you don't want marriage and children?'

Anita and I exchange wary looks, her Hawaiian eyes both questioning and sad. Sometimes this topic feels impossible, though we talk about it often. There's also a painful joke name for MSF: Many Single Females. Some of our MSF colleagues have managed the difficult act of balancing work in the field with partners and children, but they seem to be the minority. Some choose to remain child free. Others move from fieldwork to office-based MSF work in London or Amsterdam, but those jobs are scarce, and require living in the city. What worries me most is that I'll always have to choose between one or the other.

Normally, I'd try to brush off this question by saying I didn't feel a strong maternal impulse yet, maybe I never would. And sometimes I do believe that. Next I'd shift the conversation to how much I loved my nieces, and my twin nephews, who were now two years old. But this is James asking, so I tell him about an intense experience I'd had about a month ago:

'I was on a night shift in Nottingham, doing some shadowing work on the neonatal intensive care unit. This baby came in, she'd been born with her left eyeball unexpectedly missing, and the left side of her face dysmorphic from a rare congenital condition.

'It was the strangest thing: I was holding that baby, feeding her through a nasogastric (NG) tube, and I had this sudden, unexpected rush of love up through my chest. It was so powerful, so protective, and I thought: *Oh, so that's it!* That's what people mean when they talk about maternal instinct. I knew in that instant that if this was my baby, I would love and care for her, no matter what.'

Anita sends me a little smile, then nods her head. She gets it. James is quiet for a moment too.

'I hope you'll have one of your own one day,' he says. I poke his bare foot with mine, not enjoying the look of concern in his eyes.

'You're lucky,' I say. 'It's not the same for you. You've had your kids, and you can have children at any age, if you want to.'

He's quiet again.

'Not always easy,' he says at last. 'I love this boat, but I can't stay forever. My youngest daughter's about to start her nursing degree, so I'm moving back to California to help with her kids. I was a pretty fucked-up dad when she was young, so it feels right.'

He'll enjoy being with them, he adds. He'll build himself a cabin in the woods, but he'll miss this. His eyes travel over the darkening sea, tracing the spot of light where fishermen are bringing in that night's catch.

Atonement. The word pops into my mind. The word he introduced me to in South Sudan.

'Yup, so, for now, I'm retired from aid work.'

I'm surprised to hear it, happy too, and maybe envious. Despite his rolling-stone outlook, he's older and settled in a way I still don't feel.

There's a moment's silence between us three friends. The lazy flop of a fish jumping.

'So no honky-tonk man at home, Kent?' James says out of the dark.

I blush. 'Well... There was this one guy... I met him at a music festival in Scotland.'

James drags on the *shisha*, Anita lights a cigarette, and they nestle down for a juicy story. It was a four-day festival in Dumfries and Galloway,

I'd camped with my flatmates in the arm of a hill next to a river that babbled all night. We'd put on our most colourful dresses, danced, heard bagpipes playing from the pine forest above. It was there I'd met a beautiful woodsman; we'd talked, danced, spent the night in his tent. After I'd undressed, he'd made me laugh when, in a soft Glaswegian accent, he'd said I was 'a wee hottie' and 'very nicely put together'. The sex had been wonderful. When the festival ended, he went back to his small woodland community, and I went back to Nottingham.

'But it was more than just a fling.' I'm blushing, but loving telling the story. 'Because, guess what? A week later I got my period back.'

'Well, I'll be damned!' laughs James. 'The English Rose just needed to get laid!'

*

In the days that follow, James teaches us to sail, we sit on deck eating bean burritos, and we laugh or lie in the shade in comfortable silence, basking in the closeness of being together.

On the last night, as Anita takes her turn to cook below deck, James says, 'Can I ask you something, Kent? Did you ever talk to your brother about what happened to his girlfriend?'

I take a deep breath, then start to explain how I had, finally, spoken to my brother. It felt terrifying at first to break down that wall of silence. Always finding more solace in the written word, initially I wrote to him. I worried about what the reply would be, and wondered if it would harm our friendship. Like me, he's not one who enjoys talking about the deep stuff — he's very private. But actually, when we finally spoke, it went better than I expected. He didn't mind me sharing; in fact, he said it was helpful for me to bring it up and how sad he felt that I'd carried the guilt around for so long. He admitted that he felt guilty too for not including me at the time, but that he'd reached out for professional therapeutic support and had learnt to live again. And to love again, as he was by now happily married. Afterwards, I felt some lightness, but also closer to him, as if an invisible barrier had been knocked down.

All this is said quickly, because the conversation had been brief, though I feel James wants me to say more.

'Was that it?'

'Yes, but that was a lot for us. It felt like we'd finally made peace.'

'OK.' James looks thoughtful.

'You've got to understand, James, I'm British. Some of us do things differently over the pond.' I probably sounded defensive, but I knew I wasn't alone in keeping things private and bottled up.

To illustrate this, I tell him a much-repeated, much-loved family story about my grandparents. On the night before they were married during the Blitz, London was in flames, bombs were raining down, and Granny, who'd gone to the church to talk to the vicar, ended up lying with him under a table. 'I slept with the vicar' was her oft-repeated punchline. I'd always admired how this terror had been refashioned into a joke. Admired their stoicism, their sacrifices, their humility.

Granny used to say, 'Draw a line and move on.' Grandpa, based with the RAF in Malta, rarely spoke of the war either; his collection of expressive paintings of RAF planes and scenes of bombing would only come to light after his funeral a few years later. I believe these were his way of processing the deaths of so many of his generation, his friends, and of the national grief that was hidden below a 'make do and mend' mantra. In turn, my parents were imprinted with these coping skills, and I think I must be too. 'That's why…' – I could hear my voice crackling – '…it felt doubly shameful to fall apart. They'd tried to protect me from their traumas, so why shouldn't I protect those I love?'

James thought about this. 'OK, I definitely get that,' he said eventually. 'But I don't think you can quarantine horrible memories and experiences, just hoping they go away.'

And slowly, reluctantly, I was learning he was right. Trauma was a many-headed monster that sprang when you least expected it. I'd seen those old soldiers at commemoration ceremonies, crying inconsolably; I knew about men who'd come back so damaged they couldn't talk to or touch their wives. About the many who took their secrets to the grave. But British society was only just beginning to see mental health as an element of health as a whole. Mostly, though, we still just tried not to talk about it.

Moments later, James asks quietly, 'Do you still think of Mariam?'

'Every day,' I say, not hesitating.

'How do you cope with that?'

And I'm suddenly uncomfortable. I'm not ready for this, and want to move the conversation on. A big part of me wants to make James see that I'm fine now. To make him proud of me for being resilient, like he is.

'I dunno. I go running, I keep fit. I let my hair down and party. The midwifery studies really helped.'

Sitting in silence, he ponders, a dark shadow on the deck now with a halo of smoke around him.

'But when the shit hits the fan, I worry about you burying your head, working hard and partying harder – it's the same stuff as when your brother's girlfriend was killed. I wish you could find a way to actually let it out.'

My breath catches. I hadn't even seen it like that.

Anita comes up to the deck. She sits cross-legged, shoulder to shoulder with me, and listens to James.

'Listen, I'm not trying to sound like I've got it sussed. You know I've fucked up in my time, still do, but what I do know now is you're gonna have to work out how to sit with these painful feelings without reacting to them. To stop being busy and important, to make peace with them. Meditation helps me, but you need to work out what helps you.'

A pause.

'And remember the good times too, right? The people we did help.'

'I do.'

It's then I admit there's an MSF job I've already applied for, a year's contract this time. One that both scares and beckons me. I've been reading about the Rohingya refugee plight in Bangladesh, where there is a desperate need for midwives. I can't stop thinking about going.

James takes a deep breath, looking at me with tender concern. 'Great, Anna,' he says. 'But if you go, be careful.'

Did I hear this? Properly hear it? I'm not sure. Half of me was already out the door. I'd convinced myself I'd be better at it this time.

CHAPTER EIGHTEEN

Hot sun beats down on the January morning I arrive in Dhaka, the chaotic and overcrowded capital of Bangladesh. Above my head, electricity wires run like vines in every direction. The air smells of dust, dung, petrol and old rubbish.

After five days of briefing in Dhaka, I fly to Cox's Bazar, the town where my office and accommodation is based. Cox's famous beach, with its ninety-six miles of curving, silvery sand and amethyst waters, looks glorious from the air.

In our MSF office on the outskirts of town, I get more detail on the refugee camp where I'll work for most of this year, 2011. My job is as a nurse and midwife, with overall responsibility for female and pregnancy health in a refugee camp of around 30,000 Rohingya people, all of whom have fled persecution in Myanmar.

My heart quickens; clearly this will be a massive challenge. Since accepting the posting, I've had midnight terrors, when I wake with fear and doubt stalking around my bed, nightmares about catastrophic failures that will strip me naked. To settle myself, I run through the emergency interventions for a major PPH and eclamptic seizures, this time scripting how I will explain them to the Bangladeshi staff I'm to be working with. *I'm more prepared this time. I'm a midwife now.*

Although I'm told in detail about life in the several refugee camps, the truth is you cannot imagine how harrowing life is for the exiled Rohingya until you've seen it. And that, maybe because the camps are so horrific, even aid workers must be introduced slowly. I'm taken down to the beautiful Cox's beach and handed a fresh coconut to drink. Sitting on the sand, I watch crescent-shaped, wooden fishing boats bring back the day's catch.

This very mellow beginning, on a beach where tourists from Dhaka flock to go surfing and eat ice cream on lines of sun loungers, doesn't feel like the start of a new mission. The idea of 30,000 Rohingya refugees living in desperate need an hour or so's ride from here causes a background rumble of disquiet in my head, like a distant train coming down the track, but they're still just figures until I get to live them.

*

Singing wakes me at dawn the next morning, an amplified male voice calling people to prayer, which echoes eerily through the streets. I'm in an upbeat mood as I climb aboard the 4 x 4, keen to get going, excited even. My decision to do more MSF missions has made me feel much better, stronger. I have a goal again. Maybe this is my life now, maybe I don't need a relationship that works long term, because I'll always be travelling. I'm not sure where that leaves the idea of having my own family, but what I'm doing right now seems more important and it no longer feels like my friends having children are leaving me behind.

Dr Thomas, a young German about 6 ft 2 inches tall, is squeezed in the back seat beside me. With his piercings and shaved head, you might take him for a bad-ass metalhead, and I shift awkwardly away from him. Later I will see his gentleness with malnourished children, his determination to get everyone in the camps vaccinated – measles and typhoid are killers here. He's yet another lesson in not judging books by covers.

Marjie sits on the other side of me. She's the Canadian midwife waiting to hand over the maternity project to me, fiercely dedicated, hugely experienced, kind and with no obvious flaws. Later I'll learn to laugh at myself as I unfavourably compare our coping strategies – hers, staying in her room at night, knitting hats for prem babies; mine, drinking, partying and the Frenchman. She'll be a tough act to follow. *My new team.*

Saddam, our driver, takes what feels like a racing dive into the main road, which even at 6.30 in the morning teems with brightly painted lorries, goats, tuk-tuks and helmetless motorcyclists. We're heading south-east towards several refugee camps, and the specific one, 'The

Makeshift Camp', where I'll be based. 'Makeshift' strikes me as an odd name, until I see it.

As we leave the busy town behind, rice fields of tender green plants stretch out on either side of us as far as the eye can see. They are tended by women dressed in vibrant red saris, who stand up to their calves in water. After the grey of winter in the UK, the huge blue sky and bright green fields feel almost phosphorescent, as if I'm looking at a landscape painting.

Jason, my new project coordinator (PC), sits in the front. An athletically built, quietly intelligent American, his head is shaved too. In the small world of MSF, we've actually met before, on the first pre-departure training course I did in the frozen forests of Germany five years ago. His initial placement took him to Sierra Leone, where we'd lost touch, but it reminds me that MSF is like a wayward band of brothers, and we're all linked somehow. He's having a rant up front about safety procedures, telling me about the emergency kit we must carry in case of roadside accidents; how we must leave the hospital by 17.30 sharp, as the road after dark could be full of both smugglers and border guard police.

And I'm thinking *whatever*, let me enjoy this moment of beauty in the unfolding landscape, feeling a bit cocky, like I'm an old hand at this. Patches of jungle-like forest pass now, hills in the distance that glow green, and, to our right, that long dreamy coastline, just out of view. This is so beautiful, *James would love this, I need to just 'be in the moment'*. Maybe, in some ways, I'm becoming more like James and adopting his viewpoint that everything happens for a reason. *We just do our best*, those words of wisdom he gave me when I was so new and naive in South Sudan. This time, I think, I'll be the one saying these things. I even fool myself into believing I'll cope better this time with the suffering I will see.

The road we're on, scarcely more than a single-track concrete lane, is shared with a blizzard of vehicles all revving and honking. Ahead of us a cyclist, pulling eight small children in a little go-cart or 'cage', plunges into traffic. Inside the cage, the young children are immaculately dressed – the girls in smart blue pinafores, hair plaited like show ponies, the boys in shirts and ties and blue sailor hats.

I'm admiring the elegance with which Saddam scissors in and out of traffic, charmed by the schoolchildren, when in one heart-stopping second, a huge, roaring, rainbow-painted lorry hurtles round a corner and heads straight for us on the wrong side of the road, blaring its horn. I hear myself screaming as it leaps towards us.

Time works so strangely at these moments. In slow motion, I watch Saddam's arms windmilling frantically, his skullcap falling from his short hair as tyres screech. In the stretched-out seconds it takes for him to come to a stop on a hard mudbank, I hear the petrified screams of those children in their little schoolbus cage: we've come centimetres from wiping them all out.

Saddam turns to see if we're in one piece. My heart's leaping, my stomach rolling. I think I'm going to be sick. Thomas shifts his long thighs, adjusts his earring, doesn't say a word. He's been working in these camps for months already, and takes this horrendous journey twice a day. And I will be taking it too, from today onwards. Marjie, who shoots me a gentle, sympathetic smile, seems to know what I'm thinking.

Jason looks me squarely in the eyes.

'OK, that's what I'm talking about – this road is a deathtrap.' He talks about the dangers of roadside medical aid if we see a crash, of the dangers of a large crowd of people who will form around us to stare. When another large vehicle comes hurtling down the road, I grip the seat under my legs and pray.

*

Two near-crashes later, we drive slowly through the busy traffic of a small rural town called Ukhiya. With the windows wound down, the air is thick and hot from the spicy heat of chickpea patties sizzling in vats of hot oil over wood fires. People mill about, chattering, brightly greeting each other. Normally, I'd love all this: piles of exotic fruit and vegetables, bright spices spilling from large hessian sacks, sari silks hanging like bright kites, but now I'm rubber-legged and nauseous. I just want to get to the MSF hospital.

Fat bluebottle-type flies scrabble over the food, scrawny dogs nose through decayed scraps of whatever, piles of decomposing rubbish fill the streets. Above us, political slogans promising change and education hang like bunting from a cat's cradle of drooping electricity wires. Jason explains that high levels of illiteracy here mean that each political candidate must put an identifying symbol on their posters – a water jug, scissors, a sword, etc. – beside their name. The candidates, he says, often argue about who gets the sword.

'Typical guy, huh?' Thomas addresses me directly for the first time today, and smiles.

*

As we leave Ukhiya, the road and our polite newbie conversation peter out as the rice fields become stretches of barren earth. A mile on, past unmanned police checkpoints, Jason turns to see my reaction as he says, 'This is the town of Kutupalong.'

Nothing to see at first, or nothing much – just a few old fold-out tables on the side of the road with piles of rice and some shrivelled-looking onions for sale. Behind them, a scattering of low, ramshackle huts with open fronts, like small garages. A few serious-looking men sit inside the huts wearing lungis, a sarong-like garment often worn with a shirt. They watch us drive past without a word.

This town feels dead: none of the hustle and bustle of the other towns; no political bunting or banter from the crowds; just a few men staring, women with bare feet darting into doors.

Jason points to a sign at the entrance to a long drive bearing off to our right.

'This,' he says, 'is where the *registered* Rohingya refugees are housed and looked after by the UN. This is not our camp.' I rubberneck, trying to see.

He goes on to explain that the Rohingya people are one of the most persecuted and forgotten minority groups in the world. Mostly Muslim, they've lived for centuries in the mainly Buddhist country of Myanmar, also known as Burma. Myanmar authorities still contest this, claiming the Rohingya are illegal Bengali immigrants who came to Myanmar in the twentieth century. The result has allegedly been a programme of violence, murder and rape, followed by their mass exodus from Myanmar. At the time of writing, over 1 million Rohingya have fled to Bangladesh alone, where they live in sprawling refugee camps. Even the UN has a cap on how much help they can give, which is why MSF, who've been working here since 1985, stepped in to give emergency medical assistance.

A few minutes later, Jason is pointing at a heap of broken debris on our right.

'And this is the Makeshift Rohingya Refugee Camp – it's where the *unregistered* refugees live.'

I'm confused, as I'd known it would be grim, but I had a different picture of a refugee camp in my mind: long stretches of tents bearing aid organisation symbols, children playing in the shade between the tents. Images like those we've all seen on TV. But this vast, stinking landscape of decrepit shacks made from mud, plastic scraps and sticks, each one roughly the size of a one-man tent, doesn't make sense. How could a population equivalent to that of Reading live here?

Turning to Thomas, I say, 'Where?' meaning this can't be it.

He senses my confusion.

'It's those shitty little shacks, Anna, the ones without a proper roof. That is the Kutupalong Makeshift Camp.'

'Where's the hospital?' I'm trying not to look as shocked as I feel.

'There.' He points at a two-metre-high bamboo wall to our left, with three entrances carved in it. No flags flying here. No large murals with health promotion messages. Everything must be discreet in this unregistered and precarious place. The hospital's fragile bamboo walls must not look like a health point, but instead blend like a stick insect into the dirt so as not to draw the attention of authorities who may not want us here.

My legs are trembling as I step from our vehicle into the hot morning sun. *Oh God, I remember this feeling of being out of control.*

Thomas and Marjie go straight into the hospital – they have sick patients to see. Jason offers to show me around the camp first, with Amin, our Bangladeshi colleague, who speaks English, Bangla (or Bengali) and Rohingya (which I'm told is similar to the Chittagonian dialect of Bangla). His slicked, oiled hair glints in the hot sun, as he puts his hand respectfully on his chest, bows to me and smiles brightly as he explains he's a hospital supervisor. Following them along a small path between the shacks, we traipse up a hill, getting glimpses of life inside each home – single rooms with dry mud floors, toddlers sitting listlessly in open doorways, their eyes full of flies. At my approach, the children are snatched from the dirt by their mothers and held close; a young girl backs into the dark entrance of her shack. The clear message in their narrowed eyes is: don't trust anyone.

There had been a time, after my brother's girlfriend was murdered, when I had distrusted the world. But to see fear and distrust on this scale, and directed at me, was unimaginable before I'd seen it with my own eyes.

We're being shadowed by a small group of middle-aged men, who mutter under their breath in Rohingya, and send a boy to run ahead and alert others of our presence.

To my naive, ignorant eyes, these Rohingya people look very similar to the Bangladeshis I've met so far, except their skin is darker from a life exposed to the elements, their hair thinner, their foreheads more deeply wrinkled. They watch us in tense silence as we continue up the hill, where the baking sun bounces off the dry mud, no breeze, no sound. In South Sudan, children stared, but they laughed and joked too, they found ingenious ways to play with bits of wood or a bottle top. Here the kids just sit and stare.

At the top of the hill, I inhale quickly – I hadn't expected the hovels to reach the horizon, but they run from left to right as far as my eye can see. All belong to people who once had homes, maybe farms, fishing boats, schools, land. It freezes me to the spot.

The heart of the camp is an impenetrable maze, no planning or pattern to the layout, no greenery or garden space, just this mess of mud and twigs covered in sun-bleached plastic bags and rubbish scraps, hence the name 'Makeshift'. Woodsmoke drifts from some of the shacks; it's impossible to think of an open fire inside such small homes, but they must cook, they must eat.

A fly scrambles over my dry lips, the air hangs heavy with the smell of human excrement from latrines. I'm too overwhelmed to remember everything Jason said, but I do remember him saying, 'Some people have lived here for nearly thirty years.' The length of time I've been alive.

Jason assures me quickly there are improvements happening: the twenty-five new water points under construction, the building of more pit latrines, the long hut that was hoped to be used as a madrasah (a school for Islamic instruction). I can't see them yet; I can't see hope. What I see looks like despair.

CHAPTER NINETEEN

When I think of the word 'kindness', I think of Marjie, the 33-year-old Canadian midwife who sat beside me as we drove to the camps, not saying much at first.

Marjie, who is quiet and bespectacled, sleeps in the room next to mine in my new home – a ten-storey cement apartment block on the outskirts of Cox's Bazar. This building, painted pink, is called – according to the lopsided sign outside it – the Pink Pearl, and houses a floating population of twenty or so aid workers from four different international organisations. It has single rooms, cold showers, standing toilets, and water that sometimes runs red from rust; outrageous luxury compared to the camps.

Marjie insists I have one of her outfits to wear until I can get to a local tailor to run one up. I choose a plain green cotton salwar kameez (loose trousers and tunic), and a scarf I've wound several times around my neck, nervous of trailing it in the dust, or doing an Isadora Duncan in the car wheels.

Sitting in Marjie's borrowed clothes has a fitting symbolism – I have so much to learn from her, because 'Marvellous Marjie' is a legend here. Born a farm kid in southern Alberta, this stocky, smiling woman is also as wholesome and down to earth as good brown bread. Her brand of kindness has nothing soppy in it – it's the product of high skill, relentless energy, intelligence, experience and an amazing memory. (Later I'll watch in awe as she remembers the names of every single one of our 110 Bangladeshi national staff.)

As we bound down the road en route to my first full day at the hospital, Marjie surprises me by saying Bangladesh is her first assignment with MSF.

'How did you learn so quickly?' I'm sweating already in the early morning heat.

'Australia,' she says simply. 'I was like a nomad midwife there for over ten years. Way out in the outback, you learn to manage emergencies on your own.' I do the maths: she must only just have qualified then, and been in her early twenties.

Marjie feels so safe, I can't bear the thought that she'll be leaving in a week's time. I feel like begging her to stay. Instead, I must note down as much as I can get from her, and remind myself that I'm more prepared than I was in South Sudan.

Painted lorries are tumbling past our window, blasting their horns. Marjie takes no notice; she's telling me about the team of Bangladeshi nurses I'm about to work with, the forty staff I'll be the line manager for.

'You're going to love them – they're some of the smartest, kindest people you've ever met.' It takes bravery and dedication, she says, to work in camps that many locals are horrified by. Most of the local towns don't want close to a million displaced Rohingya sitting on their doorstep, any more than folks back home would.

Saddam swerves violently to avoid that morning's near collision. I'm almost on her lap, but Marjie serenely pats my arm.

'You OK?' She carries on telling me a story from the camp, face falling, eyes starting to moisten. Shortly after she'd arrived, nine months ago, a birthing woman had died of a postpartum haemorrhage in the hospital. Every midwife's worst nightmare.

'There was no blood transfusion available. I couldn't save her, and that killed me. I was warned by my PC (great guy by the way), that I might need to lose my naivety, toughen up, but I know I can't be a good midwife if I do. But the biggest success,' Marjie's face brightens a little, 'was getting the grandma in and giving her lactation training. She was fifty-three, but she stuck to it and damned if it didn't work! Her milk came and she was feeding that baby within a few days and most likely saved it.'

*

A week later, my notebook is stuffed with information, and the staff are lining up outside the bamboo hospital to say goodbye to Marjie. They give her humble gifts; they talk with tears in their eyes about how hard she worked, how much she taught them, how she never stopped smiling. When it's her turn at the front, she mutters shyly to me that public speaking's not her thing, but ends with a flourish:

'If I have ever wronged you, please forgive me.'

People often end speeches in Bangladesh with this phrase, but for her, this was not a polite, 'culturally appropriate' formality. Like me, like all of us, she was haunted by the women she couldn't save. Still is. When I wrote to her recently, she said the woman who died is still on her conscience ten years later. After Bangladesh, she went on to have close to twenty missions with MSF, in terrible situations, including Syria and Iraq during the war, but working with Rohingya women was the one that affected her most.

'The reality, Anna,' she says at the end of her email, 'is that while aid work has been one of the most rewarding experiences of my life, it's left some pretty serious scars. I am, as I see it, a high-functioning individual, but I don't sleep at night. PTSD started in the past few years. All the babies I lost, all the mothers I couldn't save, and the horrors they recounted. The fistulas, the female genital mutilation, the rape.'

She's working again, training midwives in Canada, but after Iraq, she'd had to retire for a while from aid work. 'I'd forgotten,' she said, 'how to smile.'

*

Now it's February, Marjie has gone home, and it's Dr Thomas who strides ahead of me through the bamboo hospital entrance. He's telling me over his shoulder how bamboo is in many ways a fine building material – fast to grow, easy to construct, great in the occasional earthquake because it bends sympathetically. Not so good, however, in the cyclones that can sweep in from the Bay of Bengal, causing flooding and landslides.

Following him into the hospital, I see rows of Rohingya people sitting on the long verandas. They're silent and look at the floor. I've never seen patients sit like this before; when they glance at me, they quickly look away. It's like they've collectively been sent to the head teacher and are waiting to be punished.

Thomas smiles at these people, makes a respectful nodding gesture saying, 'Assalaamu alaikum,' an Islamic welcome that seems to ease the tension, just slightly.

Waiting for me in the maternity unit is Sarika, the Bangladeshi head midwife at the hospital. Sarika, with her tinkling laugh, her delicate gestures, the way her head bobs gently from side to side in that familiar Indian style – the no that could mean yes – is one of the most traditionally feminine women I've ever met. On this morning, her salwar kameez is soft, pink and sparkly, her sequinned sandals have kitten heels, her wrists dance with bangles, a chiffon scarf is tied delicately around her neck. I'm immediately worried by this outfit, so different from the theatre scrubs we wore as midwives back home; how on earth will she keep it clean during births?

Sarika, I learn later, is way ahead of me. A lifetime of wearing ornate clothing means she can throw her scarf out of the way in a flash and pull the trousers up so the bottoms don't trail in birth detritus. We have washable plastic aprons on hand, hanging on the wall. In fact, I don't recall any moment where her beautiful clothes became soiled, despite her relentless hard work.

Sarika was the smart kid in her poor and mostly illiterate village, the girl who'd defied convention by refusing an arranged marriage, and going off to the big city to get an education. Fortunately, she chose a time when the Bangladeshi government was keen to improve dire infant mortality rates by training obstetric nurses (midwifery was not yet a recognised profession in its own right – that came later). Sarika studied hard, got her qualifications, then gained experience by working in government hospitals. Her golden earrings may bob around as she speaks, but she's a highly trained professional, fluent in several languages.

'She'll be your lifeline here,' Marjie had told me.

Following the imprint of Sarika's dainty kitten heels down a short outside path, we head to the forty-bed inpatient ward, where maternity patients are treated alongside other patients. Inside, the metal-frame beds, thin plastic mattresses and mosquito nets hung from a bamboo ceiling remind me of Leer Hospital. Next door is the children's ward, but you wouldn't know that from the noise, as it's unnervingly quiet. Just rows of kids staring blank-faced from their mother's lap, or semi-conscious from fever, meningitis or diarrhoea. No chatter, no laughter.

*

Our maternity unit is two small rooms lit by a single bulb suspended from the thatched bamboo ceiling. When I look up, a huge spider with thick furry legs and bulbous eyes looks down at me.

'Madam,' Sarika's bangles tinkle gaily as she pats my arm (she calls me Madam for several weeks before I convince her to call me Anna), 'please don't worry – this boy doesn't kill, just hurts.'

'We see most antenatal assessments in this room,' Sarika says, showing me the wooden bench covered by a plastic sheet where women lie down. Compared to the UK, the equipment is basic: a hand-held Doppler for listening to foetal heart rates, a Pinard stethoscope, a manual blood pressure cuff, thermometer, tape measure and a variety of basic medications. (A tape measure is one of our most-used items, as in the absence of ultrasound scans, measuring the length of the bump indicates whether the baby is growing properly.)

The place feels familiar, similar to South Sudan, but it's daunting to be back. Through the doorway is the small delivery room: a bleak metal bed with stirrups attached, where women come to give birth. Beside it, on a rusting, fold-out metal table, are disinfectant, cotton wool, gloves and sterilised equipment in stainless-steel jars.

Next to this humble maternity unit is a well-equipped lab, so at least we can do blood work on the spot, as well as testing urine and stool samples, and screening for infectious diseases. Anyone requiring surgery or a blood transfusion will be greenlit to a hospital in Cox's Bazar, if there's time, thinking of the woman who died in this room of a PPH. But anything else, including all births, I will have to manage here.

*

Bright midday sun catches the sequins in Sarika's salwar kameez and makes them dance around the dull cement floor. She's explaining the desperate plight of the Rohingya people now gathering quietly on the veranda. While most Bangladeshi Government health care is free to all (with the proviso that patients are generally expected to buy their own dressings and drugs, often from dodgy chemist shops that surround hospitals), the Rohingya are frequently excluded from hospitals because they're classified as illegal migrants rather than refugees. If they're found outside the camps, they could be arrested, deported, or worse.

'Without us, they have no easy access to doctors, nurses, hospitals or midwives,' Sarika says.

'Come!' Sarika calls our first patient, her voice loud and authoritative.

A young woman walks in. She leaves battered flip-flops at the door and pulls her scarf over her bowed head, as if to obliterate herself. She sits on the edge of the metal chair as though it might collapse. A strand of black hair escapes from her light orange headscarf, her ears are pierced but empty, her nose piercing has a splinter of wood pushed through it to keep the hole open, but no jewellery.

It's hard to see her body shape below the folds of her clothes.

But her name is Rashida. Because of what was to come, I'll always remember that.

Sarika, whose bedside manner is brusque, but not unkind, writes Rashida's details down on a single A4 antenatal card. She questions her in Rohingya, relaying the answers to me in English. This slow, circular process is daunting. *I wish I could speak to you. Or at the very least make eye contact.*

Rashida lives in a small squat in the section of the camp named D1. Like many women in Bangladesh, Sarika explains, her first and last name were taken from the Koran. Her parents called her Rashida Begum, meaning 'righteous or wise one', in the hope that this was the kind of woman she would become. Her parents died many years ago, old people being quite rare in the refugee camps, where over half the population is reported to be under eighteen. Rashida and her husband, Yusuf, are alone here now.

'Who is your majee?' Sarika asks. The majee (not to be confused with the midwife Marjie) is the man chosen to be the unofficial warden of

Rashida's section of the camp, and each camp section had one. If, for any reason, we need to track and trace Rashida, it's the majee we must contact. I find this reassuring in some ways – in South Sudan, when women left the clinic, we had little way of tracing their outcomes. But it also felt oppressively paternalistic.

Sarika closes the shutters against the midday sun and a temperature of 30°C. She asks Rashida to lift her top so we can feel her abdomen. Rashida nods, loosens her black blouse, pulls at the top of her black skirt.

'Her urine sample has tested positive for pregnancy,' Sarika says. The young woman's concave belly shows no signs of this. Rashida's skin is dry and flaking, her hip bones are prominent, with a pinkish scar across the right side, which looks like an old burn.

'Where did she get that?' I ask Sarika, trying and failing again to make eye contact with Rashida. I've heard already about the alleged violence towards Rohingya both in Myanmar and Bangladesh – shootings, beatings and burns. Without medical assistance, these burns left to heal, sometimes with turmeric powder pressed into them, often caused disfigurements or infections.

A short explosion of words follows. Sarika talking, Rashida shaking her head.

'She won't tell me,' Sarika says, 'but she was born in Kutupalong camp – it must have happened here.'

I'm aghast. Rashida, who is twenty-two, has spent her whole life in this bleak shit-pile place. When I was a young girl enjoying that lovely country cottage in Shropshire, she was here, and here she will stay until the atrocities against the Rohingya people end. Maybe forever.

'She's never stepped foot out of the camp,' continues Sarika, 'except to collect firewood along the road to Teknaf,' a town closer to the border with Myanmar.

My heart hurts for Rashida – no wonder her eyes are so dull, her stare so blank. She's spent her entire childhood in a camp where schooling is forbidden, where fixing your own roof can mean punishment for trying to improve your own existence. She has no passport. No country. This is what it means to be *stateless*. Unwanted in Bangladesh, but fearful of being pushed back over the border to Myanmar, where they're also unwanted. Hopeless.

Sarika fires off more information. Rashida has been almost continuously pregnant since she was sixteen years old, having miscarried fourteen times, all within the first three months of pregnancy.

Why does she keep getting pregnant then? might sound like a reasonable question, except there are multiple and complicated answers. Maybe she had no choice, maybe she's simply expected to bear children, maybe lack of education, lack of understanding. Or because her husband may expect sex and she has no power or agency to say no. Maybe because contraception is either banned or hard to get hold of, or her husband simply refused to use a condom. Leave the husband you say? But the consequences of that might be starving to death. Men are the only potential breadwinners here, and many risk their own lives by leaving the camps at night to find work in local towns. A woman with no family and no husband here is vulnerable to attack, rape, trafficking and ultimately death.

Or maybe she simply longed for a baby – something warm and alive, someone who made her feel necessary. It's a fierce desire that can grow and get stronger when you've lost a pregnancy. I was to learn this later myself, the hard way.

But what we needed to figure out this morning was why all the consecutive miscarriages? In the UK there would be tests, ultrasounds, referrals to specialist units. Here there was Sarika and me.

We do blood work, check for blood-borne viruses – nothing significant comes up, except anaemia. But I have no idea what else to offer. My first patient and I'm stumped.

Sarika takes charge:

'We will offer tetanus vaccine, pregnancy vitamins, a mosquito net, soap, we will see her every month and she will come back if she starts to bleed, have pain or a fever.'

There's a bluntness in this assessment that at first takes me by surprise. Sarika is sweet and clearly caring, but she knows the limits of help here. For instance, Rashida is stick thin, but unless someone is severely malnourished, we're prevented from distributing food, as this would improve the well-being of the Rohingya. If we did it anyway, we risked being banned from the camps completely.

It's wretched to bear witness to such suffering, but have to limit the help we can give.

Before she steps off the bed, I notice a black cord tied around Rashida's tummy. A belly chain that Sarika says is a tawiz, pronounced 'tabiz', 'To keep her safe.'

Inside the small metal amulet tied to the cord are herbs and some writing from the Koran, though some deem the talisman to be black magic rather than religious. Different religion, different continent, but with the same symbolism as those beaded teek belly chains in South Sudan. The message is: *Pregnancy is risk, you need protection*. When you're poor, you need all the courage you can get, and I perceive Rashida's tawiz as a small green shoot of hope. Maybe the splinter of wood through the nose piercing is another glimpse of hope too –the hole stays open in the hope that one day she will be able to put jewellery there. At the very least, Rashida has trusted us enough to come for assessment, I tell myself, she wants to keep herself and the pregnancy safe.

When Sarika hands Rashida her antenatal chart, a single piece of card in a plastic sleeve, Rashida's eyes light up.

'She will carry this like gold,' Sarika says over her shoulder. 'It's the first document ever to have her name on it.'

'Come!' Rashida is dispatched quickly as Sarika calls the next patient. So many more women to see, so many needs. But Rashida is under my skin, and there she has stayed.

CHAPTER TWENTY

Instinctive tenderness is not a phrase that crops up in midwifery textbooks, but Marjie was right: you're no good as a midwife without it. You're meeting a woman at the most vulnerable and challenging moment of her life. Routinely touching her in places so intimate, they're usually out of bounds for anyone but a lover. She might be yelling, screaming, swearing like Gordon Ramsey, crying, laughing or groaning most terribly – she may go to a place beyond words. She might feel herself at the very limits of her courage, her energy, a space she has never known before. You might find yourself covered in her blood; or your cheek next to hers as you hug her and tell her *you can do this*. You will shine lights between her legs, you may hurt her without wanting to; whisper in her ear, reassure her that losing control of her bowels is normal, you will tell her she's amazing! You will grasp her hand with joy, you might guide her face towards yours and say, *trust me, I will keep you safe,* you will watch her scream with joy as her first bluish and cream-covered baby is placed in her arms; you will cry with her if the worst thing happens.

While it's never OK to touch someone who does not want to be touched, in general, without touch, without gaze, something incredibly powerful and precious is gone. In a way, it's a virtuous circle because when the woman looks back with trust, it gives me strength and confidence in my skills. Without gaze or touch, I feel less able to do what I do well. I learnt this first in Bangladesh, and later while attending births behind a plastic shield during the Covid crisis.

The Rohingya women here do not trust me. They do not want me to hold their hand. They shy away painfully from even my smile. If I try to offer comfort in my old way, it can make them feel worse. This is because they have no reason to trust anyone, because they're constantly hit by impossible choices. Every single Rohingya person in this camp of 30,000 people, and in the camps next door, has a horror story to tell. *Every single one.*

Here I witness a mother discharging her desperately ill child – one we could have saved – because she was worried her neighbour would steal her cooking pot. Without the pot to cook rice, the whole family could die of starvation. And what of the many young men who attempted a painful suicide by drinking insecticide when they felt there was no hope left? Or came to us unconscious after taking *yaba*, an awful mixture of methamphetamine and caffeine often crudely mixed with cement or poisons. I have never seen suffering on this scale, and, at first, I feel paralysed by it.

Here my own emotions feel like an irrelevance, an indulgence, they make me angry, but even so, during those first few weeks, my body keeps the score. It's like a strap is being tightened around my chest and a constant pressure around the bottom of my neck. Loneliness rumbles in my chest, self-doubt echoes between my ears. This is too much, I can't do this. And I'm supposed to be leading this team. Reluctant to reveal my fears to people I don't know yet, once again I write to Anita over email, and once again she sends the right words at the right time. *Everyone feels this way in a new project. Trust you'll find a way to make things a little better, a little safer for the women there. Think about what you want to achieve in your time there.*

*

A month in, and Thomas and I have become close. Not romantically close – it's clear from the start that neither of us feels that way – but intimate in other ways. We trust each other's medical opinions, we get how crazy and guilt-making the contrast is between the relative comfort of our apartment and the camp where horrors are daily and the need endless. We know we're the privileged ones. We can get on a plane if it gets too much.

We're seeing about 1,000 people a week from all areas of the camp. About 60 per cent are Rohingya from the Makeshift Camp, the rest from poorer local Bangladeshi homes. One big problem in the maternity wing is that although we see about a hundred pregnant women a month, most Rohingya babies are still delivered inside their shacks in secret, in the dark, and mostly in unsanitary conditions. I start to wonder if it's an impossible dream for every woman to give birth in the comparative cleanliness and safely of the hospital. We don't have the space or the staff for that yet, but I start sketching out a plan for it at night. *Could a birth unit be what I hope to achieve here?*

Thomas and I work five days a week in the hospital. On Fridays, the first day of the weekend in Bangladesh, when our male Muslim staff tend to go to local mosques and the women pray at home, we work in the MSF office in Cox's Bazar, where there is a vast amount of admin to keep on top of. Ordering drugs with the help of Djimon, our upbeat but shy Ethiopian logistician, writing reports for Amsterdam, planning new health programmes.

Saturdays are, officially, our one day off. No drivers are rostered, and even though we make sure the best national MSF staff are at the clinic, there's always the low hum of anxiety in the background. It's not like South Sudan here, as all our staff are highly educated, but they still want to consult us on complex cases. We'll be eating rice and vegetables at lunch in the apartment, Jason telling us a funny story from home, or Thomas will be daydreaming about his approaching end of mission in his soft German lullaby tones, when a mobile phone will ring. Thomas will leap into the small kitchen, where there's a two-ring gas hob and a fridge. He'll speak slowly and clearly:

'Listen to the bottom of the lungs. If it is crepitus, it may be pneumonia.' A pause. 'Count the breaths for one minute, tell me how many she is taking.' He's sweating with the strain of hearing limited English over the phone with a poor connection, his brow deeply furrowed. 'Give the paediatric dose of the IV antibiotics.' It might be a sick child, a burnt baby, a snakebite.

'I want to be able to go to the hospital,' he states when he gets off the phone.

'You cannot work every day of the week. You'll burn out. Our staff at the hospital need to be able to deal with these cases,' would be Jason's calm reply.

Of course he was right, but I feel the same frustration as Thomas. My work mobile, which does only texts and calls, becomes a permanent extension of my body. When I'm not at the hospital, I never really get a day off because my phone may ring three or four times a day or night, and its shrill tones makes my chest constrict. *Who's dying? Bleeding? Convulsing?* I must find the words, speak clearly: 'Inject IV cefuroxime and metronidazole… Give paracetamol for fever.' Simple sentences. Short sentences. I charge my phone obsessively, scared it will run out of battery. I sleep with it under my pillow. Not knowing where it is sends my anxiety through the roof. But my fear is proportionate – someone could die if I miss a call.

Friday nights are not exactly party nights, not yet anyway, but nights for chilling. Inside the ten-storey Pink Pearl live an exotic mixture of French, American, Italian, Japanese and Dutch workers. All represent different organisations, but most work mainly with other groups of Rohingya people in the scattered camps between Kutupalong and Teknaf.

Although, later, things got a little out of hand, when cumulative stress caused our boundaries to expire, so far Friday nights are relatively tame: maybe a film with all of us crammed around a laptop, or someone cooking food from their home country. Maybe a couple of cans of Hunter beer – local, weak fizzy lager and, at £2 for a small can, expensive – but somehow tasting of home. We might climb up to the apartment's flat roof, floor mats in hand. You could hear the bubbling of street life from up there, the tinkle of a rickshaw bell, smell the salt from the sea or rubbish from the streets, depending which way the wind was blowing. You could drink some more beer and chew the fat and try to forget, though sometimes Thomas and I catch each other's eye in that unspoken way because maybe we'd both seen the bloated drowned child too late that day, or the woman who'd had a miscarriage after refusing treatment for pneumonia. And knowing he knows makes a difference. That same camaraderie I had grown to love in James was here as well, and I was grateful for it. I was back with people who understood, and that, at least, felt good.

CHAPTER TWENTY-ONE

'Assalaamu alaikum, Anna!' Sarika greets me in the morning. She's finally dropped the 'Madam'. She's also started to quiz me: 'Why are you not married, Anna?' Rather than wait for an answer, she happily instructs me, 'You must find a husband, Anna. A nice Bangladeshi man.' If only she knew what was to come.

But sometimes, it's also my turn to quiz her, explaining the dangers of the skin-lightening cream I've seen her pile onto her face and which, sadly, is so popular here.

Today she wears a coral-coloured salwar kameez and delicate scarf. Her hair is oiled, her nails brightly painted, and she seems to float towards me like a delicate butterfly.

After two months of round-the-clock calls, I'm starting to count down the days until my first R & R in April. I've been working long nights at a computer in the Cox's Bazar office after day shifts at the camp and hospital. Already I'm worried I'm running on empty, but I'm determined to finish a plan Sarika and I have been working on for the new birth unit at Kutupalong. Here we could employ qualified Bangladeshi nurses that we'll train as midwives, and also create an outreach education programme for the camp TBAs (traditional birth attendants). We're a good team: Sarika has a far deeper understanding of maternal health here than I do, while I'm more experienced at researching aid literature and writing a formal proposal for MSF.

Many of the one hundred births a month at the camps are attended by Rohingya TBAs, and it's them we must convince if we are to get women to birth in the hospital. Our relationship with the TBAs is complex and crucial to the success of our plan. They are the ones, after all, who depend on the women in the camps for their livelihood – their services are often paid in food rather than money. They speak the same language, they're familiar and trusted in ways we're not. Many of the TBAs are well-meaning and experienced, they've offered services when no one else has, but they are not formally educated, so we're seeing far too many women brought in with injuries and infections as a direct result of their care. We heard rumours of a woman bleeding to death while the TBA refused to bring her to the hospital, and who was buried before dawn. If the birth unit is going to work, we must find a way of involving the TBAs in a whole new way of doing things.

How to do this becomes an obsessional game of mental chess for me. Funds are so limited and the need so vast. A new unit means a new building; the hiring and training of fifteen new midwives; a completely new supply chain of obstetric medications and equipment. After a few weeks, and some false starts, I submit a proposal, fully costed and referenced, to the operational centre in Amsterdam.

Looking back, I was probably too forceful during those first tense meetings with Jason that follow. His responsibility is the whole project, not just maternity care, but I'm desperate to get this thing done. It feels like a new and separate me emerging – someone more outspoken, more determined, even if it means I'm liked less. I'm not sure what my parents would think of this new me, but I can imagine James winking at me, egging me on. I tried to channel his style of negotiation. It was never aggressive, but he was good at ignoring what other people thought of him and ploughing on regardless. 'Sometimes in life, Anna,' he'd told me once in Tam, 'you have to not care what others think to get things done.'

*

It's a boiling hot day at the end of February. I'm halfway through a ward round, aware time's running out. Pressure always mounted in the afternoon as we approached our 17.30 deadline to head home. If our driver hadn't phoned Jason by 17.45 to say we were on our way, mobiles would ring in our pockets, instructing us to head home. After nearly getting fired in South Sudan, I'm aware of how seriously MSF takes its security policy, and intend to stick to it.

Today I have about fifteen pregnant and post-natal women as inpatients. I hate that there's no space and they have to be nursed on a ward with the male patients. Some need IV antibiotics for infection, one has a severe breast abscess that needs draining, one has severe pre-eclampsia, others have pneumonia. I'd hoped to do this ward round before the antenatal clinic opened this morning, but it wasn't possible – one of our nurses hadn't turned up for her shift, so Sarika adjusted the rota and has gone home to rest before covering the night shift.

I'm checking my watch, only half an hour to go and many more patients to see, when Benita puts her head around the door. 'Anna,' she says politely, 'can you come, please? We have an emergency.'

Benita, one of our nurses, is twenty-four years old and very private about her background, but with her tilted eyes, glossy eyelashes and thick black hair is often mistaken as Chinese by foreigners. In fact, she's Chakma, one of the Tibetan–Burman people of Bangladesh, and wears traditional Chakma weave in colours of deep blue, red and orange. She's still shy with me, her English better than she thinks it is.

With a loud holler in Bangla from the hospital guard, a young collapsed woman is hauled into the back maternity room and onto the bed with stirrups. She lies, curled on her side, groaning, her long skirt hitched to her knees. Trails of dried blood stretch down both legs, staining her shoeless feet. The man who carried her in walks off hurriedly before we can learn any more.

Benita says the girl's name is Aadab. Aadab's clutching her stomach, wincing in pain, crying, 'Oh, All-ahhhh!'

One of her front teeth is missing. When her black headscarf falls to the floor, Benita bends to pick it up. She speaks gently to Aadab in Rohingya, and slowly, so slowly, we get drip-fed small amounts of information. Child marriage was common in the camps, but at sixteen years old, Aadab is unmarried, but also a few weeks pregnant. To be pregnant and unmarried is considered a big sin by many people here. More complicated, without a birth certificate, Benita wonders if this girl is even younger, but lying to us about her age.

Starting basic checks, Benita thinks Aadab's been bleeding for four days now. Her respiratory rate is startlingly high, her abdomen painful, her temperature soaring over 40°C.

'Likely sepsis with working diagnosis of incomplete miscarriage,' Benita reels off shyly but accurately.

Sepsis can still be fatal, even in the UK, so we have to work fast. It takes skill and patience for Benita to get an IV line in. Consent is complicated, as there are no parents here to confirm consent for a minor, but this is a medical emergency, so we go ahead. Aadab stops screaming as strong morphine painkillers go in. I'm putting on my headtorch, Aadab finally agrees, and we're ready to do a life-saving speculum vaginal exam, when Benita touches my arm.

'Look there.'

Peering into the vagina and towards the cervix, I expect to see some blood, and maybe dark clots of birth product. Sometimes the cervix will still be a little open after miscarriage, but this cervix is closed, and there are deep gashes bleeding all around it. Cuts. Wounds. Right up high in her vagina.

'What is that?' I breathe to Benita, having never seen such an injury.

Aadab gives a muffled cry, turns her face to the bamboo wall in shame. Benita coos to her soothingly.

After the exam is over, in the privacy of the next room, Benita takes a deep breath as if weighing up what to tell me.

'Tell me everything,' I say.

'This is a home abortion. Either she, or maybe a TBA, has given her a forced abortion with a stick. A "Burmese" stick they call it.'

I feel sick.

'Why?'

'Maybe she was raped?'

'What the fuck?'

Benita turns away in shyness at my language, which I instantly regret.

I then learn of Aadab's grim options. If her pregnancy was the result of rape, she, a stateless refugee, would potentially be forced to marry her rapist, if he was known. This was a way to save her from the 'sin' of pregnancy outside marriage. It was horrifying. I couldn't even encourage her to tell the police – she's illegal in this country, and stateless, no authority can or will protect her.

The 'Burmese' stick would become hideously familiar during this project. It's the sharpened stick that a desperate woman, or untrained

TBA, used to pummel into the vagina and up through the closed cervix in order to destroy the pregnancy inside. It's deadly because it introduces infection, damages the vagina and cervix, and leaves dead pregnancy tissue deep inside the uterus.

I'm numb as we start IV antibiotics, my mind reeling. I wouldn't describe myself as pro-abortion, as that could imply I looked upon this complex issue dismissively, which of course I don't. But I am certainly pro-choice, and believe it is a woman's right to choose what happens with her body. And surely, personal opinions aside, no one on Earth could argue that Aadab should marry a rapist because she was pregnant? Aadab, whose name means hope.

My pocket vibrates. It's 17.45.

Oh, God, no. 'We have to go.' Thomas is standing in the doorway, his eyes full of hurt and understanding.

I get into the 4 x 4.

'Fuck this place!' I cry on his shoulder in the back of the vehicle, clutching my phone as I await Benita's update on Aadab's condition. Our car swerves around a wandering goat.

CHAPTER TWENTY-TWO

'Happy birthday,' I say to my reflection in the bathroom mirror. I'm thirty today. My hair is falling out – this morning there were more long strands on the pillow. My periods have become irregular again, another sign of stress. Putting on my faded pink salwar kameez with short sleeves, I peer in the mirror – I've lost weight around my cheeks, the wrinkles around my eyes are deeper. The pressure on my chest is constant now. Jaw clenched. Feels like fingers wrapping around my neck. I feel damaged and vulnerable. I don't want to phone anyone from home, it feels too far away.

In South Sudan with James, it felt different in the end. It was tough, but there were moments of fulfilment there – like we were running a two-man hospital and not doing so badly, all things considered. The people I treated there often smiled, looked us in the eye, made jokes. This place can feel like the death of hope; there is so much that is uncontrollable. These feelings only got worse when Aadab died in the night, when I wasn't at the hospital. If she'd had access to a safe abortion, she would probably have lived. When no family came to claim her body, I paid for the burial, back in the land that had failed her. *She needed intensive care, but there just isn't one anywhere near here,* I tried to console myself, to convince myself that it wasn't my fault. But instead Aadab joined the line of souls who sat heavy on my shoulders.

This place feels like two worlds, with a border guard between them. One is our bare apartment in Cox's Bazar, with a whirring, rusted fan, a bathroom with cockroaches scuttling in the plug hole, a thin line of blood from a squashed mosquito. Late nights with glowing blue face from the office computer screen; tossing and turning on a hard bed, phone under my pillow. Evening air smelling of dust, sandalwood and flatbreads.

Chirping night insects, tinkling rickshaw bells. Crying quietly in the cold shower. Laughter. Watching naff TV series on DVD. Gut-wrenching car rides. Loneliness and, later, the Frenchman. When I wrote to Anita about him, she was the first to say it: *he will break your heart*.

The other world is the refugee camp and its constant rumble of suppressed anger. Of shame. Of futility. Of fear. It's the empty space when there's no fight left. No singing. No building. Women birthing in darkness, shrouded in fear; bloodied concrete latrines being sloshed out; a place where people go missing every day and are almost never found, where our only way to estimate the death rate is to count the graves. There is no word for 'happiness' in the Rohingya language inside the Makeshift Camp.

Clicking on Facebook, I read birthday messages from friends and family, some I should've replied to weeks ago. 'Hello stranger,' reads one. 'We'll celebrate when you get back,' says another. But Facebook has started to feel like a bad friend – all those laughing, smiling, kissing, drinking, getting married and pregnant people make me feel lonely and disjointed – and the suffering in the camp feel worse. I sort of want to reach out, but if I showed pictures of Kutupalong, that sneery voice in my head would accuse me of being the worst kind of attention seeker. The few shots I take are bland images of us, a band of young people drinking and larking around at the Pink Pearl on a Friday night. My emails home to my parents and friends are self-censored again. I say vaguely that it's hard here, but I say nothing about vaginas torn with sticks, it just feels too much. All my relationships at home are becoming more diluted as I withdraw from them and those lives move on.

Last time I googled, a news article popped up saying some Hollywood stars were injecting their wrinkles with tissue from baby foreskins – potentially harvested from poor people in poor countries like Bangladesh – and I wanted to vomit. *So don't read this shit, no one needs your moral outrage, no one likes a goody-goody, you can only be useful here if you stay strong and forget about the rest.* That's how my thinking goes now, and once again, just as in South Sudan, my world starts to divide into those who know, and those who don't, and after three months here, I feel closest to Sarika and Thomas. I don't have to hide with them, except that's only partially true. When I do feel myself falling apart, I hide in the shower, put the water on so no one can hear me, and howl.

*

On the March morning of my birthday, I arrive at the clinic wanting to vomit as usual – the car sickness never went away – but the whole nursing team is waiting for me at the bamboo entrance. They're holding out gifts and their beaming faces bring a burst of happiness. I didn't expect this, especially as many of our staff don't celebrate their own birthdays, only that of the Prophet Mohammed.

Thomas winks at me as he lumbers on towards the inpatient unit. He looks pale with exhaustion – he's days away from going home now. Sarika holds out a pink flower she grew on her tiny rented back porch in Ukhiya. She tucks it delicately behind my ear, her smile so bright, so beautiful. Idris, one of the outreach workers, gives me a large cucumber he grew in his garden. I've never known more generous people than the staff here. I've had to train myself to go easy with the compliments: early on when I admired a bangle Sarika was wearing, she took it off and fastened it on my wrist, insisted I keep it there, said she'd be offended if I didn't. Although the staff earn a respectable local wage, they have little to spare, yet food is always offered, tea always bought. These small acts of kindness can make me feel British and humble and awkward – I'm still finding my way.

'Where shall we start today?' Sarika asks, in a waft of rose water, and as eager as ever to work.

I say, 'I'd like to find Rashida.'

Rashida was the tiny, timid pregnant woman I first assessed back in February. Her light orange headscarf, her nose piercing kept open with a wooden splinter. Rashida, who'd miscarried fourteen times, but politely removed her flip-flops at the door, would now be around ten weeks pregnant, if she hadn't already lost this baby.

Sarika and I are taken into the camp by Amin, the outreach supervisor, an elegant young man well versed in local politics.

The sun is already fierce as the three of us trek into the refugee camp boundary; heat bounces and gleams off Amin's carefully combed hair. Sarika walks several paces behind him with her head down, almost obliterated by her headscarf, a deliberate act of submission, even though they are the same level of seniority inside the hospital. Cracked mud under our feet, the scent of woodsmoke and latrines in the still air. My walking boots squelch with sweat, Sarika has exchanged her kitten heels for ballet pumps. After a hundred yards or so, Amin helps me up a steep ravine to a higher tier of the camp. No trees or bushes line the thin pathway, just shack after shack made of sticks, plastic scraps and mud.

Each day, twenty-five Bangladeshi MSF outreach workers go into the camps so they can find sick people and encourage them to go to the clinic. Their role is diverse, from giving information about our vaccination campaigns to antenatal clinics. They assess nutrition, teach hygiene, but arguably their most important role is to be the eyes and ears of the camp and bring back rumours and information of disease outbreaks, more refugees arriving and local politics.

Rashida lives in an area of the camp called D1, but Amin has purposely taken a detour on our way there so we can see the smouldering remains of a large wooden frame.

'The people tried to build a madrasah here,' he says matter-of-factly, 'to attempt some education for the children. It was burnt down before it was finished,' he says, and walks on.

'Who burnt it down?' I ask quietly. The air still smells acrid, smoky.

Amin looks over his shoulder. A group of local men are staring at us. 'I can't tell you that here.' His silent nod asks the men if it's OK for us to keep walking. They know him and nod back, and on we walk, in silence.

So many secrets here. Later I hear rumours that the school was burnt down by a landowner, allegedly punishing the refugees for not paying enough rent. Unbelievably, these people pay rent in several of the refugee camps around here. Paying to live in hell.

After twenty minutes of uphill walking, Amin stops to talk to a serious-looking man with a white skullcap (tupi). Sarika stands respectfully back. The man's shirt is blindingly white against the beige mud. He has a long black beard, thick eyebrows and listens carefully as Amin talks politely to him. The pair of spectacles tucked in his shirt pocket are a status symbol – there's no glass in the frames.

'He's the local majee; he'll know where Rashida lives,' Sarika whispers discreetly – these unofficial Rohingya leaders are politician, judge and police all in one. Some are good men, others potentially mobsters, who take bribes, enable human trafficking and resist any change that might protect women.

'He's the man we must also convince,' Sarika lowers her voice, 'to get women to come to our birth unit or use contraception.'

I feel my cheeks grow hot at the thought of having to cajole and finesse for the right to give birth in safety. It's criminal how low down the pecking order these women are.

With a nod from the majee, we walk down another winding muddy path.

And suddenly we've arrived.

Rashida's squat is a doorless stick-frame home. Its roof formed from torn and sun-bleached plastic scraps and wood, the outside wall, made of mud, bears the marks of a woman's delicate fingerprints.

When Amin murmurs 'Assalaamu alaikum,' from outside, there's a flurry of movement inside, like a trapped animal looking for an exit. Seconds later, Rashida, wrapping her orange headscarf round her hair, bolts out of her home. When she darts a look to the majee and Amin, all the whites of her eyes are visible, and I'm suddenly frightened that by coming to see her, I've made her life more difficult. Would she be punished for being singled out?

But the majee has moved on, serious-faced, to his next task.

'He's a good majee, don't worry.' Amin reads my thoughts. 'I wouldn't bring you here if it would make trouble. Trust me.'

I have to trust him. There's so much here I'll never understand, it makes my head reel.

'Please.' Amin signals for Sarika and me to enter Rashida's home. He stands alert by the doorway.

Taking off my walking boots, I stoop to get through the doorway. Her home, which is night-time dark, smells of smoke. My sweaty socks leave footprints on the swept dry mud of the floor. In the corner, a small circle of stones holds ashes from last night's cooking fire, beside it a single metal pot and spoon, but no chimney. Her supplies consist of a small paper bag of rice, a bag of salt, a pile of gnarly sticks for kindling and a broken plastic bottle with half an inch of cooking oil inside.

A rolled-up bamboo mat stands in the corner; at night it'll be unfolded for her bed on the hard ground. I can't see any bed covers, or any other clothes, just a metal water pot in the shape of a football trophy and a brush made out of feathered twigs. With three women now jammed inside, there's no room to stand up, so we squat to the floor.

Rashida looks up at the ceiling, where she stores her items of importance: her MSF antenatal card, pristine and covered in its plastic sleeve; a used bar of soap we gave her; pregnancy vitamins; a mosquito net carefully folded away; and a sharp knife for cooking. This is the bleak sum total of Rashida's existence.

Sarika starts to chat gently to Rashida in Rohingya, and for the first time Rashida looks directly at me as she replies. My breath catches, nervous.

'She is very grateful,' explains Sarika. I'm initially confused, but she continues, 'You took your shoes off as you came into her home. This is very respectful. She's very grateful for that.'

So Rashida has decided to trust me because I took off my shoes, or was it something else? What matters most to other humans is often so mysterious, so hidden. There's a lump in my throat but I swallow it – not wanting to ruin this moment.

Slowly Sarika and I do a full assessment with Rashida, and this time she's more cooperative. We gently feel over her abdomen with the old scar, still adorned with the tawiz. The small bump in her uterus shows she's still pregnant, and thankfully no bleeding. Her other checks – temperature, blood pressure – are normal and recorded on her antenatal card. Information now flows a little more freely, and we're able tentatively to ask more questions. She says she's been able to buy a small amount of fish and green spinach from a local Bangladeshi landowner in exchange for collecting wood in the jungle. Wood-collecting comes with risks of snakebites and attacks from angry locals, but it's a small reassurance she's eating. Rashida's eyes are downcast as she explains that she hasn't heard from her husband Yusuf for over two weeks. He went to find work in Cox's Bazar, hoping to make rent money, not wanting her pregnant and collecting wood. She hoped that he'd found work, maybe cycling a rickshaw, or cheap labour on a building site, but she didn't know if he was safe. It was unlikely that illegal workers would have the luxury of hard hats or scaffolding, they also raised anger in the local population for undercutting the cost of labourers. What if he had been caught by the border guard and transported back to Myanmar? Or worse?

Standing in the faint light of her doorway, she looks, with her tiny frame and delicate features, like a child.

As we leave, Rashida promises to come to the clinic for another check-up in four weeks' time, a cycle of the moon, sooner if she has any problems. Although I yearn to hug her, or to reach out, I know it would make her uncomfortable. But, in a surprise gesture, as I stoop to leave her home, she reaches out and gently touches the back of my arm. I think I catch the glimmer of a smile.

I'm elated walking back to the clinic. This feels like such a breakthrough, as I'm here to help vulnerable women, and the touch of her hand on my arm feels like *the best birthday gift ever*. It's a sign that she trusts me. It makes me believe I can do some good here, and that feels amazing, and, best of all, Rashida's baby is still alive!

*

We're crossing the hot tarmacked road that leads back to the bamboo hospital, past the long queues of quiet people waiting to be seen, when a guard comes running.

'Go to Benita,' he shouts.

Running into the small delivery toom, a woman is lying on the bed, clearly labouring. Beside her is an older, bigger woman, white hair tied back in a bun.

'She's Reza, a TBA,' Benita says hurriedly, nodding towards the older woman.

'This refugee has been in labour for two days, waters have broken, but baby doesn't come.'

Benita's listening to the baby's heartbeat with the hand-held Doppler, and on hearing the 'sh, sh, sh' of a clear foetal heart rate, we all breathe a little easier.

Benita explains, 'I did a vaginal exam, 4 cm dilated, but there's a problem – I think the face is presenting, I can feel the lips.'

A face presentation is an emergency because the hyperextended neck (rather than a tucked-in head) could prevent the birth, causing injury or death to the baby. The diameter of the face is usually too wide for the finite space within the pelvis, especially for women who have themselves suffered childhood malnutrition, where their pelvis may not grow properly, causing cephalopelvic disproportion.

Gratitude to Reza, the TBA, sings in my chest. She chose to bring this woman to the clinic before things got any worse. It's another reminder of how important it is to nourish our TBA relationship. Sarika, who can see how serious this obstructed labour is, starts to rap out orders.

'I'll get the birth kit, you assess her, Anna.' She rushes to get the sterile kits from the autoclave behind the clinic. Sarika's a dynamo when an emergency requires it.

With a nod of consent from the labouring woman, Alifah, whom I've barely met, I wash my hands and put on sterile gloves. Alifah groans from a new wave of contractions. Benita puts in an IV drip and prepares antibiotics to prevent infection from prolonged rupture of membranes – plus we knew most TBAs didn't wear gloves.

Pushing my fingers as gently as I can into Alifah's vagina, I can feel the baby's head against the cervix. Yes, still about 4 cm dilated, definitely in established labour. Also, I can feel the soft squashy body parts that Benita thinks are the baby's lips, being careful not to damage anything. But then, wait! What's this? There's a strong pulse in this soft tissue. We were wrong about the lips, it's the umbilical cord.

Now it's all hands on deck – racing to save the life of this baby. Cord prolapse, an umbilical cord coming through the cervix first, is a dire emergency. Pressure from the baby's head on to the cord could cut off the blood supply at any time, killing it or leaving serious brain damage. With the cervix dilated to only 4 cm, there's no chance of a prompt, safe vaginal birth, so our only option is an emergency caesarean section. There's a flurry of activity around me, but I can't move – part of the emergency care is that I must keep my hand deep inside the vagina, with my fingers carefully pushing back the head of the baby to stop it pressing on the cord. It's a delicate but life-saving manoeuvre.

We tilt Alifah backwards with a rolled-up blanket under her bum, lift her onto a stretcher, me waddling beside her, my hands still under her long skirt. Sarika gives her a potent injection to safely stop her contractions, as Benita grabs a sheet to put over her. Thomas runs alongside me as I tell him we're taking one of the vehicles to Cox's Bazar and I'll see him back at the apartment later. He's on the phone to Jason, getting the greenlight to move a patient.

Within my emergency kit is a bulging envelope of cash for moments like this, to pay around £70 for an emergency caesarean section at a private hospital. As the driver guns the engine, Sarika and I face backwards in the rear of the 4 x 4, my hand still inside Alifah, guarding the cord. Reza, the TBA, bravely insists on coming; as a stateless refugee, this comes with risks to her too. With four bodies wedged into the back of the vehicle, we tear off down the road, swerving in and out of the traffic, full of adrenaline and fear. It's painfully awkward, jammed together in the back, but I'm desperate not to move my hand, which has started to cramp. *I will not lose another patient.*

My world has contracted to keeping that umbilical cord, that baby's lifeline, safe.

As we bump and swerve, my stomach begins to swirl. When I start to vomit, Sarika hands me a plastic bag from her purse, but I don't move my hand. The journey seems to take a hundred years.

When we pull into Cox's Bazar over an hour later, our driver sounds his horn as a constant, deafening blare. The massive seven-storey brick hospital feels imposing, and we dash in with a stretcher, watched by long queues of staring people. Strong chlorine smell from the washed tile floors, a working lift. Sarika talking in a rat-tat voice to a surgeon she knows, me running alongside Alifah, my hand still inside her, towards the theatre. Talk of blood transfusions, contact details, where Reza can sit. Sarika discreetly drops off the money.

When the theatre doors close, Sarika and I stand in an empty, silent corridor, looking at each other. For me, it's such a moment. I peel off my gloves and find somewhere to wash the amniotic fluid off my arms. Sarika stands in one of her glamorous salwars with one bead of sweat on her forehead, she's seen all this before, her shock absorbers are better than mine.

'Let me buy you sweet tea,' she says, composed and smiling. In her mind we've drawn the line on this emergency and are now on to the next thing.

*

Later that night, I'm on the roof of our apartment, drinking rum from a fresh coconut, a bit tipsy, but also stressed and distracted. One of the French team has put on some Novatunes music and about ten of us are having a party.

'Happy birthday! Bonne anniversaire!' they shout happily to me.

The phone in my pocket buzzes — a text message from Sarika. My throat is almost too tight to breathe.

'Boy baby born today to Alifah. Mum and baby safe and well.'

'Yeah!' I cry out loud. Thomas runs over to read the message.

'Yes! YES!'

It really is the best birthday gift ever. We look at each other. Wide-eyed, ecstatic. We understand each other. I can still feel my hand on that pulsing cord, and that baby lived.

Thomas tops up the coconut with more rum and no mixer. He takes my phone away. 'You're not on call tonight, Anna. I'll do it,' he says firmly, and fills his glass with water.

I feel so high. We're winning the small battles that Anita told me to look for and it feels amazing.

Grinning, shaking my head, not sure whether to laugh or cry, as Jason grooves up beside me. 'And guess what?' he says. 'You also got the greenlight from Amsterdam to make your birth unit.'

The best moment of my life to date.

CHAPTER TWENTY-THREE

This is perfect, I say to myself, taking a deep breath. I'm on leave, a few weeks later, hoping to give my brain a break from my growing obsession with setting up the birth unit, and the horror and confusion of the camps. Right now, I'm lying in my bikini in the shade of a palm tree on the beach of a Thai island called Koh Phi Phi. This beach, with its turquoise waters and silvery white sand, its coral reefs and magnificent sunsets, is paradise. I've been enticed here by the seductive images in the Leonardo DiCaprio movie *The Beach*, which was filmed nearby, and it's more beautiful than I'd expected.

The notebook I've been scribbling in is temporarily closed. *I'm here to relax.* I'm sipping a ginger tea with honey, looking at the shadows the palm leaves make on the sand, listening to the slurp and slap of the sea.

Tonight I'll sleep in a pure white bed underneath a mosquito net in the quaint wooden beach hut behind me. Inside there's my own shower with proper hot water, a really comfortable bed, and I have five more days ahead of me here at only £20 a night. It's such a romantic setting, but I'm glad there's no one sharing the bed with me because, when my inner cheerleader shuts up, I'm feeling silent and introverted. And even if I had a boyfriend, I wouldn't want to ruin someone else's holiday again by being dreadful company. Before lunch I'll swim, then wander up to the shaded outside restaurant to eat a salad of noodles and fresh vegetables. I can sleep all afternoon if I want to.

And then it comes again – the pounding of my heart, a feeling that bats are flying around my chest, the sudden weight as I lie here trying to breathe calmly, the shooting pains running between my shoulder blades, a feeling of imminent doom, just as people describe when they have a heart attack. I hate this happening, particularly with everything around me so calm and serene. I can't control it. It frightens me. It doesn't belong in the picture. I'm not ready yet to recognise this as a response to trauma.

Instead, when the chest pains start, I drink a Chang beer in the shade, which helps. Then maybe another in the early afternoon, and then I wait for the point when the alcohol makes the pain stop and I can breathe again. When the sun sets and the sea turns red, I'll wander back to the same small beach restaurant and order supper – *pad thai* for about £1. It's my favourite, containing peanuts, fresh local vegetables and green papaya. Lately, I've gone off the seemingly perfect local vegetables in Cox's Bazar market after a news article revealed that some were illegally treated with formalin as a preservative. That's what can be used to preserve dead bodies. *You have to stop thinking about Bangladesh.*

When it's dark, I sit on the beach again, or sometimes on the balcony and drink a gin and tonic, watch the small, anchored sailing boats bob on the water, trying not to think of ruptured cervixes or women giving birth alone in the camp. A few Chinese lanterns drift up to the heavens from the local town. I try to read some light novel, but end up getting sucked down a rabbit hole with thoughts of the 2004 tsunami that hit here in Thailand. Where would I run to? Would I be in any position to help others? I go to bed late, inebriated. The next morning will start slowly, hoping I will feel more peaceful, but when the chest pain starts, I order a Chang beer.

*

I'd love to do that boat trip to Maya Bay, I think, draining the honey from the bottom of my cup, maybe tomorrow. The cheerleader is back, and I'm leafing through the brochures.

Back in Bangladesh, there is, of course, another amazing beach. When I first got to Cox's, I'd go there on a Saturday evening, before the week's work began on Sunday, to find some space and recalibrate, and enjoy watching the Bangladeshi tourists and surfers. But that magic stopped working when I'd find myself surrounded by a group of twenty or thirty people staring at me unselfconsciously. At first I didn't mind, but the staring is starting to make me feel trapped. A few weeks ago, I was walking there but had forgotten to wear my scarf, and this old man came up to me, waving his gnarly fist and shouting 'Yunakarmi' or something like that. 'What does that mean?' I'd asked Sarika the next day, but she wouldn't say. Someone else told me it meant 'sex worker'.

*

Popping the top off another beer, my head is swimming. I don't want this darkness inside me. I want to merge into this beach, this turquoise sea, this blue dream of a horizon with one long boat drifting across it, not fight off images of Aadab's fatal abortion done with a dirty stick. I don't want to think about the women in Kutupalong who might have given birth that day and who I should be helping. The Thai women cleaning the bedrooms here are so beautiful, so gracious and friendly, but I can't help wondering what *their* local hospitals are like for maternity care. I guess it doesn't matter how perfect your location may be; if you're miserable inside, you can't see it.

Talking is such an effort. There's a young couple staying in the beach hut next to mine, but I'm finding it hard to make chit-chat. Or even to say 'kapun-ka' ('thank you') to the staff. At the same time, I'm so lonely. My sense of failure in relationships is tangled up with the failures and grief from my missions; the patients who had died, the impossible choices we were faced with – all this bleakness bundled into one dark cloud.

I've started drawing – large, slashing scribbles across my notebook pages, and sometimes biro outlines of women with headscarves holding their babies. They're based on Rohingya women, but remind me of Mary with Jesus. They're pretty bad, but it's a small escape.

My main good moments are in the sea, a few feet away from my hut. When it gets too hot, I wade in, and as the water touches every part of my body, I am, for a moment, released. I stretch my legs and arms, loving the freedom of not being watched, forgetting there was a time an orgasm could have brought me this.

In his book *Blue Mind*, marine biologist Dr Wallace Nichols says: 'There are numerous cognitive and emotional benefits that we derive every time we spend time by water, in water or underwater ... When you see water, when you hear water, it triggers a response in your brain that you're in the right place.' He goes on to explain how swimming can also relieve some symptoms of PTSD (post-traumatic stress disorder), which maybe unconsciously was what I was trying to do, though in many ways I wasn't ready yet.

Why am I so quick to anger now? That's another thing that frightens me. How it comes on after my first Chang of the day on an empty stomach and erupts in obscure ways. Like in the town of Krabi on my way to the island, when I saw that group of gap-year students exploring the beaches on their hired mopeds. They were tanned, gorgeous. One of the girls was wearing shorts printed with elephants, like those I've seen in the local markets. I watched her swig the remains of her beer, swing her leg over the seat and off they zoomed, laughing, no helmets. And I felt painful, hot anger – because she was taking unnecessary risks; because she felt so invincible; because she could fall from her scooter and rip up those bare unprotected legs; because she'd been offered every chance in life to keep safe, and had chosen risk; because the lives of Rohingya women, like Rashida, were all danger and no choice; because women, like my brother's girlfriend, took no risk but still died.

Some saner part of myself knows that this anger is not proportionate or fair. In fact, it's completely hypocritical, as there was a time when *I* was that girl, swinging my leg over the back of a motorbike in Ibiza, wearing only a bikini, but now, all I can see are desperate contrasts, and they make me feel sick.

I must find a way of holding these two worlds apart, but I'm frightened about what this splitting apart is doing to me. I know I'm drinking too much. On Friday nights in Cox's, my one night when I'm not officially on call, I've started to take a can of Hunter beer into the shower with me after work. Images of Marjie, the good midwife, knitting peacefully in her room taunt me as I go upstairs later, to the French NGO (non-governmental organisation) quarters to play a drunk game of cards. Their apartment is always thick with cigarette smoke, overflowing ashtrays, a great liquor supply. Seems that the hangover the next day is the only time I allow myself to get any rest.

Although it should feel like fun, it doesn't exactly – more like we're all escaping from the burden of the work here; what we've seen and want to unsee for a night. My drinking's steeped in guilt – the Rohingya don't get a night off to unwind or let loose. So we drink more to stop thinking.

*

The next day, two beers in, I'm in the sea. I like watching my toes bob on the waters, the feel of a slight salt breeze drying off my face. I fail to see the irony of my swimming while slightly drunk.

So blue. My thoughts drift away from Rashida and the birth unit to friends back in the UK, to their growing homes and babies. Career progression. Pension plans. Anita had phoned with the most exciting news – she's pregnant! She's leaving MSF, has stopped smoking and is starting a family back home. She's made the break and she's thrilled.

'He says he'll look after me.' The biggest draw of all, not to be alone. I know she'll be an awesome mummy, and it's good for her to have finished her harrowing missions in Congo. After a couple of beers, it doesn't even seem to hurt my heart, this idea that relationships and babies may not be in my future, not if I want to go on doing this work.

Blue, like the eyes of the Frenchman. Forgive the cliché, but when the Frenchman had walked into Dr Thomas's leaving party, my heart really did leap a little. Wearing a T-shirt with the sleeves ripped off and the name of some band on the front, The Ramones, I think. Silver ring, leather bracelet. His thick, dark curly hair flew over his face as he stooped to light his next cigarette. Serious face. Serious frown. When Thomas introduced us, he nodded nonchalantly in my direction, and I'd felt my skin prickle, my pulse race. In my defence, I was pretty drunk, and it was so long since I'd desired anyone, and here he was, the older kid on the French exchange, whom everyone fancied but no one dared talk to; the unapproachable singer in the rock band, dismissing the screaming groupies.

'This is Léon, a child psychologist for the French NGO,' Thomas had said, 'and this is Anna, our midwife and nurse.'

Léon looked at me, blasé, muttering through his cigarette, 'Sage femme?'

'Pardon?' I said, but not in a good 'r'-rolling French way. (I'd mentally bunked off French at school and regretted it ever since.)

He raised a thick eyebrow dismissively, his wide eyes mocking me.

'Sage femme means midwife,' he said deliberately slowly in a thick French accent, clearly bored by English people who couldn't speak French. 'It also means "wise woman",' he continued with that serious face. 'Are *you* that?'

I'm trying not to stare at the bluest pair of eyes I'd ever seen, and can't think of a thing to say. Again, a dismissive nod of his head, a deep drag on his cigarette; he slouched across the room to speak intensely with another aid worker, not looking back.

What a dick! I told myself, trying not to clock those lean, tanned upper arms, the strong jawline. But my stomach flipped over, even though I didn't want it to. For the rest of the night, I was annoyed by my acute awareness of where he was in the room, how deep his voice was, how passionate he sounded talking to his colleague in French.

Does he have a girlfriend? I immediately gave myself a mental slap. After Jack, and the mess I'd made of things with Jaan in South Sudan, I was desperate not to repeat my mistakes. *And anyway, he's rude*, I reminded myself.

We all got pretty drunk that night – we were going to miss Thomas, who was heading back to Germany. We danced wildly around the French team's apartment, most of us too far gone to remember how we got back to our own residences. I woke the next morning, with no idea of where I was, and was scrabbling desperately around the floor for my phone when I heard a French voice, tired and groggy.

'What are you looking for, midwife?'

Mortified, I looked around. We were both fully dressed, but I'd fallen asleep like a lap dog at the end of the Frenchman's bed, and he looked pretty pissed off.

'My responsibility,' I said, feeling sick and jumbled, but meaning I'm looking for my phone, my missing limb. What if I'd missed a call from the clinic? Ah, there it was! I finally found it beside a pile of his junk, and sighed with the deepest relief; the screen was empty – no missed calls.

'You are searching for your responsibility under my bed?' One eyebrow raised, as he reached for his pack of cigarettes.

And then, out of nowhere, he erupted into a deep belly laugh, his big white teeth showing, his bright blue eyes glistening with tears at the idea of me somehow misplacing 'responsibility' under his bed.

'You are funny,' he said, looking at me. It was almost a compliment, and I blushed deeply and leapt out of the room. I was glad I'd managed to avoid him ever since.

*

Bobbing peacefully on the water, close to the beach and within view of my notebook, I think about his thick curly hair, the lean jawline, the sexy way he smoked a cigarette, his nonchalance. He knew he was hot and didn't have to work too hard. *He's an arsehole,* I reminded myself – he'd enjoyed my embarrassment. Probably modelled that ciggie drag on some old French film star like Jean-Paul Belmondo. I replay our introduction in my mind, wishing I hadn't been drunk, wishing I'd replied to his teasing in perfect French. *Sage femme? Huh!* I decided he was one of those men who like making women laugh and feel stupid at the same time. *I'm definitely going to avoid him.*

CHAPTER TWENTY-FOUR

I can't remember who we're saying goodbye or hello to, but it's a few weeks after my holiday and another of those Friday nights, drinking and dancing at the French NGO's apartment, when I see the Frenchman again. Someone's produced a plastic bottle of imitation whisky bearing a label that states 'Made in Myanmar'. Over ice, it doesn't taste too bad.

Out on the balcony, I'm hoping the whisky will ease the pressure on my chest, as I think about the birth unit proposal. After initial approval from Amsterdam, I was on a fantastic high, but now reality dawns about the vast amount of work involved. First task is ordering the obstetric instruments needed for safe births, then I have a whole midwifery training programme to write. When the lorries turned up at the hospital with bamboo for the unit's construction, my stomach flipped at the weight of responsibility. *A journey of a thousand miles starts with one step*, says an imaginary James again, standing beside me.

From here on the balcony, I can see above a line of dusty palm leaves to the twinkling lights of Cox's Bazar, and even the trucks and crazy motorbikes with babies, wives and kids piled on them. Occasionally, I hear a blurt of music from a tuk-tuk's loudspeaker, or a squabble in the street as someone nearly gets knocked over.

In a clearing on the street below, there's a pile of half-broken bricks. When day breaks, women wrapped in saris, wearing no safety equipment, will spend hours smashing them into small stones and dust to use in cement. They'll squat in pulverising heat, ending the day covered in red dust, looking more like statues than humans. They're paid, I'm told, about £2 a day.

There's beauty here too, if you can see beyond the beggars, street dogs and piles of rubbish to the green rice paddies and spectacular beaches.

Also, the kindness, the generosity, the humour of so many people here. But more and more, I find myself too overwhelmed to notice. It's as if that part of me is closing down – my lens adjusted to suffering. I'm also thrown by the thought that our familiar team is disintegrating. Thomas, now back in Berlin, is a huge loss, especially when we'd grown to work so well together. Jason's off to his family home in New Hampshire and then another mission. Djimon is going home to Ethiopia.

In come the new team: Lisa, a thirty-year-old GP from New Zealand, will be my new doctor counterpart – her first MSF assignment, so in at the deep end. There will also be new project coordinators, nurses, logisticians and psychologists. All this newness will have a massive impact on our national staff too, who are naturally wary of change.

I'm on the balcony, drinking on my own, when...

'Hello.'

He's standing beside me – Léon, the Frenchman, an unlit cigarette in his mouth. When Prince William and Kate Middleton married last month, all the folk of the Pink Pearl had crammed around a small computer screen, beer in hand, to watch. When the happy couple exchanged a chaste kiss, it was Léon who shouted out in mock fury, 'That's not a real kiss!' much to everyone's amusement. He'd turned to me and winked, a big wide smile, and seen me blush. That night we exchanged phone numbers and since then, the occasional text. I don't know what's happening here, but I know I like the contact, the sense of escape. Loving that my phone is no longer solely a source of fear and horror stories. I wonder if I should warn him that I'm poisonous?

His tanned muscled arms are resting on the rail, and I'm uncomfortably aware of them. He's staring down at the street, close enough for me to hear him sigh.

'How are you, midwife?'

How am I? To be honest, I have no idea. I'm pleasantly numb from the whisky, dulling my heartache for an extremely premature baby that died in the hospital today.

'I don't know any more,' I say simply, sounding more poetic than I expect.

Lighting his cigarette, he breathes in deeply, eyes still on the horizon but nodding his head.

'This fucking place,' he says in sad acceptance. His exhaled smoke curls and disappears. I feel shy but pleased I'm talking to him.

'Where were you today?' I ask.

He sighs again. 'I went to the Makeshift Camp,' he says after a long pause. He has lovely long brown fingers. When he clenches and releases them, the beaten silver of his ring gleams and I wonder which girl, which wife, has given it to him. *I will resist him.*

'A boy was attacked by a wild elephant near there,' he says, 'and after he went to your hospital, I went to the woods to see the elephant.'

He stubs out his cigarette. When he turns to look at me, his blue eyes are clouded with confusion.

'It was a horrible accident,' I say, remembering that patient.

He shook his head.

'It wasn't an accident.'

In a low voice, he explains how he saw a gang of adolescent boys in the woods, throwing sticks and stones at the elephant, daring each other to get closer and closer.

'The elephant was terrified, that's why it stampeded. Everything here is such a fucking mess. Even a beautiful wild animal becomes a problem.'

I'm watching him speak, mesmerised, stricken, every detail of his large angled nose, his stubbled cheeks, the glossy hair he wears tonight in a top bun. This is the moment when my heart swells and I think, *I don't want to be alone any more*, because I know he gets it too – the turmoil, the confusion, the fruitless attempts to solve the unsolvable. Apart from the tent-à-tents with James, or the hugs and talks with Anita, it doesn't feel too melodramatic to accept that, maybe, I've always felt alone.

He sees me watching him and suddenly touches my cheek with his hand. My stomach flips. *Is this what he wants? What I want?* Part of me wants to bolt back to the safety of the party, from which I can hear laughter, Queen's 'Bohemian Rhapsody' being turned up, the clink of glasses, the rumble of conversation, but I'm still staring at him.

And then we're kissing, his lips dry from whisky and cigarettes. A few gentle pecks and then harder and faster, his tongue searching for mine. Normally, I hate the smell of cigarettes – too many memories of ED patients with their terrible coughs and yellowed nails – but this tastes good.

It's the taste of rebellion — sexy and adventurous. It's my first snog with a naughty boy in my year at the school disco, who'd snuck down the field to have a smoke. It's the imaginary kiss with the cowboy hero, smoke hanging from curled lips. It's me sticking a rebellious middle finger up at the medical world, which has consumed me now for so long.

At some point the kiss ends, we break apart gasping. I'm high as a kite on serotonin, my heart crashing, but, for the first time in ages and ages, for happy reasons. Heading back to the party, a few cheers and jeers greet our return, everyone's drunk and merry, and I'm blushing but loving it. We dance together, jumping as though in a mosh pit, but then in slow grooves, our hips touching, my arms seductively around his neck.

Later that night, he gets out his guitar and starts to play. *When was the last time I smiled like this?* He's great at the guitar, his strong fingers are nimble. When he stops, we drink some more, someone puts on Muse's haunting version of 'Feeling Good', and the whole room starts to sing at full volume about birds high in the sky and a new dawn.

While we're singing, he stands behind me. He winds his arms around my waist and sings in my ear. The French accent, the missing words, the slight out of tuneness make my blood sing and my heart float in space. The tightness in my chest has gone. My holiday had felt like I was hitting rock-bottom, but now I feel like I'm dancing in the stars, and here I want to stay.

*

We talk all night on the roof — about work, our families, our friends. I don't want to sleep. His piercing blue eyes trace my face as I talk. I've totally miscast him as the stuck-up, Gallic, God's-gift-to-women twit. He really listens; he's interesting and quirky. Nothing is said about when we'll see each other again. *That's fine.* I know I'll see him soon — after all, he only lives one floor above me. *I can't wait until the next time.*

CHAPTER TWENTY-FIVE

It's a new dawn. That's what it feels like, and my upbeat mood is driving me to work harder and more efficiently than I've ever done before. The proposed birth unit is actually starting to take shape, which is unbelievably exciting. Bamboo rooms have been built, new beds have arrived, the drugs ordered, and the staff hired, though not yet started. I dare to believe *this could actually work*.

On this hot May morning, wearing my most formal black and white shalwar kameez, I'm about to teach my first session to the camp TBAs. This is an auspicious day, as without their support, the birth unit will fail.

Taking a deep breath, I walk in. Thirty women sit staring back at me, looking suspicious and glum. Through small windows, I see dark clouds gathering, signalling that the dry season will soon be over and the monsoon will start. A storm is expected before the day is over and I'm already sweating from the hot, moist air.

'Assalaamu alaikum.' I'm pitching a friendly-but-formal tone. The blank faces stare back. 'Amar nam Anna,' I say, explaining my name in Bangla. A few mutterings in the back row. Faded headscarves are adjusted, a couple of coughs and bored tuts.

In front of me, a luridly pink plastic model of the female reproductive system is centre stage. There's also the bony pelvis model I brought in my backpack, the one that raised a few eyebrows at Dhaka Airport, and Marjie's knitted placenta. The room is silent.

Sarika steps in, bright, chirpy, wearing fuchsia pink. When she reels off an introduction like a schoolmarm, the gathered women sit up a bit straighter, look directly at us and nod their heads for me to continue.

It's taken two months of delicate negotiations and hard work by the outreach workers to get the TBAs here, and it's a relief so many have shown up.

Last week I held a meeting with the local imams (religious leaders) with the view of increasing contraceptive services in the camp. That also went better than expected until, at the end of the meeting, I realised with horror I'd started my period unexpectedly and had bled all over the seat cover. It was mortifying to have gushed out at this spectacularly inappropriate time. All I could do was to keep my head low, try desperately to cover my own blood, and let them all leave the room first. In a weird way, this worked to my advantage because they read it as a sign of respect, and quietly nodded their approval.

But this roomful of bored TBAs will not be a pushover. I get it. They are Rohingya women; many have skills gained from experiencing hundreds of births; their very survival is based on food donations they receive from grateful families when they tend to births in the camp. I'm encroaching on their domain; there is almost no other employment open to them. The job now is to encourage them to trust and work with us, as well as persuading them we're not going to leave them destitute.

Our biggest problem is that Rohingya refugees, unless legally residing in the country, are not allowed to be employed in Bangladesh. Instead, our plan is to match, or increase, the donations they receive from local families by giving them incentive packs that will include rice, salt, cooking oil, lentils, sugar, tea, that sort of thing. These older women seem keen to help their community, so when they realise practices such as the 'Burmese' stick are dangerous, I'm sure they'll want to change their way of working. But this is a refugee camp, not a Hollywood movie, and nothing about this teaching will be plain sailing. Having never been to school, the TBAs have little or no understanding of basic anatomy or science, most can't read or write their own names, and it doesn't look like they even want to be here.

First comes a short talk on basic anatomy, which I deliver in English while using the teaching aids and Sarika translates: 'At the end of the vagina is the cervix. This is closed during pregnancy, but in labour it starts to soften, thin and eventually open, like this.' The women stare and listen with no change of expression. A few minutes in, and one bored-looking

woman in the back row shouts out a question. She's dressed top-to-toe
in black, her front teeth are missing, and she may be forty, but looks
old and weathered. When everyone murmurs in response, I'm relieved.
Great! They're warming up, even enjoying themselves.

'What did she say?'

Sarika seems to blush, she smooths down the front of her top as if to
tidy the question away.

'Leila asked where is your husband?' she says sheepishly after a long
pause.

'Tell her I haven't got one,' I say, knowing full well that even our
Bangladeshi staff like to laugh and gossip that most female aid workers
are only in Bangladesh to find a husband because we can't find one
back home.

I feel a little disheartened. As a thirty-year-old spinster, I'm probably
an object of pity, not the font of new wisdoms. I don't even have my own
experience of childbirth to bring to the conversation. Never mind, *get
over yourself*, at least Leila's smiling now and genuinely interested, and
so are one or two of the others. There's something different about this
group; they seem to stick together, to enjoy a laugh, to be a bit feisty. It's
the first time I've seen this among Rohingya women, and remind myself
it's a good thing.

A bigger woman, with a large and untidy white bun, stands up next.
It's Reza, whom I met in the back of the 4 x 4 on my birthday. Her
question brings more rallying cries from the rest of the group,

'She wants to know where the snacks are,' Sarika says regretfully.

OK, so they've come for the snacks we'd offered in advance: the
delicious, sweet, tiny bananas sold in the local markets, the biscuits and
a drink of fizzy lemonade.

I'm adjusting to this when Benita rushes through the door.

'I need you!' she shouts at me.

Amin rushes in behind her, looking tense. He gives me a nod, says
he'll handle the snacks, so Sarika and I can go to the delivery room. The
timing is awful, but we can't leave an emergency unattended.

Inside the small delivery room, on the stirruped bench, lies a young
Rohingya woman called Mia. Benita says she's twenty-five, with three

live children and several miscarriages. She has a full-term pregnancy bump and is crying out to Allah at each contraction.

'Leila, the TBA all in black in the back row, brought her here on the way to the teaching,' Benita explains. *This is wrong, something is wrong*, all my instincts shout loudly. Mia's deathly pale, sweat drips off her panting chest, but it's the smell that hits me first. Of damp leaves and rotten eggs. My nose puckers and my stomach rolls. *She smells like the woman on the plane in South Sudan.*

'Mia has been in labour for eight days, but her waters broke before that – maybe two weeks ago,' Benita explains.

Sarika listens to her tight abdomen with the Doppler, hearing scratchy sounds of interference as we search for the baby's heartbeat. I'm holding my breath, my own pulse ringing in my ears. We search all over the skin until Mia's bump is covered in gel. Finally, Benita, Sarika and I dare to look at each other. *We know.*

The contractions still come in waves as I feel gently over Mia's tummy. Under the skin, the baby's head is engaged into the pelvis, but the body flops from side to side as I gently move my hands, making more stinking, infected birth waters run down Mia's legs. The stench is so strong that my eyes are watering, reminding me of the stench from a festering leg wound infected with pseudomonas that I'd once dressed in Nottingham.

Sarika gets in an IV for antibiotics, fluids and painkillers.

My throat's so tight I don't know if I can breathe. I listen again, almost desperate, all across Mia's torso, but there's definitely no foetal heartbeat, and it's clear her baby has died inside her – an intrauterine foetal death. Mia is now septic, her body incapable of delivering the dead baby inside.

We're racing now – the dead baby must be delivered, but it's completely stuck, despite her contracting for all these days. Benita is explaining it all to Mia, but she's delirious from fever. We try different manoeuvres to release the stuck head, but we have to be careful not to cause an obstetric fistula. We're running the IVs, but Mia's eyes have started to roll backwards, and any moment now she could enter into septic shock.

In a flash, Sarika's on the phone for a greenlight, and ten minutes later Mia's being loaded into the 4 x 4 with Benita as her escort, and Mia's husband, a slight, innocent-looking man, on board too. Dried mud flies into the air as the vehicle takes off, and when it's out of sight, a few deep breaths, a slug of sweet thick tea, and I wipe away my tears for the baby that's died. *Try not to dwell on it. Keep pushing on.*

Back in the meeting room, the TBAs have all disappeared and Amin's tidying away their chairs.

'Where are they?'

I'm desperately disappointed, tired and frustrated. We still had so much to cover.

'They ate their snacks and went back to the camp.'

I walked out and saw a second 4 x 4 in the driveway. Locking myself in it, taking off my scarf and stuffing it over my mouth, I lay on the back seat and screamed.

'FUCK!'

I wanted to cry, but the tears wouldn't come.

'Tough day here,' I text Léon, wanting his friendship, his support.

It gets worse.

*

Two hours later, we're eating lunch in the empty antenatal room, tea perched on the desk. Sarika's mobile rings – it's Benita.

Sarika's face is shocked, but I can't read the expression.

'Mia's coming back here. They refused to remove the baby.'

'What!' *Stay calm, listen.*

I've never seen Sarika like this before, lost for words, unable to ascertain why the surgeon refused to do a caesarean. Was it because Mia was Rohingya? Or because he thinks she'll die during the operation? I'll never know. *Nothing is ever clear to me here!* I want to scream.

'What do we do?' asks Sarika, out of ideas.

I don't know. Unless the dead baby delivers, we can't stop the sepsis and she will die. If we wait for Mia to deliver the carcass vaginally – *it's a baby* – she'll probably be left with an obstetric fistula even if she does survive. *She has three young children in the camp dependent on her for their survival.*

'I don't know,' I say out loud. But the voice inside me says, *Yes, you do.* I don't want to listen, to do that. It's something I prayed I'd never have to do.

Making use of all the support available to me, I call the MSF medical coordinator in Dhaka, I scour through my textbooks. With only half an hour before Mia gets back, we need a plan.

*

What I have to do next is horrendous. I'd heard about it on an MSF obstetric training course in Amsterdam before I came here, and left the classroom feeling ill. Even now, years later, my mouth is dry at the thought of it, and I have to mentally will my fingers to keep on typing.

It's called a destructive delivery, to be performed only in cases of dire emergency, and this is my recollection of it.

I'm watching myself as if I'm an angel, observing the scene from the height of the bamboo ceiling. Therapists have told me this is an act of 'depersonalisation and dissociation', a way of coping with a traumatic event. I see Mia brought in on her stretcher, Benita crying and sorry she hadn't been able to get help. Mia's cries fade as she falls asleep under a strong dose of ketamine. The oxygen compressor whooshes. The generator strains. We ensure no onlookers.

Legs gently lifted into the stirrups, Mia's mouth flops open, her eyes unfocused, but Benita coos to her anyway. I'm in sterile gloves, plastic apron and goggles, headtorch poised. Sarika keeps all our textbooks open and holds the phone to my ear for when I need support from our doctor in Dhaka.

Mia is dying, Anna. Do this to save her. Don't let her become another Aadab.

Stomach acid is bubbling in my throat, and from this lofty ceiling view I can see myself swallow it back. I'm pale. I look so small. Sweat soaks the inside of the gloves and fogs the goggles.

Sterile instruments to the right of me, a speculum examination, and I see the stuck top of the dead baby's head. The skin is white and peeling off, mushy. I think it's been here longer than eight days, weeks maybe. I suddenly panic – have we got this wrong?

'Listen again for the foetal heartbeat,' I order.

'Mia was given an ultrasound at the private hospital, Anna.' Sarika looks stricken. 'This baby is definitely dead.'

I'm looking in the speculum again, trying to make myself think in a purely practical way. A deep breath. Clenched jaw. From this position, looking down, I know I'll never be the same again. That there will always be life before this delivery, and life after. *This is way beyond the frontline. You won't come back from this.*

'OK,' I say, feigning confidence, 'I'm ready.'

Start by performing a craniotomy. Reduce the size of the foetal head by collapsing the cranium.

I can't do it! I can't do it! I won't do this!

Tilting my headtorch so I can see clearly, my hand shakes as the scalpel moves inside her vagina. I don't want to cut Mia's vaginal wall, but my hand wobbles as I feel an urge to defecate. I'm looking for the line within the baby's skull called the sagittal suture. By cutting along there before taking strong forceps, I can crush down the skull. *Crush down the skull. Please help me, someone.*

Sarika touches my shoulder. Her hand is also trembling.

We were taught in Amsterdam how a destructive delivery is never seen in the developed world, or very rarely, but it may, *it may* be a skill needed in poor countries when the risk of caesarean is too great. I seem to remember the lecturer saying she had done it once in Papua New Guinea. *It was the only way to save the mother.*

I try to swallow. There's no saliva. I'm preparing myself that the skull may be tough and I'll need to be forceful to crush it down so the body came come out. My eyes are watering from the foul smell – rotten flesh and old blood. I can't smell it from my viewpoint up in the ceiling, but I see my eyes are streaming. My bottom lip is wobbling, like it does when I'm carsick.

I make the cut.

Taking the forceps, I grab onto the newly revealed end of skull bone, then fold it back.

Like a boil being burst, the head almost instantly crumbles down and is unrecognisable as rotten brains spill forward into Mia's vagina. There's some relief that I don't have to break it or crush it, but it shows just how long this body has sat there decomposing, and I am in full meltdown disgust. My legs go from under me and I'm kneeling on the floor, Sarika behind me holding me up.

Let the dead body deliver slowly. That's what the textbook says.

Somehow Mia's body still has the strength to contract, and suddenly these waves of power and pressure come more forcefully, and the mess of bone, mucous and decomposed tissue blobs out and pools on the bed. I try not to look at a mashed-up bit of tissue that could be a little hand. Benita is rushing to clean it up, her headscarf across her mouth like a face mask, while Sarika is feeling over Mia's abdomen, checking that the uterus is tight. Somehow, maybe half an hour later, the last of the stinking placenta is born. The bleeding stops. I vomit.

It's over.

*

I remember sweet tea. I don't remember the journey home and I didn't want to talk to my new colleagues – too much, too soon. I remember Sarika whispering, 'You're not on call tonight. I will do it. I will keep her safe. Thank you, Anna.'

I remember getting into my apartment, and there, under my door, was a folded-up piece of paper.

'I am here for you, midwife.'

I don't know if I ate. I remember taking a shot of neat vodka right out of the bottle. I'm lying on my bed in a daze, staring at the ceiling.

In my next memory, I'm walking up the stairs to the French apartment. Léon opens the door and waves me in, worried about the text I'd sent to him earlier in the day. He hands me a shot of whisky without talking. He knows these camps. He knows what happens here. Then I curl up next to him, like the little spoon. He smells of sandalwood soap as his arms wrap protectively around me.

'I'll break your heart,' I hear myself tell him.

'No, I will break yours,' he says sadly.

Then darkness.

CHAPTER TWENTY-SIX

It was morning by the time I left Léon's room, and back in my own room I lay on the bed exhausted and half crazy. In moments of clarity, I knew it I'd done the right thing, the only thing: Mia was alive; her sepsis was being treated; with luck she'd be home soon to care for her other children. But when I woke and remembered, a creeping shame smothered me, as if I'd committed a horrible crime.

Although I'd never analysed it before, as a midwife, my expectation was that my hands would be used for healing, for soothing, for delivering bundles of joy. Now I'd used them to cut off a baby's head, and to know I was capable of this was to feel I carried an invisible stain, one that no amount of Lady Macbeth-type hand washing (which I did a lot in the weeks to come) or sensible rationalising could shift.

After the operation, I'd had a debrief with the MSF MedCo, another four-line report about what I'd done and why, but mostly I avoided talking to my colleagues about it. The team was new and each member was finding their own feet in the hellish world of the camps – they had their own burdens to carry. Maternity and female health was my responsibility, after all.

Anita felt like the only person I could tell. She was back in Hertfordshire when we spoke over a crackling line, and even with the six-hour time difference, she was as present and kind as ever. Halfway through the conversation, she went so quiet I thought we'd been cut off, then she told me she'd had to do a destructive delivery on twins in Congo. I'd later find out that Dr Simon had performed three in South Sudan, to save the women from 'the man with the spear', their version of the untrained home abortionists. But when Anita's voice began to falter and fade, we automatically shifted to talk about something else. I wanted to protect her – she was pregnant after all, and no woman needs reminding of the possible horrors of childbirth when they are carrying a baby. I suddenly felt worse that I'd made her revisit her own nightmares.

*

This was a strange time to be falling in love, and with my relationship to Léon so new, I told him only the briefest of details. I didn't want him to know that the hands that touched him had been capable of such an act. With him, I wanted to escape from the horror and uncertainty, and to step away from that part of myself, like one of those lizards who leave their own dead skin behind. Looking back, though, it may have been the intensity of moments like these – my desperate need to connect with another human – that opened up my heart to love again.

Léon had done his best that night with the whisky and the cuddles, and the limited amount of information I'd given him, but in the months that followed I should've said more. He was, after all, a clinical psychologist, trained in trauma. And he was in my bed most nights when he was working in Cox's Bazar. But my memories had begun to poison me – I wanted to protect those I loved from that poison too. My old self was back in the room, the one whose main coping strategy was repressing feelings, working hard and drinking more.

With Léon, the sex was amazing: an explosion of aliveness amid so much devastation, a narcotic, a way of forgetting and narrowing our world down to one of sensation and pleasure. He was handsome, confident, and when he'd yelled, 'That's not a proper kiss' at Prince William and Kate on the TV, he was tempting me with what was true. I was trying so hard not to fall in love – there was so much deep feeling, so much trouble already between us, and we seemed to live inside a very fragile bubble.

But whatever it was, it was unstoppable, irresistible. Sometimes, when we fucked, he'd shout 'Oui!' as he orgasmed, not caring who might hear; sometimes it was slow and caring and nurturing. Other times, we'd lie in bed and I'd make up the kind of stories you might find in a Grimm's fairy tale, about witches, magic and far-off lands – almost bringing us back to a childhood place of safety, where the complexities and suffering of being an adult didn't exist. There was a sweetness to him, below the façade of a man who didn't give a shit, and every time I found glimpses of that side of him, it was like panning a nugget of gold in a bleak, unpromising landscape.

It depended on our moods, or how drunk we were, or how bad our days had been. But the kissing, the sex had brought my periods back, and with him I felt stronger, more womanly, more normal. There were whole moments when I could forget where we were.

*

But it's never that simple, or it wasn't for me, because there's the other part of the lizard – the part I desperately want to bury but can't. On the day after the destructive delivery, I go back to the hospital, furiously determined to get the birth unit open. What happened to Mia is disgusting, a disgrace, *it must never happen again*. Entering the hospital, I now have a new, fake, bright smile, but behind it, I feel colder somehow, more driven – like one-third of my heart has turned to coal. Creation of the birth unit becomes an obsession, I have tunnel vision, and maybe that's the only way I know of coping with responsibilities that feel unbearable at times. I can't just sit with these excruciating feelings as I know James would do. Instead I put my head down and charge forward.

We're busier than ever within the maternity team, and once I get to the hospital, it's so full on, I barely think about Léon, and hardly ever text or phone him from work. It's almost a point of pride with me, this splitting in two. Later, therapists will describe this as a response to trauma and an assault on my sense of self, but actually, right now, this feels like a gift. *As long as I can work, nothing else matters.*

*

Mia takes over a month to physically recover from the destructive delivery. It's been a long haul for her: the huge amount of antibiotics she had for the sepsis have caused other problems, but when I see her, she's finally ready to go back to her three children. Watching her walk back up the mud track, towards her tiny home in the bleak refugee camp, breaks my heart further.

I can't talk to the staff at the hospital about these feelings. They're pragmatic, not used to things going well, familiar with lurching from one crisis to the next, and rarely seem to analyse how they feel. Sarika confides in me one day that when she was just a child, she witnessed an auntie bleed to death from an unassisted birth in her own home, and with the next breath she tells me excitedly about the TBAs agreeing to come to another teaching session. I'm often incredibly grateful for this stoicism, these shock absorbers I see in so many of our staff here. They care deeply about the women they look after, but rather than grieve what cannot be done, they appear to put their focus on what *can* be done.

Another heroine here is a woman called Prachi, who seems to know these camps inside out, as she started to work here when MSF did in the 1980s. Until arthritis set in, she was an outreach worker. Five feet tall and almost as round, she gazes at the world defiantly, or benignly, depending on her mood, through milk-bottle glasses. Her vast tummy, criss-crossed with stretch marks, she flaunts proudly between crop top and sari. Fat is beautiful in these parts, it means you can afford to eat.

Our younger Bangladeshi staff adore Prachi, they whisper and giggle that she's over 200 years old – she's maybe late fifties – but as a natural matriarch, she wields power as precisely as she paints the bindi (the Hindu red spot) between her eyes in the morning, or puts her wispy grey hair in the walnut-sized bun that sits on top of her head. It's Prachi who explains that women shave the heads of their children here in the belief that the hair will grow back thicker and shinier. Also, that the large black spots painted in kohl on babies' faces are an attempt to ward off evil spirits from their perfect children.

Part of Prachi's power is to do with her being an older woman who takes no shit. I find it comforting too when she treats me like a four-year-old: 'Pull that scarf up! Eat more lunch – you're too skinny!' Most of the staff here are so polite to me, it's unnerving, and an uncomfortable legacy of colonialism. But after chastising me, in a flash of bangled arms, Prachi will also suddenly stroke my face, be tender, call me her daughter. And that touch, that comfort, feels like a lifeline of human contact and connection. It feels like home.

Prachi doesn't have a bedside manner. In situations where I might politely ask women to hold their premature babies against their own warm skin as a makeshift incubator (there are no neonatal intensive care facilities or incubators this side of Dhaka, over 400 km away), Prachi will stand at the door of the maternity wing and bark out orders like a sergeant major and babies will – Hup! Two! – fly into their mother's arms, snug as kangaroos in pouches.

Technically, I'm her line manager, but she makes her own rules. I've found her sound asleep in the postnatal room where she was meant to be doing check-ups, a line of women waiting patiently for her outside. She chews betel nut, a mild stimulant forbidden in the hospital due to the gross red spit piles it creates on the floor, and lies and smiles at me with orange lips when I catch her. She has poorly controlled diabetes because she's so partial to *misti* – milk curd balls in sickly sweet syrup.

But Prachi is key. So many of the Rohingya women have lost their mothers that her unique combination of tough love and genuine sweetness is balm to them, as it is to me. They called her *Mashi,* which means 'auntie'. Differences of religion between the Muslim Rohingya women and the Hindi Prachi never seem to be a problem.

But rape is. We're seeing about one or two victims (or 'survivors' as some women prefer) a month, and keep a trunk of clean but worn salwar kameez for them to wear when theirs have been torn and ripped. We stopped giving women new outfits when they said it 'advertised their shame', and refused to wear them.

Marjie, my predecessor, had designed a fast-track rape referral system around Prachi. Any woman who's been raped, or beaten up, has only to whisper 'Mashi' when they get to the guards, and they're taken directly to her; and if needed, she'll call in me or Sarika to consult. One of the greatest frustrations is that we can document these violent crimes, but there is no one we can report them to. We can stitch, we can offer emergency contraception, safe abortion referral, antivirals, tetanus jabs – but when you're stateless, the police won't even listen. Each time these abused and humiliated women turn their backs to us and walk alone back to the camp, I feel despair.

*

Today, Prachi is marching up and down a row of women waiting in the antenatal area. She's holding up sketched pictures of Rohingya women experiencing different pregnancy emergencies, such as passing blood, fever, abdominal pain. Over the last six months we've made all teaching in the Makeshift Camp visual – I am yet to meet a Rohingya woman in this camp who can read or write. We've found a local artist to replace the smiling white women from UK-produced teaching tools with pictures of women who look like them.

Now Prachi points at a large picture of a condom. We knew, from the very beginning, that she'd be the right person to deal with this acutely sensitive subject.

It's during our contraceptive focus-group work in the build-up to the birth unit opening that we hear hair-raising stories of the vans that wait outside the camp at night. Of men who traffic women by promising them paid sewing work in India, and how the lure of a better life makes it hard to say no. Of how these women are rarely seen again.

Some women have explained to us that before they came to Bangladesh, a number of them were seized and forcibly implanted with contraceptives in an abhorrent attempt by external forces to sterilise Rohingya people. Another crime of genocide so far left unpunished.

It was more important than ever, then, that women had informed consent here. If our contraceptives get a bad name, all the hard work of getting permissions from the imams, getting TBAs on board, getting a quality supply of medications, will be up the spout. Quality supplies are especially important because there's a massive industry in fake drugs in Bangladesh, many being sold from shacks on the street, where they will (perhaps unknowingly) sell you a fake abortion pill that could kill you for 10 taka – that's 10 pence.

But as much as Prachi cares, she doesn't seem to dwell on these things. Life is life, up with the socks, on with the bindi and off we go. Her one front tooth winks in the sunlight as she tells me how proud her family are of her doing this work. Proud too of the nearly forty years she's been married to her husband, a schoolteacher in Cox's Bazar. As she makes her stately way towards the training room, I can hear the crinkling of sweet wrappers hidden in the layers of her light brown sari so immaculately folded into place.

*

Prachi and I are standing in piercing sunlight, about to go into clinic, when she stares forensically at my face. Her lips are pursed, her arms folded. 'You should wear more make-up,' she says, her head bobbing from side to side, chastising me. 'Maybe then you can find a husband. Nice Bangladeshi man.'

I smile politely. Léon will laugh when I tell him later; he doesn't seem to mind that my hair is always scraped behind a bandana, or my salwar kameez is often stuck with sweat to my scrawny frame. For our Pink Pearl extended family, keeping up with fashions or styles is refreshingly unimportant. I rarely think or care about what I look like these days.

Tasneem, our first patient, lives in one of the nearby villages and is Bangladeshi. We like it when locals come to us, as it encourages acceptance of our presence, plus our MSF mandate is to treat everyone who needs it.

Tasneem wears a hijab, her face eyeing me up warily. The rest of her is shrouded head to toe in black material. Prachi tells me this mother of four is breastfeeding a ten-month-old baby, and definitely wants no more children. They talk some more; Tasneem looks less tense – these conversations can be like pulling teeth in this modest society – and I feel a swell of pride. Prachi's doing a grand job. Our full contraceptive service is happening! Another important arm of the birth unit is taking shape.

Tasneem, after concentrating hard, decides on condoms. When Prachi hands her a discreet paper bag, Tasneem's eyes flicker and dip, but Prachi doesn't do shy. Now she's telling Tasneem that condoms aren't worth a hill of beans unless you know how to put them on properly. When she says, 'I will now demonstrate,' I flash back to Year 9 at school, my fiery red blush when the teacher put a condom over a Pritt Stick.

The wooden teaching penis I've ordered hasn't arrived, so Prachi reaches for the foetal heart Doppler, with its sky-blue probe. Deftly, she unravels the condom over the blue wand, showing how to pinch the end and roll it down smoothly. Tasneem watches, face serious and attentive. She asks Prachi the normal stuff: what if husband refuses to wear it? What if it comes off accidentally during sex?

Prachi answers in full, then, 'Any more questions?'

'Yes,' says Tasneem. 'Must I paint my husband's penis blue to use it?'

We all look puzzled for a moment, then Prachi translates, her mouth twitching. I look at Tasneem to see if I've misunderstood this, but a mischievous grin transforms her serious face. Prachi has started to chuckle, her belly wobbling, her arms jumping up and down, and now I'm laughing too. We're laughing so hard that Tasneem has tears running down her face and has to take off her hijab. Prachi's specs are off as she wipes hers, and my cheeks are sore.

Condoms, wooden penises, I have no idea why almost everyone seems to find them funny, but it's such a great moment, I don't care.

*

Like a dog with a particularly good bone, I take this story back from the camp to tell Léon. There's so little good news. When monsoon season starts in early June, buckets and buckets of rain pelt down, pinging off the roofs, gurgling in the gutters, and streaming down the street. Temperatures in the middle of the night soar to 25°C. I lie with him naked on top of the sheets as we hold hands and listen to the water splashing off the broken gutter outside. I stare at him while he sleeps: his soft mouth, smooth olive skin, thick dark curls that fall over his face. When he's asleep he looks gentle, all that aloofness gone; also the rudeness that can make me wince when we're with other people.

He says he's glad I don't wear make-up after I tell him of yet another chastisement from Prachi. It would slide off my face anyway in this insanely hot weather. He kisses my shiny nose, my face, my ears and tells me I'm beautiful. I don't feel beautiful. At thirty, I feel old and tired, but to have these things whispered in your ear in French is something – more than something. With him I feel on a thrilling knife-edge – the girl who's lucked out with the unattainable boy.

I wish he'd tell me more about himself. His childhood comes out slantwise, as everything does with him: the fractured childhood that

followed his parents' divorce when he was five; the grandmother he was
sent to when he was six who wasn't thrilled to have him; his young life
in Marseille. These are jumbled facts, which I may have misremembered.
He tells me reluctantly, as if too much information might make him a
walking cliché: the child psychologist trying to heal his own wounds.

In bed, he can be soft and gentle and funny.

He makes up poetry and puts it under my door. He tells me we English
are so stuffy about sex, especially when I shy away from his suggestion
of anal. He calls me (fondly) a 'white witch' because he thinks I can
somehow read his thoughts. We talk. He's distant sometimes – trauma
is a daily part of his life too. There's the little boy he'd seen this week
in another refugee camp who's mentally and physically disabled. His
parents have tied him to the floor with ropes and the boy now acts like
an animal. These parents are not monsters, just trying to keep the boy
safe – there's no help for disabled people here. Maybe the boy was brain-
damaged at birth, an injury not uncommon when births are not assisted
by a midwife. I listen to Léon's pain, his frustration, how he doesn't
know how to help this family despite all his years specialising in child
and family psychology.

While I listen, I stroke his back. In return he touches my arm when
my phone goes in the night and I reel out emergency instructions for
the patient I can't attend to. He doesn't mind that I'm driven too.
He cares enough to text me the next day to hear the outcome. For
the first time, maybe ever, *I'm not alone.* Because in my life to date,
there has been a separation between the 'me' in relationships and
'me' in aid work, and now I have finally met someone that I trust to
show my whole self to. Well, most of it – there's still so much I don't
understand.

But I don't tell him that I've fallen in love, or how beautiful I think he
is. I'm scared to break this fragile bubble, this small world underneath
the mosquito net, my first breath of companionship within this mess.

Then one night he catches me looking at him – my pupils widening,
my lips half-smiling. It's then he warns me: 'I'm a goat on this planet.
I'm just wandering. You deserve better than a goat,' but I don't listen.
I'm more like a seed in the desert that's been watered. I'm just starting
to come alive.

CHAPTER TWENTY-SEVEN

He said it first. That probably sounds petty given the weight of what was to come. But it mattered to me. With the backdrop of such bleak misery, my heart half-frozen, the month we've spent together within our fragile bubble had become both a safe haven and the most delicious space I'd ever shared. Not that I'm admitting it. *It's just a fling, a bit of fun*, is the lie I tell myself. *I'm not alone anymore.*

Léon's the one who lies in bed with me as water gurgles and splashes in the drain outside. He holds me when he tells me the news that Amy Winehouse took a fatal alcohol overdose that day. He knew how much I loved her defiance, her raw, tender voice, the songs that had been the soundtrack to so much of my life – the break-ups, the bad days in South Sudan. Her lyrics about losing at a game of love echo through my thoughts.

A few years before, I'd gone to see Amy live at V Festival. The beginning of the end, as it happened, and as excited as I'd been in advance, it had felt wrong and wicked to pay to watch her staggering and slurring all over the stage. Like paying to watch a wounded animal die slowly, or a public hanging, as they scooped her up and bundled her off the stage on skinny legs that swung like a puppet's. Vulnerable women were everywhere, it seemed. I'd convinced myself that her self-awareness made her a survivor, but she wasn't, and that felt so bleak, so futile, when she had so many possibilities. Pain is pain wherever you find it, so it was wrong again and utterly pointless to compare her to the women out here who struggled to survive with nothing, but I couldn't help myself.

Next morning, Léon took my hand and we climbed up to the roof of the Pink Pearl. Looking back, I might have viewed this half-finished roof with no safety barriers as a useful warning of what was to come, but I didn't. A row of beautiful saris had been hung out to dry on a washing line up there. They bounced and fluttered in the breeze like wet butterflies. Below us, the streets were gleaming from another downpour, the air recharged, and as we stood looking down without talking, that thought came again: *I'm not alone*.

*

The roads are truly awful now – it's rained for eight days non-stop, and our journey to the camp takes over two hours as we splash through rivers, swerve around rubble landslides, and today an upturned lorry lying on the side of the road. After being here for over seven months now, I'm learning to ignore the risks, instead playing music loudly from Dr Lisa's stereo. With an international team, it can be hard to find music that fits everyone's taste, but for some obscure reason, Billy Joel's 'Piano Man' seems to fit the bill and we all sing loudly, Sadaam chuckling quietly in the driving seat. Lisa's the new Kiwi doctor, fresh-faced but smart and dedicated. She's even starting her own GP practice back home after this mission to Bangladesh. She's questioning, she holds me to account for the decisions I make about the maternity services here (which I like), and her abundant energy is a breath of fresh air. Maybe we're also starting to get closer as we learn to trust each other's work, plus she's fun on the nights in the French apartment, proudly showing us her haka moves.

*

When I get back to the apartment after work, I climb out of my muddy clothes, take a shower, eat, and, if Léon's there, get under the mosquito net and into bed with him. This is the place where, in certain strange moods, we can fall out of time and into a kind of fantasy world, where I tell him more stories of The Witch and The Goat. He listens, hardly breathing, like a child in my arms.

At other times, I observe his grace, his boyishness; how he stoops to play games of football and cricket in the gutters with the street kids, wild wet hair matted to his head. Or we go to the beach, holding on to each other in the back of a rickshaw. We swim in our clothes as the rain splashes the surface of the Bay of Bengal, still warm and calm between the storms on an otherwise deserted beach. His bright white teeth flash in contrast to the grey water and sky. No one watches us here now, everyone stays inside, it's beautiful.

We are both, at different times, overwhelmed by this place and our place in it. What a drop in the ocean we are. When he rages helplessly, I feel his fragility.

When I ask him how his day was, he tells me, haunted and wild-eyed, about a family he's working with at a camp near Teknaf, where the mother is purposely starving one of her five children so they can all be admitted to a feeding programme. 'She had no other choice in this fucking place,' he shouts in pain, before throwing his water glass at the wall, where it shatters into a million pieces.

And then this morning comes. As always, his phone's alarm wakes us – a song called 'Nantes' by a band called Beirut. Just three notes, only a fifteen-second intro, but its haunting organ music and lyrics about how long it's been since they saw a smile – will sit beneath my skin ten years later. Outside, rain hammering on the balcony from the same broken drainpipe, the loud echoey call to prayer just ending. Room smelling of acrid mothballs and damp, where the moist air grows mould on my clothes.

I'm naked in bed, a thin sheet wrapped around me. Léon's getting dressed, his hair in messy curls, an unlit cigarette between his lips. Today, he'll be heading back to the sodden camps in Teknaf. There are rumours of a cholera outbreak and he may not be back for a couple of weeks. With only his T-shirt on, skinny bare legs poking out underneath, he looks youthful and innocent.

'I love you.'

He says it earnestly, out of nowhere, looking at me directly. My breath catches. From surprise. From a sudden belief that I *can* be lovable.

And in that moment, my world grows bigger. Instead of seeing us both as complicated masses of unknown quantities, I can see us together after we've ended our missions in Bangladesh. I'll show him my childhood home, we'll walk in the Welsh hills, we'll ignore my parents' disapproving faces as he smokes down by the garage. I'll drink red wine with him in Marseille, the town of his childhood. I'll bumble along in schoolgirl French, not caring I can't understand the conversation around the table because *we are in love*. Actually, I'll learn French, I'll start today! Where is that vocab book he gave to me?

Looking further, I can see our first child, a boy, with my green eyes and his wild curls and skinny legs. Anita and I will raise our children near each other, they'll be the same age. And it's like a switch turning on – I want to be pregnant. This deep yearning for a child, in my belly, in my uterus, like a period pain. All these feelings just below the surface, bubbling silently like lava all this time while I repressed them – kidding myself that I didn't want children – when now I see how incredible it could be. Actually, my maternal instinct was just waiting for someone to share it with.

Anything is possible, says my hardened heart. My periods are back, my breasts seem to tingle and I wish I hadn't had a contraceptive coil fitted a couple of years ago. But more than this, his declaration gives me an overwhelming feeling that somehow it is all going to be OK. We are in love. *And he said it first*.

'I love you,' I reply, honestly and with relief, unaware yet of how many versions of love there are and how many unrealistic conclusions I'm racing towards. In the next breath, I fully expect him to say we'll be together forever, no matter what. Does that sound delusional? Mad, even? Maybe, but my thinking is that after all this misery, how could we possibly let go of something so unexpected and so beautiful?

It's like watching the sun go out when I say I love him too. His face looks set, his blue eyes narrow slightly. He starts to say something, but he changes his mind, and in a flash, he's dressed and out of the room with just a peck on my cheek. I see this, but I'm not ready to feel it yet. Instead, I lie on my back, drunk with love.

*

Over those next few grey and rainy days, I text him a lot in excitement – it feels like the universe has decided to give me a free pass. The birth unit is almost ready for its official opening, and the newly hired nurses are forging ahead with their midwifery and MSF guideline courses. The TBAs are still coming to teaching sessions, and not just for the snacks, as Ramadan has started. I tap these messages out to him on my old phone, making jokes about the buckets of fake blood I'd made with red food colouring for estimating delivery blood loss, how we'd used Marjie's knitted placenta and umbilical cord on training sessions for complex births. *We're full steam ahead*, I tell him merrily. One evening I even try to call him in Teknaf a couple of times, but the phone rings unanswered. *He must be really busy.*

Sarika notices the change in me. 'You look happy,' she says. 'Are you in love?' Prachi teases. I say nothing – pre-marital sex is often frowned upon here and I don't want to give the international workers a bad name. It's never easy to talk about sex here, let alone the enjoyment of sex, even with broad-minded Sarika. In Bangladesh, men can have multiple wives, and marital rape is not usually seen as a specific punishable crime within law, which Sarika explains often leads to an assumption that men can have sex whenever they feel like it.

But now I have love in my heart, I'm hoping that the flash memories of the destructive delivery will fade, along with the heart pounding and that horrible feeling of guilt clawing its way up my neck. I'm relieved to feel on top of them, and this gives me the illusion of having the strength of ten workers. I'm spinning so many plates, but they're all up in the air and it feels good. *I can do this.*

*

During the next week, the rain is constant and torrential. Rohingya people are coming to the clinic with bare feet, wet mud up to their knees. Women are carried to us with saris stuck to their skin, covered in red blood mixed with clumps of grassy mud. Every home in the refugee camp leaks, and streams of muddy, shitty water flow down the side of the hill. I think about Rashida, whom we saw at the hospital last week, her seven-month pregnancy still going strong, and wonder how she survives these awful conditions. Her husband Yusuf has been missing for over four months now. I want to tell Léon about all this, it feels like a great relief to have someone to tell, but when his replies become more and more sparse, it's back to scribbling in my diary at night by headtorch. And I'm pissed off with him. *Where is he? What's he doing?* But I can't bear to be alone again, so I don't push it. The needier I am with him, the more distant he becomes, so I tailor my mood to his. *I have to be more aloof.* I sit on my hands to stop myself texting him, and write in the evenings instead.

*

One month later, it's August, and Léon and I are still playing a painful game of cat and mouse. We share what feel like amazingly intimate moments of sex and storytelling, then he pulls away and goes silent. I tactically retreat until his concern sparks other thoughts – maybe he isn't good enough for me, or I've found some else – and we repeat the cycle. The moments of separation hurt like hell, and when he returns, we argue, we drink. He shouts, I shout. I smoke when he does now, an act of defiance because I know he hates it, though I hate it too. I've never argued like this before, I've never smoked before. I don't recognise myself. This anger I have learnt to show doesn't help me here. Then somehow, we make up, and the 'up' is wild, intense, consuming.

Somehow, within this chaos, the birth unit starts to come together – all the supplies are here, the staff are ready and keen to go, we've just got to put everything in place. We're so nearly there. I just have to keep pushing on. To keep spinning those plates. *Just keep going.*

*

For the last two weeks, Léon's been away again from Cox's Bazar, but he hasn't been in touch once. Something is slipping away and I don't know how to fix it. When he finally walks into my room unannounced, I'm all geared up either for a fight, or to plead with him not to ignore me. At the very least to talk so that I can understand the weird dynamic between us now. But he's already drunk, slurring, looking thinner than I remember, more tired. Taken aback, I look at him more closely, and I'm suddenly worried. His left eye is swollen.

'What happened?' I ask, seeing his familiar contradictory impulse between intimacy and secrecy play across his face. But soon he's howling with pain, downing more whisky and lets me peer at his eye, where I'm shocked to see a creamy white abscess covering the previously piercing blue. Finally, he admits that when he was in Teknaf, the rain had partly washed the road away, trapping him there, so he'd had to reuse his contact lenses over and over again, and now his eye was severely infected.

That night, I treat him with eye drops, antibiotics and analgesics. He howls in pain, refusing to go to a local hospital, but also hating me nursing him. I start to panic that he could be septic, like Mia, that he could die right here in my bed.

'It's nearly my end of mission,' he mumbles, apparently to comfort himself, and taking another large mouthful of whisky, he falls asleep.

CHAPTER TWENTY-EIGHT

Léon is so ill the following day that I insist he gets seen at a specialist hospital in Dhaka. He agrees with great reluctance, furious with me for overruling him and speaking to his bosses on his behalf. At the private hospital in Dhaka, the doctors are so concerned that they want to admit him immediately, but he refuses. Instead, we fly back to Cox's together, armed with medications and him even more monosyllabic and morose, refusing to hold my hand. My stress is sky-high too – all the responsibility to nurse him now falls on my shoulders, and he is so ill.

My alarm goes off every three hours, day and night, so I can insert his eye drops, and Léon's scowl shows how much he hates me looking after him and seeing him so depleted. He wants to be the professional, not the patient. At one point in a fever-fuelled rage, he shouts that the eye drops have made things worse, glaring as if I've done this to him on purpose. The angry, abandoned child he once was is back, and I've lost my lover. In turn, I'm overwhelmed, unsure if my concerns about him developing sepsis are proportionate, but then remembering how we live in a world where I see deaths from sepsis on a daily basis. I'm fighting to save him, but sense it's destroying what we have between us. I hate becoming like a mother to him, a mother he rejects. His scowling look says, *I don't need you. I don't need anyone.*

Eventually, when the infection subsides, a kind of peace returns, and we spend our evenings like old people, cuddling in silence or doing jigsaws. Surreptitiously, I watch him, knowing something is very wrong – he's a smaller version of the quietly magnetic, self-aware man I met on the balcony at that party. One night, drunk and unhappy, he tells me he feels he's mostly failed here in Bangladesh. Making children feel happier and stronger has been his life's work, but here it was just too difficult – all those broken hearts, broken minds, shattered families.

His perceived failure wasn't true – his focus groups with the Rohingya on food security and malnutrition actually led to big and long-lasting positive changes about how aid there was perceived and delivered – but the sense of failure was true for him.

When his replacement, another French psychologist, arrives, he hands over his projects without any comment to me. From then on, he spends his nights smoking silently on the balcony, drinking beer, or playing the guitar to himself. All this time, I'm uncomfortably attuned to his emotions – the subtle movements of his lips, the tension in his brow, the wary way he looks at me sometimes, as if half-hoping, half-dreading to get the old story back. Mostly, he just looks defeated.

Me – I'm like a farmer begging to save a beautiful and valuable crop, but when September comes, there are only two weeks left of Léon's mission for this miracle to happen. I'm still hoping the end of the monsoon season will cheer him and clear his head, and we'll be back to how we were. The second rice crop of the year is waist-high in the fields, markets are full of enormous jackfruit, the reducing monsoon means the sky is intermittently a brilliant blue with magical rainbows. Yet all Léon talks of, unconvincingly and flat-toned, are the friends he'll visit in Paris, the food he'll eat. One night on Messenger I reach out to James, who was online, and his reply was simple:

'Buddha said, no one saves us but ourselves. No one can and no one may. We ourselves must walk the path.'

'Pah!' I thought; actually I *did* save him, but of course that wasn't what he meant.

It was around this time that I saw, intermittently, that I was as trapped as Léon – trapped by my fear of not wanting to seem vulnerable, particularly in front of those I loved.

'When will I see you again?' I eventually burst out, annoyed at how squeaky and scared I sound, but with my own mission ending in two months, I need something to hang my future on. My replacement, a UK midwife, will soon arrive. In one of the emails we exchange, she asks me to be honest about what the hardest part of my job is. That made me chew my pen. In the end, I give her broad strokes – how hard it is having to discharge mothers and babies back to the camps, how helpless she might feel at times. I pass on James's warning: *We can't save everyone.* What I can't bring myself to say is, *You will never be the same again.*

'When will you see me?'

Waiting for Léon's answer, I hear the hum of rickshaw wheels, the 'thump, thump thump' of those women breaking bricks. He considers my question for what feels like a long time.

'I will be here about,' he says at last.

What the hell does that mean? If he's trying to sound mysterious, it's not working. I'm too raw, too mad, too desperately literal, too tired. In saner moments, I know I'm trying to build bricks with straw; at other times, I hope I can still save us and *love will win.*

*

Léon leaves on a Tuesday morning. We try to get up early to have movie-like goodbye sex, but somehow it doesn't happen – he's not hard or I'm not wet – maybe both. When it doesn't work, I jump off his lap and throw on my salwar kameez, scraping my hair into a messy bun, anxious to get to the hospital, where I have sick patients waiting for me. The birth unit is only two weeks from its official opening. *That comes first.*

When it's time to say goodbye, we hug awkwardly, the 4 x 4 in the street below revving and ready to leave. Our eyes brim with tears that don't fall.

He has one night in Dhaka before flying home. When I get back from the hospital that evening, I race upstairs and into my room, desperate to check my phone in private. Did he text to say he's safe? Instead, there's a scrawled note on my bed next to his guitar:

'I watched you run down the stairs to get to your car this morning. You didn't look back. You will be OK my Sage Femme Witch.'

What does that mean? OK until we meet again? OK forever? That thought is a punch in the belly. The guitar makes me angry. It's the most precious thing he owns, but *I don't want a fucking guitar. I can't even play it. I just want him!* History feels on a loop here – the grand piano that Jack gave me before I went to South Sudan. Unusable musical instruments, instead of what…? Words, promises, vows? *But don't forget how patiently Jack waited for you.* Maybe…still searching through my phone for the missed call…this is your punishment.

*

I never heard from him again. Well, not really. The occasional text, the odd email. Eventually, I had to unfriend him on Facebook, as it made me so mad seeing him interacting with other people and yet totally silent to me. Even now, after ten years, it flashes up occasionally that he's looked at my LinkedIn page, or I'll search for his name on Twitter. *Is he happy now? Does he have children?* No idea. After that Tuesday morning, he was never part of my life again.

I had no idea love could end so quickly. My whole body ached with the loss of him, and to start with I didn't think of the most obvious things – that there might be a wife, a girlfriend, a whole other life waiting for him at home. Aid workers are not necessarily promiscuous, but when you work for extended times under extreme stress, liaisons that can feel so charged, so life-changing, often have an end-of-mission sell-by date. There's also a culture of 'what happens in the field stays in the field': I had heard certain men say to women, 'I'm Loki single,' (for which you can substitute Nairobi single, or Cox's single) and vice versa. So maybe he was the same as the others, but I couldn't believe it then, and I still don't.

Instead, I beat myself up: *maybe if your boobs were bigger, he would have fought harder for you; maybe you're too needy.* Later, when I'd finished raging at him for all the things he couldn't give to me, I turned the barrel on myself again for being so stupid, so gullible. *He told you he'd break your heart. He said he was a goat, and goats are nomadic, grazing wherever they can find sustenance. Why weren't you paying attention?* Whatever the reason, it hurt like nothing has ever hurt before, and even now, years later, I'll find myself in a busy department store back in the UK, thinking of something totally unconnected, and 'Nantes', his alarm clock music, will come over the loudspeakers, just those fifteen seconds of organ music, just three notes, and I'll feel my knees give way, because, in a flash, I'm back there under the mosquito net, laughing, our legs entwined, reaching out for him.

*

Léon's leaving marked the beginning of dark days for me. On the face of it, nothing changed. I still turned up to work, put in long hours at the hospital, smiled at colleagues, gave everything I could to patients, and was, to use the jargon, high-functioning in my grief. It's something I've witnessed many times since in overseas colleagues and in NHS staff – this urge to battle forth when a personal life is broken into pieces, usually to everyone's detriment.

Now, when I wasn't on call, I would drink until I was sick. It was the only way I found that stopped me feeling like I was sinking and suffocating. My drawings became scribbles of endless caves and hunched figures. I stopped communicating with nearly everyone back home, apart from Anita, dear faithful friend, the one I didn't have to pretend to. Her frequent short email replies didn't offer an answer, or even advice, just reassured me she was there.

Nights, I'd drink vodka and lie motionless on the bed, staring up at the mosquitoes buzzing on the ceiling, half-listening to the rain outside, half-listening for him to phone or run up the stairs. *Are you there, my witch?*

And then, out of the blue, the flashbacks returned, as sudden as poison gas, and I couldn't stop obsessing about the women I'd treated. What could I have done better? Who had I let down? Aadab, so cruelly murdered with a 'Burmese' stick; Alifah, with her cord prolapse on my birthday. In this state, I could feel her breath on mine, smell the sick bag, the metallic smell of her blood. But it's Mia who haunts me most, me hacking her baby to bits, and no amount of vodka shots can take those images away.

I'm drowning. All my spinning plates are crashing to the floor. *I'm going to die.* This is the most mentally unwell I've ever felt, but I don't think about reaching out for help, or confiding in those I work with. Unconsciously, I assume this is just the price you pay for being an aid worker, for falling in love, for making these choices.

But there is a lifeline among the painful memories. Sometimes Rashida's small, childlike face will bring me back to the present. Rashida, who patted my arm that day I went to her shack; who trusted me. Rashida, with the splinter of wood through her nostril, her precious antenatal notes filed in her thatched roof. I have no idea why she's become my conscience. God knows, enough people have let her down in her life. I could leave tomorrow and she probably wouldn't notice – but Rashida, now in her final weeks of pregnancy, is calculated to be one of our first patients at the birth unit. As a midwife in the UK, I felt my role to be one of preserving health, but with Rashida, it feels like an urgent fight, a vigil, to keep death away. Every step of her danger-stricken pregnancy has been watched over by me, aware of what I can and can't do to keep her safe.

I've shown myself to be weak, stupid and gullible, more desperate than I ever imagined it possible to feel, but I do have my job, and I am still good at it, so when the fog clears, I know I want to help her deliver this child. It's the invisible cord attaching me to sanity. Her unborn baby is my ray of hope, as well as hers. A faint ray, after fourteen miscarriages, but still there.

CHAPTER TWENTY-NINE

I've been away from home for ten months now. Léon has been gone a week and still no word. I haven't slept for three nights. I have a headache, but I didn't drink last night because today is the official opening of the birth unit, and I'm heading out the door fast, leaving my messy room behind.

At the hospital, I give Sarika my brightest smile. She's dressed for the occasion in maximum bling – a coral-coloured sari, gold bracelet, large nose stud. Her lips are painted, her glossy hair oiled and worn down to her waist. Prachi looks me up and down with mock scorn, taking in my pale face, my faded old salwar kameez, the spot on my chin caused by stress – I'm an insult to Max Factor and womanhood.

'Are you OK, dear?' Sarika studies my face: 'You look tired.'

'I'm fine,' I say, 'just trouble sleeping.' I can't tell her I've had the same obstetric nightmare for the past three nights, the one in which I'm trying and trying to tug a dead baby out of a mother. *Stop thinking! This is a day of celebration.*

It really is, because our new birth unit is amazing. We have a dedicated maternity ward with new beds and record charts hung at the end of them; privacy screens, brand new obstetric instruments, new autoclaves to sterilise them in, bright walls adorned with teaching diagrams and murals, ceiling fans that work.

Sarika and I look around like children in a sweet shop; neither of us can speak. The still-functioning kernel of me – the worker, the midwife – is overjoyed. *We did it!* Nothing will ever be perfect here, but compared to the empty, unloved room that was here before, this progress is profound.

'This will show that women matter!' Sarika bursts out, her kohl-rimmed eyes filling with tears. 'It helps *everyone*.' Emotional outbursts are not her style, but she has lived the horror of neglected women's health for so long, and she knows how something as seemingly small as the right contraceptive, at the right time, can save a life. By creating this space where women were nursed away from other patients, we could provide some form of dignity and privacy. This unit is one shining thing to come out of all the chaos of the camps, and my stupid broken heart.

My final teaching session with the TBAs is about to start. I take a deep breath, but when I walk in, they're all on their feet. Leila is at the front, the TBA who brought Mia to us, and Reza, who I spent my birthday with. They all form a circle and dance and sing around Sarika and me. Touching our heads, they look up to the sky in prayer, chanting words I don't understand, and I'm delighted, amazed, embarrassed – I spent all these months thinking they hated us, distrusted us, and now they're dancing with me.

'They say you are their daughter now,' Sarika laughs.

'Now all we need is a safe first birth,' I smile back nervously, because everything depends on this.

*

It feels as if the stars have aligned in the scariest way possible when, two days later, it's Rashida who arrives to give birth. So far things have gone smoothly at the unit – we've already had two live births, and the news has spread fast that women can give birth here twenty-four hours a day and for free. Soon we expect to have a hundred births a month.

But with this one, I'm brimming with nerves and excitement because the odds are so stacked against her. How wonderful it would be if Rashida could leave holding her first baby in her arms. If she doesn't, it will be her fifteenth loss.

On occasions like this, it's crystal clear to me why I'm here – first, to help deliver this baby if that is humanly possible; second, to bear witness to Rashida's suffering. When the fog clears, *témoignage*, the philosophy that first drew me to MSF, feels very simple. The word means to bear witness, but then to testify and to speak out.

Rashida's carried in unceremoniously by two men, who have bundled her into a big sari. Her bare feet stick out at the end, her much-mended flip-flops left at home in the rush. Her eyes, huge, hungry and scared, flicker towards me. I want to hug her but I know better now.

'We're glad you're here,' Sarika translates into Rohingya.

It was Leila – the TBA with no front teeth – who made the decision to bring her in the early stages of labour, proof that the TBAs are starting to trust us. When Leila collects her incentive package of rice, lentils and other food, I want to punch the air. The system is working. Of course, all labours will continue to be high risk in this environment, but if we can see women before their labour becomes complicated, we can improve the outcome, save lives and link the baby to our vaccination programme.

We've given Assma, one of our new midwives, the job of caring for Rashida one-to-one, with Sarika and me on hand for assistance. Assma does a full assessment, plots the progress of the labour on our new birth charts, a tool called a partogram, which we could rarely use previously as women were only brought to us when the labour had become life-threatening. We still don't have cardiotocograph (CTG) machines, the standard monitoring equipment for higher risk labours back home. Having never seen one yet in Bangladesh, even in private hospitals, it would be a huge undertaking to introduce them here, but I've been in discussion with Amsterdam and live in hope.

*

Rashida shoots me a terrified look as Assma gently palpates her abdomen; she's primed for heartbreak. When the shutters are closed, she lies there – tiny and vulnerable on the bed in a circle of artificial light – waiting for the universe to decide. It doesn't look promising, she's two weeks overdue but her bump is tiny – if you were to pass her dressed in that black, neatly darned skirt, hair wrapped in the familiar faded orange headscarf, you wouldn't even guess she was pregnant. A tracery of stretch marks fans out from a badly healed scar on the right side of her belly – she never did tell me how she got it. That splinter through the nose hole is still her only adornment, her ear lobes pierced but empty.

I hold her gaze, trying to say, *we are here for you, we will keep you safe*. Keeping women safe was, after all, my ultimate goal, my core reason for being here. Assma, competent and focused, bends over her, using the Doppler to listen to the heartbeat. I'm so pleased with how the new midwives are performing – their skills will make or break the unit. Holding our breath until we hear the *shhh shhh shhh* of the baby's heart, Rashida's eyes widen, her pupils dilate, a look seen so often in expectant mothers. Her mouth turns up at the corners in a small, tentative smile.

*

Four hours later, Rashida is panting and close to delivery. Her childlike hands open and close with each contraction, revealing callouses on her palms from carrying firewood. When her tawiz, the talisman around her belly, starts to dig into the flesh, we get her permission to cut the string that holds it there. In the next contraction she grips it, calling out an anguished, 'Yusuf!' the name of her absent husband.

He's been gone for months now – arrested? deported? dead? No one knows and probably never will. There will never be a record of his death, just as there will be no official government record of his child's birth – should it live.

*

By early afternoon, Rashida's groans have reached a new crescendo. 'Oh, Allahhhhhh!' she cries at the peak of each uterine contraction. Sweat runs off her forehead, and in the cool breeze from our ceiling fan, Assma is checking, calming, soothing. Rashida squats to the floor and bends over the bed as Assma rubs her back. Mobile labours here are just as effective in promoting normal birth as they are back home. Leila, the TBA, has chosen to stay as a birth partner, which is great. She helps Rashida to stand as the contractions make her toes curl from pain; she hands her clean water to sip.

Rashida doesn't ask for pain relief. We don't have gas and air, and rarely give stronger analgesics, mainly because women don't ask for, or expect, them. But also these drugs always add more risk to births already so compromised. We could argue about the morality of this for hours, maybe we should, but if we were to give an opioid drug such as pethidine and it, in turn, caused breathing difficulties for the baby at birth (when we have only limited neonatal facilities), we could potentially be responsible for that baby's death. Of course, I still struggle at these ethical crossroads.

'Alllaaaah,' she cries again. My scarf is soaked with sweat. My own heartbeat rings in my ears. *Please, please, please God — a healthy baby this time.*

*

It's mid-afternoon and we're so close now. To be honest, I'm finding it hard sharing this labour with Assma. I want to do it all myself, but this unit has to run well when I'm not here. Now it's 15.30 hours and the clock is ticking — not quite curfew, but nearly. I'm desperate to see this birth through. *Please,* I silently pray, and I hear Sarika muttering 'Bismillah' under her breath — an invocation to God.

And then, at 3:50 p.m., a beaming Assma says in a half-shout, 'It's here! The baby's head! It's coming! And there it is, stretching the vaginal entrance, the membranes still covering the baby's hair. When amniotic fluid gushes onto birth table, we're all reassured to see it's clear, no signs of infection or meconium poo. Birth waters that strangely remind me of the smell of sperm, or fallen leaves in autumn. Mopping them up with a new supply of clean sheets, keeping the birth hygienic and safe, I tell myself, *this is a normal, healthy labour*, to stop myself rushing in to help Assma.

The baby's heartbeat is strong on the Doppler, no signs of distress at all, but is it me? Why can't I shift the feeling that something is about to go terribly wrong. I prepare the injectable drugs we'll need to safely birth the placenta, as Rashida has several risk factors increasing the risk of bleeding. *We're ready.*

'Ahhhhhhhhh,' cries Rashida. Her bowels open, and simultaneously, a thick head of hair is crowning. I rush to clean her up, Assma's gloved hands are poised, ready for the baby, Sarika instructing Assma in Bangla. Rashida crying out again in Rohingya, an almighty push that stretches her perineum over the baby's head, and hallelujah! He's born, all mottled and purple, which is normal, with a thin covering of creamy vernix. Assma gets a clean towel and firmly rubs him down to stimulate him.

And then the wrong tone: her thin voice saying, 'He's floppy,' rubbing up down, up down, with the towel. I know this tone and grab the resuscitation trolley, another new addition to our unit, where there's a stethoscope and a tiny resuscitation bag and mask ready. Assma's hands are shaking, but in English she recites the instructions from our training. 'Keep the cord attached where possible. Towel down vigorously. Put on a hat to keep baby warm. Listen for breathing and heart rate.'

And then, for a moment, she seems to falter, this first-time midwife faced with a baby who could die.

'Give five inflation breaths,' Sarika says clearly, her eyes trained like a pistol on Rashida. When I hold the tiny mask in the right position over the small, floppy baby's face, his eyes are closed, his skin still mottled, no movement. Sarika cuts the cord. The frail little ribcage flutters – I've seen birds on the lawn die like this – but wait! Two more gentle inflation breaths, and suddenly a little bit of movement and signs of life. A moment later:

'Waaaah'!' he yells, a sound out of proportion to his tiny size. And then again, 'Waaaah! Waaah!' And we watch the blue skin pinking up. He's probably less than 2 kg – in England he'd be dashed off to a specialist neonatal team, but here skin-to-skin contact and early breastfeeding will have to do to keep him warm and his blood sugar up.

He's lifted up and put directly onto Rashida's awaiting breast. The tiny orange hat knitted by my mum looks bright and joyful on his head, and Rashida's crying, I'm crying, we're all crying and the baby is wailing loudly too. *He's alive. He looks healthy.*

'Yusuf,' says Rashida, naming her son, simply, quietly. Normally, in the absence of a husband, a brother or uncle may name her child, but Rashida has no one.

It's Assma who speaks next in a carefully neutral voice, 'The bleeding is heavy now – too heavy,' and you can hear a pin drop in that room. It's never over until it's over, and until the placenta is born, Rashida is at her most vulnerable. Blood is mixing with the amniotic fluid and trailing down the legs of the birth bed. *OK, keep calm, Anna. We expected this. Give the next line of drugs.* We continue to give an array of medications to contract Rashida's uterus and birth the placenta. This is a clear protocol – something I've done hundreds of times and will do hundreds of times again. *Next, the oxytocin infusion, another injection of ergometrine, then misoprostol rectal tablets.* Rashida, who's cuddling baby Yusuf in joyful disbelief, has no idea things are going wrong.

'Estimated 1,000 ml blood loss,' Sarika instructs me clearly. It's a PPH – postpartum haemorrhage. Panic claws my throat, and for a moment, I'm a total blank, a paused film with white noise.

It's Sarika who moves the moment on. She scrubs her hands, dons sterile gloves, reaches in and manually removes the stuck placenta. I'm watching the twinkling coral-coloured scarf poised delicately over her shoulder. I'm noting the crazy contrast to her bloodied gloved hands. I hear her speak calmly to Assma, relaying the instructions in Bangla and in turn in Rohingya to Rashida. And it's all over in a matter of seconds – the placenta out, the bleeding stops, and the scene has resolved itself to a cooing Rashida and baby Yusuf.

I'm so relieved, but at the same time aware of my own disturbing mind fog at the end; it's never happened before like that. My heart's running crazily fast, like an over-revving motor, alert for the next emergency that doesn't come.

Rashida beckons to show me baby Yusuf nuzzling at her breasts. Her nipples are small, but he's found a way to latch. She pushes something into my hand, and when I open my palm, it's her tawiz on a gnarly bit of cord. Her talisman filled with words from the Koran that she used to give a sense of safety, of protection. Maybe her most treasured item, yet without a word, she closes my hand, wanting me to keep it, and I'm left totally speechless.

It's stopped now, Anna, it's over. I want the joy to stay, but I actually feel physically sick at the thought of discharging them both back to the camp, where Rashida's anaemia and Yusuf's tiny size could bring a host of new complications. There were a million ways we couldn't protect her. It's no comfort to recognise how much we had achieved with this safe birth. Or to know that if Rashida had birthed alone in the camp, without access to drugs, she might have bled to death and been buried by morning. The fact is that as soon as they leave the hospital, I can't keep them safe.

CHAPTER THIRTY

I'm home again. Anita runs towards me at Heathrow arrivals. She's smiling.

'Where are we now?' she says, her eyes moist.

As we hug, her eight-months-pregnant belly pushes gently against mine, and I'm uncomfortably aware of my alcohol-fumed breath. Anita's dressed in a stripy top, with stylish pregnancy jeans tucked into winter boots. She looks at me squarely.

'We have a spare room,' she says, eyeing my hollow face and backpack crammed with dirty clothes. 'Stay as long as you like.'

Her words feel like a plug being pulled. I've been working in Bangladesh for nearly a year, pushing on, fending off the next emergency, witnessing horrors, nursing my broken heart. My alcohol intake is far too high, I have nightmares, night sweats, none of which I admitted at my Amsterdam debriefing. I am so, so tired, I want to sleep in her comfy bed and hibernate for a hundred years. *Maybe I'll never wake up*, because I have no clue what I'm going to do next, little money saved, no job or home to go to. No relationship to work on. Now I'm thirty, I feel too ashamed to go back and live with my parents, *again,* though I know they would take me in. Hannah and Jen, my former Nottingham flatmates, had also moved on and were living with committed partners.

Just breathe, Anna, the James in my head is telling me.

'I'm not doing any more missions for MSF.' My heart flips in my chest – someone else seems to have uttered this firm statement, except it's true. I can't go on feeling so wobbly, so unwell. I can never be a good mother like this, and seeing Anita's rounded tummy only confirms what I want now. And it's a shock, because I never had this feeling in my freewheeling twenties, when what I most wanted was to be free, to party, to achieve, to find love and all the rest of that impossible list.

What do I want now? I don't know, but as much as I regret it, my time with MSF is over.

*

Back in Anita's countryside kitchen, steam from our teacups swirls up to the ceiling. Outside, autumn has left the trees bare, the sky hangs grey, dew clings to the grass.

'How was handing over?' Anita asks, watching me carefully, knowing how much I hated letting go at the end of a mission.

Ten days ago, I'd handed over the reins to Judith, an experienced midwife from the UK, born in Trinidad and Tobago. She's bubbly, kind, efficient and with a laugh that fills the room, especially when Sarika started to call her 'Madam'.

'When I told Judith we had no CTG machines for monitoring the baby's heart rate, she'd looked how I must have when James first showed me his dentist's chair,' I said.

In that sense, handing over had been tough: Judith had no idea how hard we'd fought to get the services up to the standard I was leaving her with. Anita smiled when I said this. She'd had to hand over her final project not long ago, so I didn't have to explain the complicated mix of relief, guilt and grief involved.

Next, I tell Anita about the staff leaving party, of how Sarika, Benita and Prachi had pulled me into the back room, giggling like schoolchildren. Prachi laughing so hard her belly jumped up and down like a blancmange. Sarika with the air of a conjurer's assistant, pulled a dazzling sari out of a paper bag, and then the whole midwife gang had attacked me from all directions, laughing joyfully as I undressed down to my tatty and holed knickers and non-matching bra, revealing Rashida's tawiz now tied around my belly. They dressed me in a bright pink crop top and wound the sari in place with fifty safety pins. Prachi, with a cry of triumph, had me pinned down at last for the eyeliner and bindi spot, Benita painted my toenails and brushed my ratty hair before covering it in oil. I was embarrassed, appalled, loved it. These colleagues, these friends, these wonderful, brave, funny women, who'd taught me so much. It felt like an initiation ceremony, except I was leaving, fatigued and so conscience-stricken.

Finally, as I'd left, Sarika pressed a thin quilt into my hands – a *kantha* she'd made herself from three layered saris, sewn together with hundreds and hundreds of tiny delicate stitches.

'To help you sleep,' she'd said simply. And we'd cried together. It must have taken her hours and hours to sew this beautiful thing, which I didn't feel I deserved.

At the end of my staff party, and the end of my speech, I'd used the same words as Marjie had: 'If I have ever wronged you, please forgive me,' and then I sang, probably mangled, the Bangladesh national anthem: *Amar shona Bangla, ami tomar bhalo bashi* – 'My Bengal of gold, I love you.'

When Prachi leapt to her feet and sang lustily, everyone joined in loud and proud. Their voices mingling with the downpour of rain that beat on the tin roof, and the rivers of mud pouring down the hill.

*

Anita's small spare room becomes my home for nearly a month. Some days we cook together, walk in quiet corners of Hertfordshire, or sit with a cup of tea and talk. I drink red wine in the evenings, she sips herbal tea and tells me proudly she'd given up smoking before getting pregnant. We share brief snapshots of my life in Bangladesh, hers in Congo; nothing too heavy – her baby is nearly two weeks overdue – a tacit understanding between us both not to stir up the sediment of bad dreams.

On other days I can't leave my room. I lie unmoving, staring at the ceiling, or write angry, unanswered emails to Léon. In the room next door, Anita moves, dreamy and heavy, around what will soon be the nursery, folding little babygrows, piling nappies.

As if stuck in a horrible cliché, I stay in my PJs, listening to Adele singing 'Someone Like You' on a loop, sobbing until my face aches. When Anita sees my bloated features in the morning, she hugs me sweetly.

All the stress has somehow tangled together into one poisoned ball – the trauma from the births, the grief at leaving, the heartbreak. It attacks me when I sleep. When I wake, *I don't know what to do.* For the first time ever. MSF had been my main focus for most of my adult life – to be a nurse, then a midwife, get qualifications, work away, no matter what. Now it all feels over.

*

When Anita's baby safely arrives in the early hours of a dark winter's morning in a clean NHS hospital, I'm privileged to be there to watch the head crown.

After a week of loving, calm days as she breastfeeds, or we walk the local parks with the pram, I tell Anita it's time for me to go. 'Stay as long as you like – don't let this little varmint boot you out,' she says, adjusting her daughter's ridiculously cute hat.

But after a month of treading water, I feel I have a choice – to go under, or to see if I can work again. And Anita, with a new baby and a relationship, has her life to live now. I know I need to leave so that she has space to do this.

*

By May 2012, six months later, a pretty good imitation of a normal person is walking towards her day shift at Nottingham City Hospital, headphones constantly on, blasting loud music. I've gone back to renting friends' spare rooms, working long NHS shifts and drinking red wine in the bath – listening to the haunting and beautiful music of Bon Iver, staring at my tawiz.

Now I say yes to every party invitation or new bar opening in town, or drink with that guy, who might be any guy – chasing the 'click' so the pain goes away. I'm left hurt and confused when one guy takes ketamine at a party for fun, before he spins out in a grotesque, dead-eyed 'K-hole', reminding me painfully of the anaesthetised women I'd worked with overseas.

One desperate night, alone and unable to sleep, I invite Léon into my bed after banning him for months. Picturing his soft dark curls, the sweet sharp smell of him under the mosquito net, I make myself come. Sleep follows, but so do the tortured dreams.

*

It's weird being back in the NHS full time. I promise you it's nothing like *One Born Every Minute*, the TV show where midwives sit with their feet up eating cake and having cosy chats a lot of the time. Truth is, it's scary in a new way: the patients' level of expectation, the increasingly litigious world, where one mistake can see a midwife in court.

Of course, I appreciate the emergency call button that's always within reach, the abundant supply of quality drugs, the clean space and endless safety measures. But partying hasn't helped my tiredness, and although I'm still professional on duty, I'm wobblier than ever behind the scenes. Night shifts and disrupted sleep only seem to worsen my mental health. My nightmares are back with full vengeance, on a black roiling loop that shifts between UK emergencies and those in the camps, sometimes even back to baby Mariam and her rolling eyes in South Sudan.

Last week at work, when a man shouted at me for being late with his wife's meal by five minutes, was it me or my imagination that shouted back, 'Fuck you'?

In my new maternity ward, we have beds for twenty-six mothers, and usually help deliver about fourteen babies a night on the separate delivery unit. During my last night shift, we had three women just back from a caesarean section, who required monitoring every fifteen minutes, plus premature babies who needed regular temperature and blood-sugar checks. This is critical, life-saving work, but with only two midwives and one support worker on duty for the ward, there was no time for any of us to take a tea break, or even a wee break. When I stayed longer with the woman who was bleeding heavily, I couldn't help the woman who buzzed me for breastfeeding support, leaving her feeling neglected, or even abandoned. And me feeling frustrated and upset.

It goes without saying, it's safer here in the UK than in many countries overseas. And, of course, things like a food menu would be an in-your-dreams luxury for the refugees, but I feel angry that we're still not giving the level of care we could actually give. All it would take is to hire more midwives and not leave us so stretched, but we're told there's no funding for more staff. *We can do better than this.*

All doctors, nurses and midwives fear making a mistake, killing someone, but in my present state, I'm haunted by it. Think about it, I sometimes warn myself, what is the worst, the saddest, most reprehensible thing that can happen in a hospital? It's a baby dying who didn't need to. And you could do this – kill a child, destroy a young couple's happiness, leave scars on their lives that will last forever. So I'm extra careful, hypervigilant even. I don't stop for a break. I smile, I work hard, I stay on way past the end of my shift. There's still a huge buzz when babies are born and cry, but I'm walking on eggshells, scared all the time and very tired.

*

Helen Loewenstein, my new friend at the hospital, is the one you'd want to appear at your bed if you were having a baby. She's Mensa-smart and kind, beautiful and seemingly unflappable. When her boyfriend's away, I stay in her spare room between shifts. We drink together, share snatched meals, she tries to make light of her chaotic shift last night – when she was working on the delivery unit and responsible for five women labouring simultaneously, who should all have had one-to-one care – but I see the hurt and exasperation in her eyes. I tell her how a dentist recently asked me if I took drugs – because of my ground-down teeth – but I haven't. I'm not into that. My clenched jaw has started to wear down my teeth. We both marvel, with bleak irony, at how the staffing 'happened' to double on a day with a hospital inspection, and how that made such inspections more of a pantomime than a helpful tool to identify struggling hospitals.

Over a bottle of wine one night, Helen and I joke in a painful way about the many patients who ask us, 'Do you have your own children?' What they think is a seemingly reasonable question to ask women in their thirties is brushed off with a smile. 'Nah, not yet!' or 'Hopefully one day' covering the painful internal conflict.

Something is accelerating inside my empty womb, something really unfortunate for a boyfriendless midwife – a calling to be pregnant, and a yearning to hold a growing baby. Helen is feeling it too: this bittersweet ache when we watch new mums meet their babies, hoping one day it will be us, knowing nothing is guaranteed.

*

Life comes to a head at a house party before Christmas 2012. My new flatmate Faith and I head there, each armed with a bottle of wine, and me planning to drink every drop until the fear leaves me. It's over a year now since I was with Léon – I don't like the idea of being single again for Christmas.

Faith looks like she's having fun. She's laughing in the hall, a man has just slipped his arm around her waist. In a profound moment of illumination, I see Faith, my roomie, my tribe, as being vulnerable, and whisk in to save her by telling her he's married.

But actually, not everyone wants saving, and a few hours later I find myself being asked to pack my bags and I'm out on the street, mortified because, somewhere along the way, I've lost my tawiz as well as my bed. Surrounded by houses all twinkly for Christmas, smelling of wine, I scroll through my phone for somewhere to stay, but can't bear to land messily in a home where there are kids preparing for Santa. It's Helen who takes me in. She picks me up, cooks for me, lets me lie down for a couple of hours in her bed.

'Are you OK?' she asks, sitting on the end of my bed as I sob loudly and uncontrollably. My tears aren't because I'm now homeless, but something much deeper.

'When I was eighteen my brother's girlfriend was murdered...' I hear her breath catch. She looks confused. 'But I've got to stop feeling everyone is vulnerable because they're not, are they?' I plough on. She still looks confused, but I can't seem to find the words to explain myself. All I can feel now is failure and emptiness.

*

Maybe I should've stopped there, but a day later I'm back on a night shift on a busy delivery ward. I'm running between labour rooms all night, helping a colleague here, transferring a woman to the ward there, my throat tight and my heart pounding. At 3 a.m., Kiara comes in to have her third baby. Her family came originally from India; she was born in Leicester. An hour later, everything is going smoothly – the unborn baby's heart rate is normal, and with each deep grunt, Kiara's vagina stretches open naturally. I'm feeling pressured, but know I'm doing a good job.

A few more pushes, the baby's head starts to crown, and he's out! Baby is helped up to Kiara's breast, just as the placenta naturally starts to birth. Honestly, it's as smooth and amazing as that, everything just naturally falling into place. There's a small gush of bright red blood that's smeared a little on Kiara's thigh, but only a normal amount for a delivery, and now her uterus is contracted so the bleeding has stopped.

'I wish all births were that good!' Another cheerful midwife has appeared. I try to smile too, but I'm frozen, staring at the blood on the white sheet and the small splattering of blood on Kiara's brown leg.

It's like a camera flashing brightly in my face. I blink, and when I open my eyes, there's only blood on skin, and I'm falling backwards. *I can smell rain and woodsmoke.* Staring at the baby, I can see it's alive and crying, but in my heart I feel *the baby is dead.* Grief pushes me down. *This is Mia's baby.* For a moment, just for a moment, I am straddling two worlds – the world in front of me is a UK hospital, but all my other senses, just as real, feel and smell the Rohingya camp. I can hear a cry for Allah in the monsoon rain, and in my heart I'm fully back there. Then in another moment, the feeling has gone. I blink.

'I need to step out a moment.'

Kiara and her husband are blissfully unaware, cared for by the other midwife, who steps in. Walking out into the car park, pitch black around me, my breath billows out in the cold night air.

'I'm scared,' I say out loud to myself. This has never happened before – being awake in two worlds. That sense of impending madness, which has haunted me for months, is here now. Panic starts to rise, not knowing what happens next, until finally, my sensible self is jolted to the fore:

Stop! I can't live like this any more.

CHAPTER THIRTY-ONE

I'm thirty-one years old, sofa-surfing, skint, single, unable to sleep without torment and in an unhealthy relationship with my midwifery career – in short, lost with no anchor.

Over the last year, since being back in the UK, I can't remember a weekend without a nauseous hangover, or the guilt and loneliness of another loveless fling. One-night-stands are so desolate – they feel almost like love, but never are. When I'm drunk, I smoke cigarettes, although I'm absolutely against it. I can't remember how it felt just to breathe without the weight of the world on my chest. I don't recognise myself.

The flashback I'd had at work really scared me.

My GP has diagnosed stress, despite me clearly explaining symptoms of PTSD – he said I looked 'too well and too young' for that – and signed me off work for the whole of January 2013. He wants me to start antidepressants, but I don't feel depressed. My boss at work, Sarah, has been kind. I've been very honest with her about my experiences, but when I'm signed off, there's no follow-up until I go back. I've never taken sick leave before, except when I broke my ankle, and I never missed a day on my overseas missions, so this enforced rest feels alien and guilt-inducing.

Some of my friendships back here need attention. My long stints away have diluted our closeness, and friends' lives have understandably moved on, and anyway, I'm rubbish company because I don't feel like smiling and chatting. I feel like I'm in a deep, dark cave. I struggle to tell my family about this, instead just give them broad brushstrokes about my sick leave, saying I'm 'stressed' and taking some 'time out'. I'm too proud to move back home, too ashamed of being seen like this. I don't have the vocabulary to describe what's happening inside my head, yet instinctively, I know this is the real rock-bottom.

I want to be the strong one. In a moment of insight, I wonder if this is how Léon felt when he'd withdrawn from me, humiliated to be the wounded healer.

*

One morning, I saw an advertisement for a local Buddhist centre in the Post Office window. *A place of peace and public benefit in the heart of the city,* the handmade flyer said. And maybe, in that moment, something like a self-preservation switch got flicked, because I knew I couldn't go on like this. Also, the rent's cheap: only £300 per month for a room, bills included.

Yeah, yeah, it may be a con, I thought, tearing off an address strip and putting it in my bag, but I walked straight there as if my life depended on it. Half an hour later I was standing outside a Georgian house, a place where snow lay in tidy piles, the greenhouse had some glass missing, and the stone Buddha on the icy drive had snow on his belly.

Walking through the stained-glass door into a hall that smelt of sandalwood, I felt, momentarily, something I hadn't expected – strangely elated and connected to James. If James, the former alcoholic, heroin-baby hippy had been able to flick the switch, surely there was a chance for me. James was, by now, back in California, babysitting grandchildren, while his daughter studied for her nursing degree. 'Payback time,' he buoyantly reminded me when I Skyped him a couple of days later.

*

Lekmo, a barefoot, Bristolian Buddhist nun, greets me in the hall with a gentle smile, her blonde hair shaved close to her head. I take off my battered pumps and follow her into a large prayer room, where my toes sink into a plush cream carpet, and where, underneath the golden statues of Buddha, the offerings on the altar this month have a blue theme, including flowers, a glass goblet and, somewhat mysteriously, a Yorkie bar.

I don't question it, as it's already a relief to feel I'm stepping out of the turmoil for a bit. Lekmo's explaining, in her soft Bristolian burr, that if I stay here, I don't have to become a Buddhist. The rules state, however, that I'm not allowed to drink alcohol on site, to smoke, or engage in any activity that Buddha wouldn't approve of. In this moment, I know my drinking and smoking will stop – they were just making me miserable anyway.

'What you do off-site is your business,' she adds with a cheeky twinkle in her eyes. The other part of the deal, she continues, is that I attend morning meditations when I'm able. Each evening there are discussions on mindfulness, anger, grief and how to live a peaceful life in a busy world.

Sounds good to me. I follow her burgundy and saffron robes into the communal kitchen. On the enormous fridge, there's a long list of chores – hoovering, cleaning loos, washing up – all fifteen residents are expected to do.

Next, Lekmo shows me a tiny room with a single bed, small wardrobe and window with a view of the city-centre backstreets. I put my two backpacks down. Everything I own in the world is inside them.

I'm surprised she even has to ask me if I want to stay, because this feels weirdly like coming home, a home where I hope to get my head straight in a healthy community.

Well, healthy-ish, because one of the biggest takeaways of my time there was how none of us quite fit our labels, or our ideal selves. Take the one about nurses, who are generally hoped to be self-sacrificing, pure, endlessly kind, sort of like the best version of your mum, but with extra training. Or the nun label – dedicated, quiet, asexual, sparing with laughs, whereas the nuns (and monks) here are funny, flawed humans. From the nightly discussion, I hear how they've all had their own struggles with loneliness, or jealousy, or looking for happiness in the wrong places. How Lekmo used to be called Janet and was trapped for years in an abusive relationship. But the difference here seems to be that this community wants to be open with their struggles; they had found the language to explain their human flaws, and aim to work on them with a healthy support system.

*

If I sound like I jumped, clean-heeled, into a new life at the Buddhist centre, I'm giving the wrong impression. At night I had to force myself *not* to open the MSF vacancies page on my laptop, like an addict avoiding the alcohol aisle in the supermarket. Reminding myself that I couldn't just box up this pain and fly away with the illusion that I was leaving it behind and hoping it would magically disappear. I was good at leaving. But I knew, this time, I had to stay. A couple of days later, feeling desperate, I'd Skyped James again.

'I'm so scared, James,' I said. 'I'm in a black fog and I don't know what to do.'

'Don't be scared, Anna Banana,' he'd said. 'I promise you, if you sit with these uncomfortable, painful feelings, they'll pass. It won't happen overnight; just eat well, sleep lots, go swimming, walk in the woods, or by the river. Forget work. Do all the things that keep you healthy. When you're ready, the answers will come to you.'

'Yeah, whatever,' I said. I sounded as vacant as I felt – too disturbed to take it all in, but I prayed deep down that he was right.

James is kind enough not to remind me how I'd once teased him about all his omming first thing in the morning. For me, it's definitely a struggle at first to leave my narrow bed early and sit quietly amidst the new tribe – the robed nuns and monks, the ex-alcoholic who hid booze in his room and smashed up the café one night, the lazy guy who complained continuously about the chores. I sit there fidgeting and trying not to look at the clock. *This omm thing is never going to shut down the mad monkey of my brain.* My mad monkey is thinking I might go out to watch a band that night, and drink a bottle of red wine.

But slowly, slowly, things start to change. I actually begin to look forward to nothing more than sitting cross-legged in a quiet room, as the meditation starts with the same repeated verse: 'count your blessings'. Something is definitely shifting inside me. The concentration it takes to observe only my breath, to scan my body from head to toe, somehow seems to interrupt my flow of adrenaline and anxiety, and bring my baseline vibrations down a notch. There are moments when I even glimpse a kind of peace, one that doesn't need alcohol or sex to get there.

I thought a lot about James then, and talked to him too. How annoying his South Sudan meditations had once seemed, when there was always so much to do. But how actually they'd given him strength, clarity, endurance.

'You have to find your own way in this,' he said one night on a crackly line. 'Don't just sit there and make the noise. Find which meditation method works for you,' and I finally understood why he'd never asked me to sit and om with him. I had to figure this out myself, and what was starting to work best for me was simple: just tuning into my own breath with my eyes closed.

Mindfulness was also helping me to solve the miserable mystery of why I was always the most drunk at friends' weddings, or why I'd slept with another awful guy. For years, I'd convinced myself these were my happiest times, my necessary escape, but now it became as clear as blooming daylight that they were just a form of avoidance. A distraction from myself.

My parents come to visit me. I think Mum's secretly worried I've joined a cult. It's interesting that they seem more concerned about my stay at a Buddhist centre than they were about my going to a conflict zone – maybe they found one experience more imaginable than the other. But as Lekmo welcomes them to the café, and Dad's handed a piece of coffee and walnut cake, they start to relax a little. I still find it hard to be vulnerable in front of them, which is my hang-up, not theirs, but I'm pleased to show them I'm settling in and getting healthy again.

*

It feels like a mark of something when one day I unearth a scrap of paper in my backpack with the address of the mental health unit in Amsterdam and, for the first time, decide to speak to them. When I do, I confess I'm struggling with anxiety, hallucinations, flashbacks and a perpetual sense of extreme foreboding. I don't tell them about getting drunk or the one-night stands. Or how my body aches from inescapable guilt, how feeling toxic makes it hard to form new friendships. MSF then organise and pay for twelve sessions with a specialist trauma therapist who practises cognitive behavioural therapy (CBT), and who, by a great coincidence, lives only a short walk from the Buddhist centre.

Up until now, I've hated the idea of talking to strangers about my experiences, thinking I might infect and harm them too, so this is a big deal for me. More than this, my Britishness recoils at the language of therapy: 'taking time for myself', 'speaking my truths'. It sounds like self-indulgent, ego-stroking.

My therapist does not use these words. She's an expert in military PTSD. She also works with sexual violence survivors, and it's she who explains that therapy is actually a lot of hard work. Crucially, because she's older, stern, robust, I don't feel like my experiences can harm her. After a couple of awkward first sessions, where I worry more about which chair to sit on, or what my body language unconsciously tells her, she cuts to the chase.

'So tell me about the nightmares you're having.'

And the boulder shifts. In that hour I spew forth the memories of the dead baby trapped in Mia's body, how it had rotted her insides, and mine too. How I'd hacked that baby to bits; my fear, my repulsion later; the guilt that weighed me down so much that sometimes I didn't know if I could breathe; of how I feel poisonous, unlovable, but in contradiction both selfish and privileged. I tell her about the friendships I've lost, the bad choices I've made; how I don't recognise myself any more.

After that exhaustive session, she starts to explain depersonalisation and dissociative states. She hypothesises that this may be why I can only remember the destructive delivery as if I am watching it from a viewpoint up in the ceiling, and how this is a form of self-protection.

'To remove oneself from the moment that is causing acute distress is a primitive defence against emotional pain,' she explains. Making sense of my own reactions helps, a little.

After the session, I feel so exhausted that for two days I can barely move from my bed.

The next session feels worse. We delve into *why* I wanted to do aid work, the 'saviour complex', which can develop as an unhealthy coping mechanism for trauma, and I finally link the murder of my brother's girlfriend with the profound impact it had on me.

'You are not responsible for the safety of every woman you meet,' the therapist tells me. 'Can you see that?' This leaves me shocked and open-mouthed. For years I've felt on some unconscious level that I was, and it was so obviously completely irrational when spoken out loud.

'Society as a whole is responsible for the safety of women, not just you.' When she looks down at me through her glasses, I feel a bit foolish. Like a child. Had I gone around thinking I was some kind of crusading angel? Importantly, though, her cutting words are helping.

'You are human. You succeed and you fail. But you are not solely responsible for everything you witness.'

'But what if nobody is doing anything either?' I reply, tears running down my face and reaching for yet another tissue. For a moment this silences her.

'You need to work out how to live in a world of injustice and pain, and see the love and the joy. We all do.'

In the weeks that follow, the therapy, backed up by my calm life at the Buddhist centre, gives me an internal feeling of movement, like spring coming after a long winter. I can see colours again, feel a lightness in my day. I catch myself looking forward to things, a sense that I have things left to do – like falling in love, having a baby, learning to enjoy my work again. My therapist offers me no direct answers, but just saying this stuff out loud, as I had also done with James, removes the veil of guilt over it. There is structure to her replies, I have topics to think about at home, she challenges my unconscious patterns of thought that I didn't even know were there. She speculates that my love for Léon was actually a form of limerence, a mental state of obsession born from the stress of the refugee camp, though I secretly refuse to believe it was anything less than innocent love. I'm encouraged to read the work of Primo Levi, a Holocaust survivor, who managed to write his account of Auschwitz with a gentle voice.

'Have you tried writing these memories down?' my therapist would ask.

If I sometimes still get that old feeling again of being exiled from myself and having pieces of my jigsaw missing, I try to think: *this too shall pass.*

At our last session together, she poses the question of whether I would want to have children.

'Yes,' I say without thinking, my heart stirring. 'I left MSF because I want to have a baby, and I want my baby to feel safe in this world.'

'Can you not see,' she replied kindly, 'that this is what *you* need to thrive too?'

*

Around the time when the oxtail daisies and yellow rattle started to burst from the concrete behind the Buddhist centre, I found a great job in the NHS, working with women and families living with HIV. I loved it because we could see results – really good ones – in preventing the transmission of HIV from mother to baby. Our small caseload meant I could get to know the women really well, and fewer night shifts helped with the nightmares, though they still came sporadically. New friendships had blossomed too. I'd grown to love some of the folk I lived with: the Mexican woman with a growing pregnancy bump, the melodeon player who happened to use a wheelchair, the Hungarian monk. Wonderful, earnest people.

It's amazing too how much money you can save by not partying. One day, when I'm watching the ducks on the canal in Nottingham, I see a battered old narrowboat lolling in the water, with a For Sale sign on it. It's fixty-six feet long, and the curtains are a bit Miss Havisham, but it has a stove and room for a bed, and views from its small windows of water and willow trees and swans.

With my heart pounding, and money saved from my salary, plus a loan, I put in my offer of £25,000. When it's accepted, I dance around my tiny room at the Buddhist centre. My boat is called *Malahat*, and it's perfect for me: structurally sound, with insides that need completely stripping and replacing – good mindfulness practice, I'm thinking. There's a wood burner that just needs the flue replacing. I sew new curtains on my mum's machine, even lay new flooring, all while listening to beautiful piano music on my laptop, 'Casual Acquaintance' by David Keye. The rising and falling of the delicate music helps transport me to a place of calm, just as the water does.

My parents are relieved in a way; this is the first step to my own permanent home that I've ever taken. My boat is my new anchor, I can afford to live here without needing to increase my hospital hours, I can write or watch the seasons unfold outside, acknowledging I have always felt much better when close to water. And although my parents see it as a permanent home here in the UK, for me it has a different symbolism, as my yearning to travel and help women overseas still hasn't gone. With a boat home, *if* I do go overseas again, I can just lock her up and she'll be waiting for me when I get back.

CHAPTER THIRTY-TWO

My new life aboard that scruffy old boat was, in many ways, perfect, and I felt happier and calmer than I had for a long time. Over my two years on board, I could see the seasons unfold outside my windows; a mother duck patiently teaching her babies to swim, the swell on the riverbank after a storm, and I went to sleep to the sounds of lapping water.

My cycle to work was along a pretty towpath lined with wildflowers and willow trees, and I enjoyed my job as a midwife to women living with HIV. It covered both Nottingham hospitals, felt important and meaningful, but didn't completely consume me. For the first time in ages, I had the sense of taking back control of my life: I wasn't drinking or smoking, I was making friends with the eclectic bargee community and taking my family out for scenic canal boat trips.

It was a mystery to me why I still felt something missing, some sense I had unfinished business. Maybe, in part, it was because the way I'd left Bangladesh last time had been so messy. So when, at the end of 2014, I saw an online advertisement for a short teaching assignment in Bangladesh, I knew this was the missing piece of the jigsaw. The job was to teach on a new midwifery programme for one month. It was to be the first time Bangladesh had ever specifically trained midwives and recognised them as autonomous professionals – a massive and thrilling step forward for the country, and one I wanted to be part of.

Although I'd like to say that I thought long and hard before applying, I didn't. Essentially, I was qualified and hungry again, knowing this training of local midwives meant countless women in the future would have safer births. It represented huge progress, but now, my thinking went, I wouldn't be a frontline caregiver any more, so I wouldn't be swallowed by the cause.

When my inbox pinged with the email saying I'd been accepted, I trembled like a retired racehorse, feeling the old mixture of nerves and excitement. My placement was to be at an NGO hospital in Cox's Bazar, called Hope Hospital. This was actually a hospital I knew well, as I used to refer women there for obstetric fistula repair when I was based in Kutupalong. The assignment was to be voluntary and for one month only, this time working with Bangladeshi female students, though unfortunately not connected to the Rohingya plight.

Although it felt sad to lock up *Malahat* in January 2015, and to say goodbye to my fellow bargees and the ducks I'd watched grow from chicks, as I packed my textbooks, my fake blood, my knitted placenta, and the hats my mum and her friends had again kindly knitted, I felt different this time. Older. More sensible. This is a short assignment, I told myself. I'd teach for one month and travel for two. I was excited at the idea of teaching, and yearning to see my Bangladeshi friends again, this time in calmer circumstances.

Digging out my old and faded salwar kameez, I washed them and hung them on the deck to dry. When Anita, sleep-deprived from motherhood but worried about me, phoned to say goodbye, I replied in my most sensible voice, 'It will be very different this time.'

'Well, good luck with that,' she joked, then added more seriously, 'I'm still here if you need me.'

*

Sarika and I run towards each other at Cox's Bazar airport. She puts a garland of bright orange marigold flowers over my head, then scolds me for not staying at her house. Despite her infinite generosity, I know I want privacy this time. One day later, and I've rented a room in central Cox's Bazar with two new flatmates, both Australian aid workers – Jim and Kacy. They work in town and are mostly out.

The next day, Sarika and I drink sweet tea together at a local café on the beach. We ride there in a tuk-tuk and I see what I was too freaked out to notice in the end last time: how beautiful Cox's Bazar is – the bright colours, the spice and vegetable markets, the elegant crescent-shaped fishing boats out to sea. So much emotion, so many memories. When my knees start to tremble, I remind myself to *just breathe*.

Sarika says I look much healthier. She does too, plumper in her cheeks, brighter material in her outfit. Later, over dahl and chapattis, she tells me excitedly of her training in Amsterdam with MSF, how she came back and met and married a man from Dhaka. As a sign of respect, she refers to him as 'my husband' rather than by name, and tells me I can call him Bhai Juaan.

Her other great piece of news is the new MSF brick hospital that's been built at Kutupalong to help with the ever-growing influx of Rohingya refugees fleeing Myanmar. She wants me to come and see it for myself, meet up with old and new staff there. But I can't, at least not yet. I know I'll mind not working there any more, and feeling instead like the genial visitor, or, even worse, the poverty tourist taking pictures but doing nothing helpful. Realistically, I'm frightened of poking that snake again and inviting the nightmares when I feel so much stronger. I ask Sarika about Rashida, wanting to know if she and baby Yusuf were safe. But she doesn't remember them, as she's seen thousands of women since that time, and I have to try and accept that I will never know.

Sunset that night is gorgeous: an explosion of fiery oranges and reds that melt and slide into the sea. When I take a short walk back along the beach alone, I feel strong, an intrepid traveller forging my own path, this time without the protective arm of MSF. Excited too at the thought of teaching in two days' time. But as the sun sinks and the sky turns to purple and blue, I think about Léon with the old ache, the old sense of shock. This was where, over three years ago, we walked, laughed, splashed in the water, and now he's gone, but the phantom limb still hurts.

I'm so sick of thinking about him, I stand up and throw stones with all my might into the sea. *Enough! Let go! Move on!* I hurl another, it sinks and the water closes over it.

*

This time, my work is a safe place, and once I start, there's a beautiful regularity to my days teaching at Hope Hospital. Maybe a yoga routine in my apartment at sunrise – nothing fancy, just a few rounds of sun salutations to reset the calm button; sometimes breakfast of puffed rice, which is meant to be an accompaniment to a main meal, but with UHT milk tastes almost like Rice Crispies. Evening chats with my companionable flatmates, early nights, much better sleeps.

At the hospital each morning, my fifty Bangladeshi student midwives turn up to the classroom – polite, pristine in baby pink salwar kameez or saris. They shout, 'Good morning, Madam,' enthusiastically, then sing the Bangladeshi national anthem, me trying to join in, which makes them laugh.

Each student has been purposely selected (and fully funded) from poorer communities that have limited access to health care, and where births are not attended by a trained professional. After they graduate, these women will consolidate their skills at a local hospital, before returning to their own communities to spread the access to a trained midwife.

After morning introductions, we spend the next three or six hours filling buckets with fake blood for estimated blood loss, running through neonatal resuscitation with dollies and baby bag and masks. We might also get out the adult resuscitation dolls and practise cardiac-arrest drills. This teaching of practical skill-drills for obstetric emergencies is the area of health I feel most passionate about. It's no good just reading about this stuff in textbooks; you have to feel the heart-pounding moment, be able to think while adrenaline courses through your body. All the while, the promise that each of these women will save countless other women during their careers gives me hope. I know now that I can't go back to fieldwork if I want a family. This feels like an important next step, although I'm not sure the yearning for frontline work ever really goes away. Because nothing compares to the sense of achievement, of feeling so necessary, of having blood up your arms and saving a life in a context of such extreme adversity. Saving a life when that life would almost certainly have been lost without you.

*

Tonight, Thursday, is the start of the weekend. I'm up on the roof when it happens, having a few drinks with Jim and Kacy. These evenings are more sedate than the Pink Pearl hoolies, but just to be sure, I add a hefty dose of tonic to my gin.

There's music playing, the Venga Boys of all things, and a few people milling about, when I see him across the room. He has the biggest, most infectious smile I've ever seen. Bright white teeth, a charismatic laugh that carries across the rooftop. His thick, curly black hair reminds me of Léon's.

Mercy, a woman I know from the UN, introduces us.

'This is Ali, he's our surf instructor out here.'

A number of aid organisations arranged extracurricular activities, such as surfing, to destress their workers.

Ali smiles at me. We chat. He can teach me to surf if I'd like that, he says, handing me his business card.

I'd seen the Dhaka tourists surfing when I was here before, but MSF had discouraged it on the grounds that water sports here were often unregulated, and if we got injured, our whole project could grind to a halt. But now I'm feeling buoyant. Defiant. I'm a free agent now. I can make friends with Bangladeshi people; I *can* take those surfing lessons. After giving Ali my number, we plan to meet the next day. That hair, that smile, are what I think about that night as I drift off to sleep.

CHAPTER THIRTY-THREE

It's hard to imagine a brighter, more dedicated or harder working group of midwives than the ones I taught in Bangladesh. Their passion and motivation were deeply rooted: many had heard stories or witnessed the horrors of sisters, aunts, close friends suffering or dying in childbirth at home because there were no midwives; of babies dying because there was no basic resuscitation at birth. To get comprehensive training, to earn their own money, was for these midwives a privilege, not a right, in a poor country where equality is still, for many, an impossible dream. To watch them learn, and later to see them graduate in 2018, was a joyful experience.

I was sad to say goodbye to their beaming, friendly faces, but glad that this time my experience had felt so completely satisfying. Instead of dashing away in shame and panic, this time I felt safe enough to stay on in Bangladesh for a couple of months to sightsee. I also wanted to learn to surf.

One image from this time stays in my mind, and still has the power to make me laugh. It's my second or third surfing lesson and I'm paddling after Ali, my surf instructor, through the roar and glitter of the waves. He's wearing Day-Glo orange board shorts and a blue rash vest that clings to his dark brown skin, showing an impressive set of muscles. Paddling ineptly behind him, I'm slowed down by my full-length black T-shirt and leggings, worn to satisfy local modesty.

And then this happens. In one lithe twist, he jumps from his board, swims under water, then bursts to the surface, swinging his curly hair from side to side, making water spin like diamonds in a halo around his head at the exact moment a shoal of flying-fish leap across the sky behind him. It is so perfectly corny, like a shampoo ad, or a scene from a Hollywood movie, but I know I'll never forget it, the way certain pictures live in your mind forever.

Ali's a patient teacher, kind about my initial lack of stamina and clownish pratfalls. When finally, after a couple of weeks' practice, I stand up on my surfboard and find myself rushing through the sea, I'm ridiculously happy, shouting, 'Wooohooooo!'

He's also grinning from ear to ear, as if we've both found the keys to the kingdom.

My teacher soon became my friend, and it was during many talks while waiting for waves, or sometimes over sweet tea in the little bamboo shelter on the beach, that I learnt in snatches his remarkable life story. He was born into a poor family, the youngest of ten children, five of whom died before they were five. The family home was a couple of roads back from the beach in a town called Inani, near Cox's Bazar. In 1991, when a huge cyclone hit the area, his whole family prepared for their fate by sitting in a circle on the floor, holding hands and praying to Allah. All of them survived.

Fate stepped in again when Ali was eighteen years old. His father, the breadwinner, had recently died, when Ali saw surfing on one of the town's first TVs. As he endeavoured to learn the sport, he happened to catch the eye of an American Christian missionary, who recognised that he was good enough to surf competitively in Indonesia and America. Surfing had both found him and healed him. Later, it emerged that the sport was a good way for the charity to introduce Christianity to this predominantly Muslim community. Although Ali didn't convert, the charity still gave him a world of opportunities to surf, to travel and to learn English. He returned a local surfing hero.

*

Sarika has warned me that some of the surf boys here don't have a good reputation. Some, it's rumoured, seduce foreign women in the hopes of getting a visa, while others allegedly sell sex for money, but Ali's not like that.

He refuses to take money for our surf lessons. He asks if we can spend more time together. I'm happy – something is building between us, and by now I'm mad about surfing. When my teaching job ends, I'm down at the beach as often as I can, pleased that I can now stand on the board for a few seconds maybe two times out of five. My plan, before I leave, is to visit the cities of Chittagong and Sylhet, all the touristy things I couldn't do last time under the MSF security rules. Looking back, they seemed fuddy-duddy, as Bangladesh is such a beautiful place to explore, and Ali says he'll be my guide.

*

I still have an almost nightmarish recall of the night it happened. I can see the wooden crescent fishing boats returning from their day's work, see palm trees drenched gold by the setting sun as Ali and I paddle out to sea, comfortably companionable by now, our arms spooning through warm water. He feels like a proper friend. I've tried to be open about my former aid work and its impact on me, but my stories are heavily edited because he says he's squeamish, plus I don't want to monopolise the conversation. What I do know, though, is that he understands poverty and lack of access to health care, but his outlook is so buoyant. He's told me he longs to have children, a stable family, everything I want now.

Swimming beside him towards the horizon, my heart feels alive and happy. When we meet, I feel it growing, this glow, this extra energy. Sarika was wrong to group him with other surf communities who have a bad reputation. He's different, he's travelled, seen a bit of the world, but is clearly devoted to the elderly sweet mum he's already introduced me to.

*

Now I'm watching a wave form on the horizon. Ali spots it long before I do; it's a good one and the swell is growing.

'OK,' he says encouragingly, 'start paddling.'

Belly down on my board, I feel the pulse of water gathering beneath me. Upper body strength isn't my forte, so this feels like a challenge, but the last waves that rolled in along the beach were gentle, the perfect surf for beginners.

'OK, stand up.' The wave starts to rise, I feel its pull under me. I clamber up, stand and nearly make it all the way to the shoreline, where I fall inelegantly in shallow water a few feet from the beach. I'm laughing as I come to the surface, glad the leash around my ankle stops my board escaping.

'One more try before the sun sets,' he says.

My arms are tired, but I start paddling, keen to nail this surfing before I leave, and maybe to impress Ali with my dedication.

'Board pointing out to sea,' Ali reminds me. The wind has changed direction, the gentle waves look bigger and stronger.

I'm hungry as well as tired now, as I lie on the board waiting for the next wave, half wishing we'd called it a day and I was eating fresh fish and rice at the local restaurant we'd planned to go to later. I can taste salt on my lips, see bigger waves splashing on the beach, hear the dream-like murmur of the Bangladeshi couples strolling along the shoreline as they watch the sun set.

'OK, now paddle.' The big swell rises, I push extra hard, though my arms are aching – faster, faster. Then I stand up! In one triumphant surge, I ride that wave all the way back to the beach.

'Woohoo!' Jumping off my board, elated, I turn back into the white churning water. I feel the leash tug my ankle, but I'm laughing and waving to Ali, and miss the next big wave as it rises and curls in a roar. When it crashes down on me, the sideways board flips and its pointed end slams full force straight into the middle of my neck.

The thud is sickening as I whirl and fall under water.

I don't know which way is up.

Bubbles, swirling waves.

Shooting pain in my neck.

When I flounder helplessly to the surface, Ali is next to me. I try to tell him what happened, but I can't speak. *Something is really wrong.* I can see the whites of his eyes. Touching my neck, I expect to see blood, but there isn't any.

I think I've broken my neck – that 'thud' was really loud. A sense of drowning, of suffocation, as I finger the rings of cartilage at the front of my neck.

Ali unties my leash and helps me to the shore, where a crowd is gathering, staring.

'Don't worry, she's fine,' Ali waves them away.

Fuck, fuck, fuck. When I try to talk, still no sound, and I don't know what to do. Something is seriously wrong with my neck.

Think, Anna. My clinical voice of reason breaks in. Pretend you're assessing a patient.

It's darker now and my wet, salty clothes are growing cold. Lying flat on my back on the sand, mosquitoes swarm around my exposed ankles. Closing my eyes, I feel down the back of my neck and spine starting at the base of my head. I've done this hundreds of times to patients in ED, the initial check to see if any vertebrae are painful. *I'm not paralysed.* Then out of the encroaching dread I have a moment of clarity: *there's no medical help here. You know that. The MSF hospital can't offer anything for neck injuries, the local hospitals aren't good. You're on your own.* Ali, still trying to laugh it off with the crowd, is non-medical.

'You're fine,' he says. 'Just a shock. Let's go for dinner.'

I don't listen to him and I'm back in my own world, eyes jammed shut, entirely focused on my second self, a trained professional, staring down at the frightened person on the sand giving a medical handover. *Background: blunt trauma to the front of the neck. Situation: unable to swallow, cough or talk. Assessment: no evidence of a broken neck, no paralysis, no bleeding or swelling. Patient is able to breathe. Recommendation: given the context, watch and wait.*

My biggest fear now is that I'll be taken to a local hospital and they'll harm me further. Suddenly, I understand why MSF kept a protective arm around us. I wish they could help me now, but they can't.

When I'm strong enough to stand, I stagger, with Ali's support, back to his room. A single overhead light bulb shines on cement walls, spiders' webs, life-size posters of him surfing. I sit on his bed. When I take in a breath, I hear what the textbooks call an 'audible inspiratory wheeze', or a 'stridor'. *Shit, shit, shit,* my scared self interrupts, *this is really bad!* A stridor is a symptom of an acute airway obstruction. At this point, in the UK, I'd be in a blue-lit ambulance on my way to a hospital, where I'd be given inhaled adrenaline and maybe a surgical airway called a tracheostomy.

There's no way I can get to the nearest specialist ear, nose and throat (ENT) hospital. It's in Dhaka, 400 km away.

Two hours later, Ali's pacing the room, head in his hands. He sits beside me, begs me to let him take me to hospital, but I write 'no' on a scrap of paper. Instead, I scribble out prescriptions for steroids and anti-inflammatories in writing I don't recognise. Five minutes later, he's back from a local pharmacy shack, with drugs I know might be fake. Crushing them into powder, stirring in a little water, I manage to trickle them down my throat by repeatedly lifting the back of my tongue.

'What now?' he almost cries. I think he's picturing the fall-out if a foreign tourist dies in his family home. When I look again in the mirror, I honestly don't know – my trachea looks deviated out of place. *I'm going to die.*

When darkness falls, I bundle pillows and a jumper on the bed, so I can lie at an angle. The nurse voice alternates with the panic and dislocation in my brain. *You must keep your heart rate down, let the anti-inflammatories work.*

I'm so frightened at first during that dark night, and then, unexpectedly, the meditations I learnt at the Buddhist centre come back to me in a weird, warm rush of clarity: *count your blessings.* I lie there, observing only the sensation of my breath going in and out of my body, and I feel like a deep-sea diver going down through layers of panic and darkness until I find a quiet place with a sense of overwhelming peace.

I don't want to die, but if this is the end, accept it. Don't be scared. Whatever else has gone wrong, I think I've been lucky to have lived the life I wanted, a meaningful life. I've got things wrong, but my intentions were good. This feels like leaving the party too soon, but if this is it, I refuse to be scared. It's a feeling of my life rushing before my eyes.

I'm aware as I write this that were I to read it in another person's account, I'd think it sounded too simplistic, too fake-inspirational. But all I can say is that it was true for me during that extraordinary night, and it saved my life.

*

My overnight meditation, and the drugs, have improved my breathing, but flying to the specialist ENT hospital in Dhaka, 24 hours after the injury, in a small, unpressurised plane, I can't grasp what's real and what's not; it all feels so unbelievable. I remembered a morose Léon needing emergency medical aid, and have a feeling that I'm in *The Truman Show*, or worse, I've died and am in a speechless purgatory. I still can't speak, swallow or cough, but there's still no visible bruising on my neck.

Initially, the doctor seems to think I'm faking the silence. 'Let's take a look,' he says patiently. He puts a small camera down my throat as I try not to gag. I focus on the long black hairs bursting from his earholes. When the images come up on his monitor screen, he sits bolt upright, clears his throat and scribbles furiously on my medical records.

'Madam,' he turns the screen towards me, 'you have a large laryngeal haematoma, it covers over half of the throat, and comes between your vocal cords. I'm thinking the cartilage at the front of your neck is also fractured.'

This diagnosis is a shock, as a laryngeal haematoma – usually the result of a car crash or strangulation – is rare and comes with a reported 40 per cent fatality rate. Sometimes it's missed in UK emergency departments because there is no external bruising. But weirdly, I'm almost relieved. There *is* something there, and we can all see it. Years later, I still occasionally look at the scan, or read my medical report, just to reassure myself that it was real, because there was a moment, before I got a grip in the middle of the night, when I was listening to my stridor and the sounds of the crickets in the dark night outside, wondering if I had finally gone mad.

In the UK, I'd be referred at this point for MRI and CT scans, but in Dhaka, my doctor gives me a large bag of medications, instructions not to speak for at least another two weeks, and not to fly home until I'm healed. Was he right? That night, from my hotel room in Dhaka, I send the scan and medical plan to a group of my UK medical friends on Messenger. This is so unprofessional, but I don't have many choices. Ali, still trying to make light of it, says I have a burger stuck in my throat.

My medical friends all message back quickly. They say they're worried, but agree this sounds like the right course of treatment. Next, I email my family. I tell them I'm injured but OK, have a friend here looking after me, and will be home in a month. I don't want to worry them. After all, I'm still alive. Alive and back to my old ways of secrecy and silence, of glossing over bad things, of telling half-truths.

CHAPTER THIRTY-FOUR

When Ali suggests on our way home that I move in with his family, I'm too sick to think of the ramifications – also too confused. I'd had only twenty-four hours without being able to access medical support, but I crumbled inside to imagine the stateless Rohingya, some of whom could never access medical help. The thought of spending the next couple of weeks, speechless and unable to eat, on my own in a foreign hospital or lodgings is frankly horrible. What I do feel is an invalid-ish gratitude for his strong male presence and kindness. He's the one who rescued me from the beach, who let me spend that night in his home rather than abandon me to the local hospitals. When I feel ready to eat soft food again, he's the one who provides my first meal of rice pudding, cooked by his sister, and brings me sweet tea from the market. So he was kind, but in a dangerously short time I'd cast him as my knight in shining armour, and as author Bessel van der Kolk identifies, sometimes trauma comes back as a reaction, rather than a memory.

All around us is Ali's extensive family. His mum is elderly and frail. I call her Amar Juaan, a respectful greeting that means, 'My mum is my heart'. In return she calls me Shona Monee, which means 'My gold and diamonds'. She has bright white hair caught in a tiny nut-bun, and a cackling laugh. Her house is on one floor, with brick walls and a tin roof. Each of its five small rooms houses one of Ali's siblings, plus their spouses and children. There are seven children in the extended house, more at his older brother's house in another area of Cox's.

Every morning his mum, who has arthritis, wakes early for prayers, then hobbles on her stick to each family's room to catch up on the day's

news. In the afternoons, she likes to watch Indian melodrama on TV —
the bit I saw had an evil twin coming back to seek family vengeance.

No one questions my staying in Ali's room, or at least not in front of
me. Perhaps they believe that his overseas work allows some bending
of the usual rules about modesty. He's also in his thirties — old by
Bangladeshi standards to be single. Occasionally, when Amar Juaan flashes
me a hopeful gleaming smile, I think that like most mums she wants him
married and happy. My parents seem relieved I have a support network
here. I've even posted a picture of Ali and me together on Facebook, so
people at home see we're in a relationship. They're pleased, they say, to
see me happy.

*

When we slept together for the first time, I felt weak from days of not
being able to eat properly, cautious because of the thin walls of the house,
and strange not being able to talk. I had a desperate desire not to feel alone,
and to feel connected to someone again. Sadly, looking back, I was perhaps
unconsciously worried that if I didn't please him, he might leave me.

But as soon as we'd had sex, I realised the condom I'd given him
had come off inside me. Under normal circumstances, I'd have got a
morning-after pill at the nearest sexual health clinic, but my near-death
experience had impacted me; this wasn't 'normal circumstances', and
my decisions became less thought-out. I could have gone to the MSF
hospital, it wasn't far away, but I worried that the staff, and I, would
be embarrassed. This is absurd looking back — I was their teacher on
the importance of family planning. Instead, I decide to go for sexual
health screening at a UK clinic when I get home. In the meantime, I lie
in bed, a symphony of mixed messages flashing through my mind, but
ultimately leaving it up to fate. I'm in love, I know that, so let's see what
happens.

*

Four weeks later, at a time when I can whisper and have short
conversations, my nipples feel as if someone's brushing stinging nettles
over them and, for the first time ever, my breasts fill my bra. When two
blue lines on a pregnancy test confirm what I already know, I'm elated.

I'm alive! I'm pregnant! I'm going to have a baby! It's a relief in many ways – alongside being thrilling and scary – as I didn't even know I could get pregnant, not for sure.

When I tell Sarika, she's polite as always, but reserved, warning me not to do or say anything until I'm twelve weeks pregnant. Ali thinks otherwise. He says we should marry straight away, before my bump shows, so as not to shock his conservative relatives, who, incidentally, don't expect me to convert to Islam.

Then, out of the blue a few days later, he actually gets down on one knee at sunset by the palm trees along Cox's Bazar beach. He tells me he loves me and will never leave me. Yes, there'll be mountains to climb he says – one of them being the visa he'll need for the UK – but we'll be a family together, no matter which country we live in. And I love the idea of being a citizen of two countries – it feels like a way of reconciling my two worlds. I'm ecstatic that I've found a way to have a partner, to have love, and still travel. To no longer be alone.

A warm wind is ruffling his shining curls, as he says all this with humble devotion while holding my hand. I willingly say 'yes' before Ali even has time to stand up and brush the sand from his knees.

We've known each other for less than twelve weeks.

*

One amazing thing about being pregnant is this new optimism, this state of believing *anything is possible*. When I phone my parents that night, they sound a little stunned, but – hats off to them – they say they're delighted. Questions follow: where will we live? where will the child be brought up? When I tell them we'll aim to live mainly in the UK, probably on my Nottingham houseboat, but travel each year to Bangladesh, there's a sense of relief. Looking back, maybe these weren't conventional choices I was making, but they were structured: marriage, babies, a stable home. They could recognise and support these decisions maybe a little more easily than my flighty years of running from disaster to disaster. I told them how I couldn't wait for them to meet Ali, and how important they would be in this baby's life.

Plans are quickly made for my parents, my brother and sister to come to my Bangladeshi wedding. My new voice, still a little whispery and half-volume, but determined, cuts out before the end of the phone call, but I'm hanging on to this good feeling for dear life. When the line goes dead, I look at Ali and smile excitedly. I've done it now. It's real.

And yes, of course I get it now, how crazily impulsive this sounds, but after being so nearly dead a matter of weeks ago, I'm in love with life, with hope for a new future. Also, my danger meter is skewed: so much of my early adult life, my twenties, took place at breakneck speed, that an instant wedding feels no bigger or scarier than stepping into another country for an earthquake, an emergency, a torturous birth. When danger feels normal, or so I rationalise, surely this baby, this marriage, is one of my better steps into the unknown. James and Anita both say they're thrilled for me. They laugh at my impetuous decisions, but they are supportive – they can see how happy I am.

*

One week before we get married, Ali and I move into a small room two roads behind the Pink Pearl. Our room is bleak – concrete floor and walls with a squat loo and cold shower, but it's cheap and private, away from the thin walls of the family home. It's also a short walk to the small eco café on the beach where our wedding will take place, and I head there to talk to the chef who's planning the food. Sarika's already picked out a beautiful purple and green sari for me to wear and some sparkling flip-flops. Ali's chosen orange flowers for my hair, and his sister is excited about doing the traditional henna patterns on my hands and arms. The date we've chosen, at the end of April 2015, works perfectly for Ali, as there'll be a surf competition hosted by the Christian organisation who originally sponsored him, so all his international surf friends can come, as well as his family. My closest Bangladeshi friends – Sarika, Benita, Prachi – can make it too.

I'm sitting at a table outside the eco café, drinking coconut water and furiously scribbling these wedding plans into my diary, when it happens. As I stand up to leave, something doesn't feel right inside, and I wonder if it's just nerves. I'm seven weeks pregnant now.

Back in our room, I go to the squat loo and in one heart-stopping moment see a small trail of fresh red blood on the tissue. The colour is bright and sharp against the grey backdrop of the room. I know, of course, that some women do bleed a little in pregnancy, so I'm already praying it doesn't mean a thing. *Watch and wait.*

*

Midnight, and half an hour ago a deep period-like pain sent me back to the cement bathroom. Squatting over the drop latrine, a clot of blood plopped down the hole. Staring at the black space, I'm in shock for a few minutes, watching the cockroaches scuttle away. Not wanting to accept what I know to be true, as a trickle of blood slides down my leg. My longed-for baby has gone, and in the most unceremonious way possible. When I crawl back into bed beside Ali, he asks, 'Are you OK?' I simply say, 'I'm not pregnant any more.'

For the rest of the night I'm awake, wanting to curl up and die. My family will arrive for the wedding in a few hours and my belly is still cramping. If my bleeding doesn't stop, I could end up in hospital. But the other pain, a grieving to my core, is much worse because I wanted this baby *so much* – for itself, and also because it had the power to change my rootless life.

I'm also kicking myself for not even considering that I could miscarry – so stupid when I know one in four women do. And in this moment, I think of Rashida. How did she survive fourteen consecutive miscarriages when it hurts like hell?

It's a long, hard night and I stare at the stranger lying asleep beside me. Light is creeping through the calico curtains of the room when I make up my mind. My body is yearning for a baby, Ali is committed to making a family with me, so I'm going to carry on with the wedding. I'm too tired, too shaken to think of any other way.

I'm looking at my wedding pictures as I write this. Me, in my new purple and green sari, garlanded and smiling radiantly. Ali so handsome in a jewelled suit. Sarika is there, and my parents. My family knew of my miscarriage, but Ali's didn't, so it became our unspoken secret.

And, in the way of these things, I still have some good memories of my wedding day: watching friends and family dancing to awful music by the Venga Boys; Ali's mum, wearing the new purple cotton sari we'd bought for her, happily tucking into a plate of fresh seafood and rice; my young Bangladeshi nieces sitting on my lap, as Ali and I sat on the traditional 'throne chairs', my family beside me. I don't remember much else, except falling into bed, bleeding, married.

CHAPTER THIRTY-FIVE

Did I marry because I was in love, or in love with *the idea* of being in love?

Was it a projection of my love for Léon, or fear of loneliness?

Was it a yearning to be happy, maybe; a moment of madness; a response to a near-death experience; the grief of miscarriage?

Was it pride, not wanting to turn back? Or was it visions of a quiet life by the sea, my toddler leaving footprints in the white sand, my husband surfing the waves? My two worlds connected?

When I look back now, I can hardly recognise the woman I was then. The marriage that felt so right was actually a massive, blinkered, bounding leap into the unknown and away from the self-awareness I thought I'd gained. Although I've never regretted meeting Ali – I try not to regret anything I've done – it was unbelievably naive to suppose this would end in happy ever after.

*

By early May 2015, sooner than expected, Ali is granted his UK visa. Our plan now is for him to join me on the houseboat in Nottingham. He'd smiled when I'd shown him pictures of *Malahat* before we'd married, said he loved the idea of living on the water. We'll also go back to Bangladesh regularly to see his family, every winter hopefully, as I find those months so grey in the UK.

On the morning he arrives at his new home, watching him unpack two pairs of jeans, two T-shirts and one pair of shoes from his otherwise empty suitcase, my heart contracts for him and I have my first uneasy feeling that we might be very different creatures out of the water than in it.

God knows what he really felt as he stepped aboard *Malahat*, looked intently around and said, 'Oh yes, nice.' I'm pretty sure the idea of carrying the toilet to be emptied each week at the marina sluice will fill him with horror, so I silently make a vow always to do this job. Ever the optimist, I watch him pull himself together, flash a white smile and say, 'So great for fishing!'

Romantic, yes, but I was realistic enough to know that this old canal boat with its tiny cabin and old wood-burning stove might be a far cry from his imaginings about a fancy life in the UK.

During the day I start to worry that he's lonely in his new life. I'm back at the hospital, working as a midwife to families living with HIV. It's a job I love, but I must work extra night shifts to fulfil Ali's visa requirements, as I am his sponsor. He can't work until he gets his next visa, so while I'm away, he spends his time exploring the city, fishing in the river, or attending the local mosque. My brother kindly buys him a good bicycle so he can be more mobile.

There is a bittersweetness to these days. As Ali starts to adapt, and later to love, the UK, he slowly sells off his business back home and Bangladesh loses one of its own. If he minds, or misses his family, he doesn't say.

Yes, we'd done some talking, but it seemed easier when we were bobbing on our surfboards, waiting for the waves in the Bay of Bengal. Now the daily demands of life in Nottingham – work, rubbish collection, boat maintenance, slop-dropping – are changing us. We're closing in on ourselves like hermit crabs. Although I try several times to talk, to prise him out of his shell, I learn you can't force someone to open up if they don't want to.

There was a sweetness to those early days too. Days when I'd come home and change from my hospital uniform into jeans and T-shirt, and some of the glow and gloss of romantic love remained. I'd see him sitting on the roof of the boat, fishing as the sun set around us. We'd drink tea and watch tiny cygnets cheeping as they followed the mummy swan down the river; we'd walk hand-in-hand along the wooded riverbanks, catch the blue flash of a kingfisher; we'd giggle at our own in-jokes. During these good times, I felt smug that I'd found love in the most unusual way, but still managed life's goals of a husband and a home.

*

Summer turns to autumn, and then comes that cold, windy day in October. We're in the maternity department of Nottingham City Hospital. It takes a while for me to unbundle from layers of warm woolly clothes and expose my swelling belly for an antenatal scan.

I am five months pregnant. My second pregnancy. This baby was conceived after just one menstruation following the miscarriage.

Hope and cautious happiness flutter in my chest as I hop onto the table. So far, everything's going well: the routine scan at twelve weeks confirmed the baby is growing and that there's no bleeding or infection. Soon I hope to take some time off work to enjoy this pregnancy. Although I still love my job, it's been challenging working through weeks of pregnancy nausea, and being around threatened pregnancies all the time can be tough as I'm constantly reminded of the risks.

*

The ultrasound gel is cool on my abdomen, it tickles as the sonographer starts to move the probe over my belly. Looking at the monitor, I'm relieved to see the baby's heart beating away.

'Woohoo!' I squeeze Ali's hand in the darkened room. We're both excited. Maybe today we'll find out the sex of the baby. I've really tried to enjoy this pregnancy, to block out my memories of traumatic births, as I want this little one growing inside to be bathed in the loving hormones of serotonin, oxytocin and dopamine. There's so much we don't know about the impact of stress on babies *in utero*, but what we do know is that stress and anxiety aren't good for their development. I've found a short meditation before bed is helpful, and trying not to think about anything deeper than this pregnancy and its well-being.

Happy vibes only. In a weird way, when I do think of all those torturous pregnancies I've witnessed, I feel I've paid my own penance with my miscarriage. Now it's *my* turn to be a mummy.

*

Reading pregnancy ultrasounds has never been a skill of mine, but I can see the outline of the baby's head, the silhouette of a face on the black-and-white pixelated screen, and I coo over the picture. The sonographer seems to be taking a long time scanning the head, but I don't say anything, caught up in the joy and wonder of seeing my baby. Next, two little arms, two little legs, all a good size for a five-month pregnancy. Now we're back to scanning the head again, this feels odd. My pulse starts to rise.

'Anna.' The voice of the sonographer is threadier than when we first came in. Her tidy brown bob sways from side to side. 'I'm not sure how to tell you this.'

Gripping Ali's hand for dear life, I hope that I'm somehow hallucinating and actually everything is fine. When my throat constricts, I can feel my carotid pulse pounding against the old scar tissue from my neck injury. *Something is wrong!* I scream internally but I'm frozen into silence, trying to work out what it is.

I look closely at the scan of my baby's head. The sonographer shows me the brain.

'There are no ventricles here across the brain where there should be.'

What the fuck are brain ventricles? I don't know what that means. Is my baby brain-damaged?

Ali looks confused. He's never seen a scan before or been in a medical facility like this. He doesn't know what's 'normal'. Turning to him, I try to explain what I too don't understand.

'There's something wrong with our baby's brain.'

'Let me see if I can find a consultant,' says the sonographer. She leaves us alone in the darkness. Ali sits looking dumbfounded. 'Oh, no,' he finally says, and whispers a prayer in Arabic.

Although I don't know what's wrong, I do know a problem with the brain is always serious. While we wait, I curl into a ball on the examination table. Gel smears over my pregnancy jeans, and from somewhere I hear the desperate cry of a woman mourning her baby. I've heard this sound in Nottingham ED, in maternity wards, in South Sudan and in Bangladesh. It takes me some time before I realise that howl is coming from me.

*

We go home that Thursday with no more information. There's a problem with my baby's brain, but no consultant can see us until the following

Monday. In the taxi home, in a sleepwalking nightmare, I stare out of the window at the grey city.

Back on the boat, I lie in bed, feeling the water rock and lap outside. *Surely they wouldn't send me home if it was that serious? But isn't anything to do with a brain really bad? Maybe this is all in your head.* I lie there awake all night, part zombie, part manic thinker, feeling completely alone. Although I try to speak to Ali, he's trying not to worry until he has to. He wants to follow the hospital's instructions and wait until Monday.

By Friday morning, I'm in a real state: my pulse is crashing, I haven't slept a wink, the walls are caving in around me. Calling the maternity department where I work, I cry to someone on the phone:

'I don't know if my baby is going to live or die. Please let me see a consultant today,' I plead, snot bubbling from my nose.

*

Somehow, the person on the phone gets me into the foetal medicine department at the hospital that afternoon. Many things are a blur now, but I do remember my hands shaking as I lifted up my top for the repeat ultrasound, still in the clothes I wore the day before. Ali's there, his head in his hands. Our consultant's eyes are kind, as is her voice; she makes us feel she has all the time in the world, and now she's concentrating on scanning the head of our baby. Her language is clear so we can both understand.

'See here.' She points to the screen. 'This is the growth that shouldn't be there. It's very big and it takes up most of the space where your baby's brain would normally be.'

'What does that mean for my baby?' I ask through a stream of tears.

'It's hard to say until we've carried out an MRI scan. But this is very serious.'

*

Another hospital, this one on the other side of the city. I don't remember how we got here. Ali hasn't spoken for the last two hours. I'm wondering if he's thinking of going back to Bangladesh, that I'm a dud wife. I'm alone, lying on a bench, as I go into the doughnut-shaped entrance of the white MRI scanner. Silently, I talk to my baby: *whatever you need from me, whatever I can do to help you and keep you safe, I'll do it. I promise.*

*

Another consultation room, this time with a foetal medicine midwife. She's offered us both tea, but I'm too strained and nauseous to swallow. A neurosurgeon is also present, and so is our consultant – her face is kind, but her eyes look sad. She's stayed past her normal working hours to give us the results of the MRI. I try to stop myself crying for a moment, to take a calming breath so that I can listen to what they're saying. While they talk, I rub my tummy protectively.

'There's a brain tumour called a cerebral teratoma. It fills most of the space inside your baby's head, squashing the brain.'

I don't catch all the information – my heart is breaking into pieces. I can't breathe. *Your baby is still inside you, Anna; it needs you to keep breathing. Just breathe.*

'This next image shows a cyst around the tumour. It tracks down the baby's throat, stopping any airway from growing.'

What did I do wrong?

'This type of tumour is normally not genetic, just a one in a million, awful event.'

What happens next? A life of needing extra care? I'll move out of the boat so I can get a hoist fitted, maybe move back with my parents for support. Whatever I need to do, I'll do it.

When I manage to say, 'What are the chances of survival?' Ali looks up, hopeful.

Simply and clearly, the team delivers the verdict.

'There is no chance of survival.'

CHAPTER THIRTY-SIX

For the four weeks that followed that first abnormal scan, I felt I was living an awful existence like Schrödinger's cat, with my baby simultaneously alive, but inevitably dead. Every time a woman passed me and clocked my pregnancy bump as I walked slowly along the towpath, then shone me a 'good-luck' smile, my heart shrivelled a little more. Signed off from work, I existed in a state of perpetual grief, as the news from every subsequent scan and appointment seemed to grow more terrible.

'Your body,' I was told during my weekly appointment at Nottingham City Hospital, after another ultrasound, 'is creating too much amniotic fluid because your baby can't drink and excrete the fluid as it normally would.' The tumour, they said, was also making the baby's head grow too big, and there might come a point when I couldn't give birth vaginally.

Although my baby's head wasn't that big yet, it could ultimately make the pregnancy a risk to my own life. On the face of it, the choice was simple – though no one should ever have to make it – to continue the pregnancy, knowing the baby would die anyway, or to deliver early for my sake.

In moments of lucidity, Ali and I talked about our options. When he turned to his family for advice and support, they resoundingly said we should deliver early to protect my life. He also got support from his imam at the local mosque in Nottingham, which had become his family away from home. When I turned to my midwifery texts for reassurance, many articles suggested that the younger foetuses are, the less pain they experience. Some of my support also came from friends, who I'd grown distant from over the years, but who instinctively came to sit with me beside the canal.

My parents came to be with me on a beautiful, warm autumn evening. We sat holding steaming cups of tea outside *Malahat*, and for the first time in my life, I was completely open and frank with them about my grief. I cried my heart out, and they cried too. This was the first time I'd ever seen my parents cry, and in some weird way, it forged a new bridge between us.

*

On the night Ali and I decide to start my labour at six months, knowingly ending my pregnancy, I sob myself to sleep in waves of crushing chest pain.

Technically, this is an abortion, and there may be people reading this who disagree with my choice on religious or ethical grounds, but what choice did I have? One saying stuck with me: sometimes mothers suffer so their children don't have to.

*

On my last day of being pregnant, I try desperately to keep my baby peaceful and calm inside me. I lie in my bunk on the houseboat, watching water patterns thrown onto the ceiling by dappled sunlight. I hold my big belly, whispering, *I'm doing this because I love you. Please, forgive me if I'm wrong.*

*

When Ali says he doesn't want to see me in labour or see the baby, I'm not angry with him – it's his choice to make in an impossible situation. I also know from the births I've attended in Bangladesh, that men are rarely present, regarding it as the woman's realm. He'll have to live with his choices, just as I will with mine.

When I tell Anita I'm nervous about birthing alone, she says,' I'm coming,' stepping forward without a second thought, and I'm forever grateful to her for that. She now has her own two children at home, a partner, a job as a nurse, a busy schedule. But she's there at the hospital entrance as I walk towards it. My legs feel heavy, as though I'm trudging through mud. Her eyes are already red from tears, her arms open wide.

'Where are we now?' I say into her hair as we clutch each other tight.

Helen, my midwife friend, is another light shining in the dark. She's changed her shifts to be with me for the induction of labour.

'I will keep you safe, Anna.'

*

Rage burns in my blood when I see a gaggle of ten pregnant women at the hospital entrance, all smoking. *This is so unfair! I did everything right and my baby is dying.* But there is no such thing as 'fair'. I know that now. Was it fair to Mia that her baby died inside her? Or to Aadab, who died alone after an unsafe abortion following rape? At least I have a hospital for a safe delivery – I must stay grateful for that.

Walking into the labour ward, the department where I work, knowing I'm here to see my baby die, is like walking through hot, burning lava.

The room for stillbirths and dying babies is at the far end of the ward. I hang my head low as I walk the long corridor – past the beautiful large pictures of babies on the walls, past the screams of labour coming from the fourteen other birth rooms, past the cries of healthy newborns. It feels like torture, and seems so cruel to make me birth here. Also, I don't want the couples leaving with their bundles of joy to see my grey swollen face. It's not fair to ruin their moment.

'This shouldn't be you,' says Rosemary, a kind midwifery sister, as I pass the nurses' station on my way to Room 1.

'It shouldn't be anyone,' is all I can say.

*

Now Anita holds my hand. Helen does a vaginal exam and inserts the misoprostol tablet that will start my labour. It will work in conjunction with the mifepristone tablet I was given to swallow two days previously. The insertion is uncomfortable, but I can't feel pain; I'm numb. Maybe I expected a fast birth, but it takes over thirty-six hours in the hospital to get into full labour. Anita sleeps on a Z-bed next to my hospital bed. We talk about my baby – I still don't know its sex. We talk about South Sudan, about Congo and Bangladesh and her children. We try to remember the successes. We talk of love, we watch TV, we lie in quiet reflection. I cry. She cries with me.

'I don't want to do this,' I shout angrily.

'I know,' she says softly.

Helen stays with me through the day shifts. She explains again the process, she gives the next doses of vagina medication, she bears witness to my grief and doesn't turn away. I trust her. Other midwives are there through the night. I don't remember everyone but I remember their support and of not feeling alone.

*

By Sunday morning, I'm getting wave after wave of powerful contractions. I'm so hot, it's a relief to be with women I trust to be naked in front of.

'Do you want any pain relief?' asks Helen gently. Most women I've worked with in the UK who are delivering babies known to be dying do so with strong analgesia or an epidural. This is absolutely their choice. But I don't want to take a single thing. Maybe I'm grief-numb, though the contractions have me shouting 'fuck' at the top of my voice in a very vocal labour. Maybe it's because after seeing so many births without painkillers, I know it's possible, and even a way for me to commune with the women I've cared for – to find kinship in our suffering. It's possible too that I'm unconsciously atoning for all those times I couldn't offer painkillers to women in their hour of need.

But what I feel most is that if this is the only time I will get with my child, I want to be fully present, not semi-conscious.

At nine o'clock in the morning, after a night of full labour, my waters suddenly go – a flood of dry-leaf-smelling, yellowish liquid – with corresponding pressure in my bottom, a feeling like I want to poo.

'I don't want to do this! I can't do this!' I shout loudly, scared.

Helen's voice is calm, reassuring, determined.

'Yes, you can, Anna. You're doing this because you love your baby.'

Another midwife is called in – Jayney, a sweet and kind woman with short blonde hair. I see tears in her eyes as she gives me encouraging words.

'Ahhhhhhhh!' I scream. My body seems to open wide, like I'm splitting in half.

*

'Anna?' It's Helen's voice carried in the darkness. 'Anna, look at me.'

Opening my eyes, Helen's face is full of love and tears.

'Here's your baby.'

I'm scared in case I feel repulsed by own child, but looking down at the tiny bundle being handed to me, I see the most beautiful baby girl I've ever seen in my whole life. Tiny, lighter than a bag of sugar, purplish skin, closed eyes. She's the most amazing baby I've ever met.

'My darling baby girl.' I immediately stop screaming and take her to my chest, cooing as all new mums do. Love courses through my body. Real love. Unconditional love. Bursting from me.

'Fatima,' I call her, a name Ali and I had talked of for a daughter. 'It means one who is perfect, and the mother of all women,' he'd explained one quiet evening on the water, before we'd known our baby was poorly. It was perfect.

'I'm so sorry, my darling girl. I'm so sorry I couldn't save you.'

I still can't believe that after all I know about childbirth, all the signs and symptoms of problems I've searched for in other people, my own baby will die of something I hadn't even heard of. A one in a million chance.

Baby Fatima wriggles a little on my chest.

'She's alive!' I say out loud.

Staring at her, I'm in awe: she's so peaceful, so perfect. There's no fight to get a bag and mask on; no run to the neonatal unit; no one pulls the red emergency button. I know she will die – there's no physical way to get an airway in – it just feels like a miracle that she's born alive at all.

For thirty minutes, I hold Fatima to my chest, talking to her, stroking her pretty, tiny face, admiring every curve of her eye, the daintiness of her nose, until, at last, she stops moving.

'She looks so peaceful,' says Anita.

And she does. Out of the whole horrendous time, that's the one beacon I can still hold on to – that I don't believe she suffered. Later, in dark days when I'm full of regret, Helen's words will come back to reassure me: 'You gave Fatima more love in her short life than some people get in a long lifetime.'

And for the first time I understand what James meant when he said, 'Maybe bearing witness to these lives is our most important role here.' During my time in need, Anita and Helen are with me. We all know my baby will die, but they are travelling with me, suffering with me, carrying me, keeping me safe from the horror of doing this alone. And in some dim part of myself, I know this will help me survive.

*

It's nearly two hours since the birth and my placenta still hasn't delivered. Fatima has been cuddled by Anita, gently wrapped by Helen, and lies in a cot at the end of the room. They've taken photos of her for me, which I hope will show how beautiful she is, not how poorly. It's unbearable to think others might find pictures of my precious baby disgusting.

I know full well the risks of an undelivered placenta, so I walk the room, I squat to have a wee. I tweak my own nipples that are already lactating. I'm given multiple doses of drugs. Nothing works.

After another hour, Helen admits, 'We need help with this.'

When a senior consultant comes to my assistance, I ask for Fatima's body to be taken to another quiet room.

'I need to manually remove your placenta,' he says, solemnly.

I nod in agreement, feeling myself slipping back into the blackness of grief. I don't care what happens to me now.

'I suggest you have some strong painkillers.'

'No,' I say vehemently. 'I don't want anything.'

Tentatively, he gloves up. I lie on my back, letting my legs flop apart. He reaches high inside my vagina, up to my uterus. I feel him use the gently sawing motion of his hand that I've used so many times overseas. My placenta starts to plop out, but because I'm preterm, it's broken into little bits, so he scoops them into a tray with a bloodied glove.

When my breasts start to leak the milk that's not needed, I feel weirdly grateful to them for rallying to the cause, though it feels like they're crying white tears when my arms ache to hold my baby to the breast, to feed her.

*

Eight hours later, I'm on my way home, hanging my head low, wanting to disappear. Helen has given me a carefully made memory box with Fatima's hand- and footprints inside, which I clutch on my lap. Years later, I'll be grateful for this, but right now I don't want it; all I want is my baby and nothing can soothe that savage pain.

A specialist bereavement midwife, Mandy, comes to the boat to see me. She talks about post-mortems, funeral plans, and how the hospital will help us to pay for it. She's sensitive and kind. Ali and I both decline the post-mortem for different reasons. He believes the body suffers pain until the peace of burial. I've seen post-mortems in my training and can't bear the thought of my perfect baby being the one on the slab.

Fatima is buried in a beautiful, multi-faith burial ground just outside Nottingham. It's a grey, rainy day. Ali has prayers read from the Koran, while I stare blankly at the rows of tiny baby gravestones. Mandy holds my hand, sheltering us both under her black umbrella.

*

A week later, I'm starting to pass small bits of placenta onto my sanitary towel. Next thing I remember is my parents are here, looking concerned, driving me back to the hospital. When Ali says he doesn't want to come, I have to remind myself that his baby died too. Then I'm on the ward where I used to work, a drip in my arm. The next moment I'm being wheeled out of theatre where the remains of my placenta have been removed under a general anaesthetic.

I'm in a confused, drug-fuelled fug as I come to. My belly is flat but I'm lying down in the familiar theatre recovery area where I work.

'How is my baby?' I ask the recovery nurse, wrongly thinking I might have had an emergency caesarean.

Mum squeezes my hand as I curl up and cry, remembering Fatima is dead and now buried. My milk has dried; my breasts have started to shrivel away, another sucker punch, like I can't keep hold of anything, and I might never have another baby.

*

Later, people, meaning to be kind, will refer to Fatima as 'my dummy run' or as a miscarriage, or that 'everything happens for a reason'. Friends will cross the road to avoid me because they don't know what to say. I will be told I've had an abortion, or, because Fatima was born at six months, they will shrug her off as if it doesn't *really* count as having a child. But this is not how I experience her loss. For me, Fatima was, is and always will be my daughter. My firstborn. My first true love. And I will always be her mummy.

CHAPTER THIRTY-SEVEN

Sitting beside Ali, quiet and numb on the plane that flew us back to Bangladesh, this feels like my season in hell. My baby is dead. The loss of her, of all she might have been, sits like a dead weight on every movement of my body. I'm still bleeding, and not eating or sleeping well.

Because Fatima was born alive, though premature, I'm now officially on maternity leave. We're going back to Ali's family; the thought of a cold winter in England is unbearable. Last time I'd flown here it was as a visitor, a helper, a privileged person with a purpose. This time it's my turn to fall through the net.

On our first evening back, I see Ali relax back to his old, joyful self as we dip our toes in the warm waters of the Bay of Bengal. It's beautiful here, with golden light softening the heat of day and Ali tries to take my photo.

'Please don't,' I say quietly.

'But we have to show everyone you're OK now. Don't let them worry. Be brave.'

He wants to put this picture of me on Facebook, to reassure everyone at home. But I don't want to 'be brave' and pretend it never happened, because I've never known pain like this and I've got to find my way through it. There are my new reserves of strength to draw on, so I won't go on a self-destruct mission this time: no drinking or partying, no reaching out for sex with strangers or to exes for physical comfort. I need to face it, this grief, let all my spinning plates fall, and when I'm ready, see which ones I can pick up again.

What I don't know then is that I'll never be the same again. My love for Fatima is bound up with a sense of loss that will change through time but never leave me. I can't have one without the other.

*

Count your blessings, the phrase from the Buddhist centre, comes back to me again as a new source of strength. I've worked out there are at least six ways that my midwife Helen, and the wider NHS, saved my life over the period of pregnancy and birth of Fatima. These include access to an accurate scan that picked up Fatima's brain tumour; referral to an experienced consultant who recognised the risks to me; safe drugs to give birth; antibiotics after the birth; a skilled professional who manually removed my placenta; and the safe surgical removal of remaining birth products. These are all things women around the world don't get if they have no access to a midwife, and why over 800 women die each day because of pregnancy and childbirth. And why the woman on the plane, back on my first day in South Sudan, was so awfully injured from her undelivered dead baby. Although I can't do much about the hollow feeling in my uterus, I'm still grateful for the care I received to stay safe, to stay alive.

Ali's family are kind. They don't fear suffering. When the men walk off to take tea and talk at a local stall, the sisters clutch me to their chests under the shade of the mango tree. They cry with me; they wail words I don't understand and point to the heavens as if Fatima now resides up there. I hear of their own losses, of how Ali's mum, Amar Juaan, was the informal and untrained attendant at the birth of all her grandchildren because there were no midwives. Of the miscarriages, of the stillbirths, of the toddler who drowned in a local pond. Their public grief for my daughter reassures me, it makes it real, unlike the silence I've received from the management at the maternity department where I've worked on and off for over five years, who have sent no condolences. I know they care, I know it's a symptom of working in a ridiculously busy unit, but if *they* can't get support right for baby loss, who can? This leads to my fear that somehow I've misunderstood what's happened – that a preterm baby loss is not *really* a baby loss, though I know simultaneously this isn't true.

*

Ali's family are disappointed when we say we won't stay with them. They're so welcoming and warm that a large part of me wants to accept, but my urgent need for a quiet space is stronger, and they've accepted my choice. Ali and I rent the same kind of cheap room – squat toilet, cold shower – we got before the wedding. This one has a mattress on the floor with a mosquito net above it. It has a lone TV in the middle of an otherwise empty room.

Some days I don't get out of bed, but lie zombie-like, watching American blockbusters on Indian movie channels. Sometimes Ali sits with me, sometimes he's out all day and I'm alone to sob until I'm dry. He'll come back with chapatti cooked by his sister that I dip into syrupy tea, or some samosas, tiny bananas and a green coconut to drink. Sometimes I speak to my family or friends from home on video and Messenger, but I don't track who I've kept up with, or what birthdays I've missed.

'How you bearing up there, Kent?' says James kindly over a video call. 'Been kinda worried about your radio silence.'

I tell him how much my body hurts, my heart, my uterus, but also how I'm not trying to distract myself from that. I'm going to sit with it, accept it even.

'I'm not gonna throw some sanctimonious Buddhist quote at you, Anna Banana, not at this time.' This makes me smile. 'But I love you, OK? And I know how much you loved your Fatima.'

*

After a few weeks like this, I walk along the beach at sunset again, and for the first time feel the warm breeze on my face, hear the giggles of children running in and out of the water. The elderly man with the crinkled face laughs as he sells me tea from a large vacuum flask.

During the daytime, I start to sit with the women of the family in the shade of the mango tree, with Ali's dog happily slumped in the sand by our feet. We shell peas together, or strip leaves from coriander plants, or peel sweet potatoes, ready for the big cooking pot over a single-ring gas stove. Sadia, my twenty-year-old niece, translates for me, as no one else speaks English.

'Misti aloo,' I say, practising my Bangla for 'sweet potato', which makes the women, my relatives, smile and laugh encouragingly. It's a different language from the one I learnt with the Rohingya women, and from the Chittagonian Bangla I picked up from the Bangladeshi staff, and feels like starting from scratch again.

We sit in a circle, each draped in different coloured salwar kameez: bright pinks, blues, me in green, our scarves on our laps. When one of the men comes into the courtyard, we cover our shoulders or hair.

We eat a lunch of rice and vegetable dahl as a family and with our fingers. My sister-in-law Salma, who munches raw chilli with each bite of food, sits cross-legged beside me. Sadia, my niece, shows me how to make the clay stove on which we'll cook the aubergine later over hot coals for a brinjal bhaji. She takes my hand and draws henna over my palm; the physical contact is soothing. Some days she combs my hair and puts coconut oil on its ratty ends. 'No stress, auntie,' she says. 'We will look after you.'

*

After two months of this gentle living, I get my first period. It's December 2015, and I feel my first pang of homesickness, knowing Christmas is not widely celebrated in Bangladesh. Also, I long to sit at Fatima's graveside in Nottingham, but wonder if that's because I've watched too many films, because that's not where I feel her most. I actually feel connected to her when I lie on my back, calm my thoughts and put my hand on my abdomen – that's where I knew her.

Today in the market I bought a silver 'Fatima's hand' pendant, a protective symbol. I tie it around my belly – my new tawiz, my teek, my talisman – and if I need to remember all that's gone, and what brought me here, I run the thread and pendant through my fingers.

I'm not ready to go home yet, or to work as a midwife. I'm worried that this time I'll scream at the small numbers of pregnant women smoking at the hospital entrance, when deep down I know they deserve compassion and care. That they have their own stories and challenges.

But I must work soon: it's always been my lifeline, but when I suggest to Ali that I could do some teaching at the Hope Hospital, he frowns and says, 'You must rest. You must eat. Then you can work.'

But I'm no good at doing nothing, plus I don't like being told what to do, and the divide between us that started out as an invisible mist keeps growing. So when Amar Juaan gets ill from a bad chest infection, I'm eager to nurse her. With Sadia's help, we change her bedding, cook soft food and make sure she doesn't get any pressure sores. I take time to comb her hair. I hang her bright nightie on the line to dry after it's been handwashed, where it flutters like a butterfly. She murmurs sweetly, 'Thank you, Shona Monee,' and gently touches my hand.

*

January 2016, and it's almost as if nothing has happened. My belly's flat and so are my breasts, and my periods have started again. Ali and I slept together soon after the surgical removal of my placenta, a bad idea medically speaking until I'd fully healed, but it felt like one of the few options we have left to be close. Clearly, we're grieving in very different ways, which isn't unusual in couples suffering the death of a baby. But I'm holding tight to the threads of our relationship because I can't bear to think of losing something else.

I'm watching the news again. One hundred babies in Brazil have been born with microcephaly (very small heads and severe brain injury), possibly caused by Zika virus, which is carried by a certain type of mosquito. Bangladesh has the same mosquito, and one confirmed case of Zika, so I grow to hate even more the mosquitoes that swarm around our ankles when we walk by the beach at sunset, or when I help Amar Juaan take her evening medications and inhalers.

*

It's the end of January and the days are heating up again. I'm lying naked on our mattress on the floor, covered only by a sheet, when I catch Ali looking at me quizzically. Following his gaze, I see my breasts are slightly bigger, the areola slightly darker.

'You're pregnant,' he says, smiling.

And immediately I know it's true. My third pregnancy in less than a year. My midwife brain knows this isn't the safest of situations, but right now that doesn't register. Since the birth of Fatima, my longing to carry a child again has been almost animalistic, despite the bittersweetness of pregnancy. Also, I've felt the growing burden of knowing that I must soon go back to full-time NHS work to keep Ali and me afloat if we are to live in the UK. But suddenly, none of that matters. *I'm so happy to be pregnant.*

Ali is praying now in the room next door. He's kneeling on the floor facing Mecca. In the street outside, an amplified male voice calls people to evening prayer. Lying on my back, a big smile spreads over my face. I'm touching my tummy, holding my tawiz, silently praying to the universe that this time I will go home with my baby. I whisper, 'I will look after you, my little one, I promise.'

CHAPTER THIRTY-EIGHT

Aisha was born in October 2016, in a warm birthing pool at Nottingham City Hospital. It was across the hall from the room where I'd birthed her sister, Fatima, and held her for the first and last time.

Jayney, the sweet blonde midwife who'd helped with Fatima's birth, was with me, as was an independent midwife called Nicky, who was my anchor. Nicky knew about baby loss – her first daughter, Penny, was born with a rare kidney tumour and died at nine days old. It was Nicky who brought me poems, birth mantras and centuries-old invocations during my pregnancy.

We invoke the women who have gone before us: mothers, midwives, wise women:

Be with us. Remind us to trust our bodies and to surrender our fears and worries. Remind us to simply be with our awesome selves – powerful, creative, yielding and wielding.

Nicky had encouraged massage and aromatherapy, anything to help me focus on the joy rather than the trauma of birth. Of course, I was helped along by the surge of positive pregnancy hormones within me.

I'm not claiming that being a pregnant midwife was all plain sailing. In general, we probably know too much, and in my case, some expectant mothers, seeing my bump, would ask me excitedly if this was my first baby. I would hear myself say 'yes', and then have to silently apologise to Fatima for dismissing her existence, but I didn't want to scare them – this was not the time to remind expectant mothers of baby loss.

When my labour started, around two in the morning, I told Ali to go back to bed, and between mild contractions I swept, mopped and polished the boat. This seemed to help my adrenaline settle as I adjusted to the pain. When I needed company, I sent WhatsApp messages to my mum, sister, Anita and closest women friends, wanting to connect to them. I also listened to the soothing music of Arvo Pärt, which I'd once heard at a UK birth.

I'd given great thought to having my baby on the boat, but if I had a PPH or another form of obstructed labour, I knew no ambulance could get down the narrow canal path. It's Ali, around nine in the morning, when I get more vocal as the contractions ripple through my uterus, who insists that I go to hospital. Rachel, a close friend, comes to pick me up. She laughs as I try to ask her about her son James between my labouring grunts. It's a circle of life moment: James is my godson; I was one of Rachel's birth partners when he was born. In these safe surroundings, I couldn't imagine having to walk barefoot through landmined fields and snake territory to get to a hospital, as the women in South Sudan had to do when in labour.

At the hospital, I sink into the warm and welcome waters of the birthing pool. Beside me, in another circle of life moment, is the frayed teek I'd been given after delivering Moses, my first baby in South Sudan. Its red, white and black beads are my talismans today. Next to it my Fatima's hand tawiz, which I've temporarily removed and aim to slip back around my hips one day.

Six hours go by before my labour reaches a crescendo and my waters go. Then, in the next grunt and howl, at 4:30 in the afternoon, Nicky and Jayney, with tears of love in their eyes, are telling me I'm amazing and are lifting my new, glistening, beautiful bundle of Aisha out of the water and onto my chest.

It had been quite a day for all of us: me shouting 'Fuck!' as I rode the mountains and canyons of childbirth, all of us giggling as I swam in the natural high of endorphins between contractions. Maybe in memory of Fatima, maybe because I'd witnessed so many births without pain relief, I opted not to have any drugs, and this too was respected and supported.

When Nicky, Jayney and I talk about this day, they always beam with love, and say it was a joyous day for them too. As for me, when I look at Aisha, I'm so humbled by love. I still can't quite believe she's mine, though not mine of course, I don't own her, but she was born through me and I am her mummy.

Aisha remains the best thing that has ever happened to me.

*

'Where are we now?'

Anita's the first person to visit after Aisha's birth. She still lives in Hertfordshire and is mother to two young children, with a third now swelling her belly. *Malahat* rocks gently on the canal as we look at each other in amazement.

We're both laughing as she holds Aisha. She examines her closely, shakes her head in wonder, holds her up to the light like a precious jewel in a moment of pure and undiluted joy.

*

Anita is still my rock and confidante; so is James, who video-calls me every couple of months from the log cabin he's built from scratch in Oregon.

It was with Anita that I commiserated in 2014, when we watched horrific footage of Leer Hospital in South Sudan burning to the ground after an attack. That important safe space and all the hard work that went into it were lost in what felt like moments, leaving only dust and ashes.

Anita was also the one I phoned in 2018, when Aisha was two and my marriage was falling apart. By then, I'd sold the boat, hoping life on land might save us. When it didn't, I bought a small terraced house in Weymouth and set up life as a single mum, our new home only a short distance from the sea. If I sound flippant about my divorce, I don't feel it. I desperately wanted my marriage to work and fought hard to save it. But when it became unbearable, for everyone's sake, it had to end. Looking back, I'd always unconsciously assumed marriage and babies were part of my life's goals. But now that's shifted, and I recognise that being healthy, mindful and a good mum comes above most else.

*

And now it's autumn 2020, I'm thirty-nine years old and in my bikini. Inspired by other Dorset locals who swim all year round, I'm about to have my first dip in the spine-shrivelling cold sea. The UK is on the brink of the second Covid-19 national lockdown, so the sea swimmers are particularly determined. *It's fun,* they insist.

King George III, around 1789, was a regular swimmer at Weymouth, where he would change in a heated hut before he and his bathing machine were wheeled into the shallow waters while his band played 'God Save the King'.

There's no fanfare as I inch into the water, just goosepimples, purple legs and biting cold around my ankles. I'm thinking George III probably chose July for his swims, not a grey day in October, and actually, didn't he end up being called 'the mad king'?

I'm not yet immersed, but I'm already regretting this. Weymouth's famously long, shallow sandbank that leads to the deeper waters seems to go on forever. If it wasn't for a small person, my daughter, sitting on the beach urging me on, my warmly clad parents laughing and waving alongside, I'd be tempted to give up and do the walk of shame back for a coffee at Oasis, my favourite beach café.

But on and on I stubbornly walk, until plop! The sand shelf gives way quite suddenly to deep water – water so cold it makes me yell. A few seconds later, as the shock wears off, every cell in my body starts to vibrate, as if I've been given an electric charge. Kicking my legs wildly, I look around at the rocks and cliffs of the Dorset coast and think, they were right. *This feels wonderful*. I am alive. I came through. There's a huge sky all around me, and best of all, back on the beach, my fierce little four-year-old is sitting with my parents, shrieking, 'Go, Mummy!'

When I get out, Aisha watches me impatiently while I towel myself dry. She can't wait to show me the sandcastle she's made with Granny, the moat dug by Papa, my parents, who I'm now closer to than ever. Laughing and shouting, she pulls me down to the water's edge, where several slipper limpet shells have been left by the small waves.

'Mummy, Mummy! Look, look, *look!* I found a good one!'

She examines each shell closely, lifts them for my inspection; if they pass, she presses them into the top of her sandcastle.

And looking at her, my heart bursts – I've never known love like it. At four, she's a bundle of fun and contradictions, giggles, stubbornness and surreal questions. I pull her for a hug in my towel, I breathe in the smell of her hair, watch every line of her face. Her smile that looks like mine, the long lashes that look like Ali's. Loving her helps me to accept what came before – without it there would be no her.

Although this feels like the happiest I've ever been, I accept now that I am still my own bundle of contradictions. Occasionally, there are still bad dreams. Or I'll find myself on a train obsessing over where the exits are, or what I'll use as a tourniquet when the crash happens. If I don't recognise these unhealthy 'catastrophising' thought patterns quickly enough, I go quite far down the rabbit hole and can have a sensory picture of the broken bones and the blood. I'm getting better all the time at recognising them early, though, and mostly use my breath and grounding techniques to come back to the moment.

There are no tidy conclusions to be drawn, only for me a few moments of understanding along the way. The first is this: if you step out of your previous life and become an aid worker, you will probably be changed in some way forever. Everyone will experience this differently, but I had a light-bulb moment when I read the work of psychotherapist Alison O'Connor, who has written about 'moral injury' for the journal *Therapy Today*.

Historically, moral injury has been used to describe the damaged mental health of military personnel, arising from traumas they experience during active service. Alison describes it as 'a state of profound emotional and psychological distress resulting from the violation of a person's core moral values. This often results in shame and guilt … leading to a loss of identity. Or even life meaning. Some call this a "soul wound".'

It makes sense to accept that many humanitarian aid workers may suffer similarly. Our job is to help, our mandate 'to save lives', but sometimes the situation is so impossible that we can't. What's more, we stay and witness the suffering that follows our inability to help. I hate labels and pathologising perfectly normal human responses, but the descriptions of moral injury described so accurately how I'd felt, and sometimes still do, that it was like another piece of the jigsaw being put back into place.

I also know now that making peace with a moral injury is a long, slow process. That my own mental health couldn't be simply fixed by an act of will, by chanting, by mindfulness, although these all helped in ways that partying and sex never could. Therapy helped, writing things down helped, taking time out of my midwifery career helped, great friends like James, Anita and others helped, my new-found openness and connection with my family helped. I had to learn to let people in. And it goes without saying, Aisha has unknowingly helped too. Loneliness has been such a big part of my life, but I've realised the root of that was a sense of being evicted from myself – I was looking for completeness in my romantic relationships but, clichéd as it sounds, I had to find it within me.

Maybe most importantly, learning to forgive myself for all I wasn't able to do in such extreme situations has also helped, as did accepting that I am human, with human frailties and flaws. And slowly, slowly, this has come to feel like a realignment of the different parts of me. While my life is not perfect, there is joy and I feel present, healthy and grateful to be here.

Now Aisha bundles me bossily into a towel, crawls onto my lap; she fixes both my arms around her waist, curls my hands around her fingers. Looking out to sea I take a deep breath, smiling. Soon we'll all head back to my little terraced house for a late, 'socially distanced' Sunday dinner. My parents and I will drink a couple of glasses of red wine as Aisha plays with her toys, as we listen to 'Redemption Song' by Bob Marley. Then we'll video-call with my sister and brother, Helen and Dan. We're unaware yet that impending Covid-19 lockdown restrictions mean it will be over six months before we see my parents again. Or that I'll choose to cold-water swim weekly from now on, even in temperatures of minus 1°C, to keep my head metaphorically above water when working on this new 'frontline' as both an NHS nurse and midwife. Swimming will come to help me process the anger and fear I feel at times when forced to work in the Covid-19 pandemic without proper PPE. I'm a single mum now, I can't accept death as I once did after that surfing accident. Being submerged in water will help me to process the angst of working in a stretched maternity unit in an ever-litigious world, where those of us patient-facing will bear the brunt when services don't meet women's needs. It would even help me to cope with my worst fear – that a patient could die under my care because of gaps in the system. Swimming will also provide space for me to admire the dedication and bravery my colleagues show on a daily basis, and to appreciate the heroic women birthing amidst this pandemic.

During lockdown, between my shifts and swims, Aisha and I will video-call her relatives in Bangladesh, her cousin Sadia showing us what's in the cooking pot that day, her auntie Salma teaching her Bangla. They're familiar faces to her, and we're grateful she got to meet them in Bangladesh before this pandemic, and to meet her now late grandma, Amar Juaan.

I'll also video-call with James, chatting about everything and nothing, sometimes touching on these PPE and staffing shortages. He'll be sitting in his homemade cabin in Oregon, and I'll be rolling my eyes in Weymouth as he says, 'Kent, there's the world as it is, and the world as you want it to be.' Yeah, James! Right – whatever! I think, knowing deep down he's probably right, but also understanding that should never stop us fighting for improvements. 'Without the truth, we have nothing,' I say, lovingly mocking him back with his own words. James is now working within care of the dying, giving comfort and medical support to people in their final hours. I'm in awe at him for this, knowing how important a 'good death' is, smiling that he is now a *midwife to the dying*. But he never lets me praise him; instead he'll shake off my admiration with a joke: 'You see 'em in and I see 'em out'.

My favourite part of the day is when the evening grows quiet, the battle to brush teeth is over, the mess of toys is put away and Aisha snuggles into my chest for a bedtime story, under the delicate needlework of the kantha quilt Sarika sewed for me. Aisha loves stories of incredibly brave people who do incredibly brave things, never seeming to worry about their safety, like the snail in Julia Donaldson's *The Snail and the Whale*. I'm not that person, never was, and one day when she's old enough I'll tell her something of how it was: of the amazing things I've witnessed, of the mistakes I've made and learnt from, and some of the truly brave people I met along the way. Maybe we'll talk about how it is 'OK not to be OK', and how breathing gently can help with feelings of anxiety, how mindfulness can keep us grounded. I hope to teach her how anger, when used consciously, can be a healthy emotional expression, how it can keep us safe if we are in harm's way, as I first learnt in South Sudan. I will tell her about kindness – ordinary, everyday, bog-standard acts of kindness – such as being with friends when they need you, how this trumps bravery every time, and how much of it there is even in our flawed world. *Look for the helpers,* I will tell her when world events may seem big and scary.

As we snuggle, her eyes start to close, her breathing becomes slow and regular, my fingers will find the tawiz still tied around my belly, tracing the outline of the Fatima's hand pendant. It reminds me of all the amazing women I had the honour to work with in South Sudan, Haiti, Bangladesh and here in the UK. It also connects me to the only space where I knew Fatima, and that simple cord with the silver pendant is a thread that holds all these intense and important experiences together. It brings me peace. And my heart starts to soften, my dreams open to the idea of love again, and I smile, as the rest of this story waits to be told.

AFTERWORD

This memoir is drawn from my extensive diaries, letters home to family and friends, situation reports and vivid memories. Every extraordinary birth described in this book has happened in real life.

I began writing a diary as a teenager, when my hormone-fuelled entries swung wildly between which boy I wanted to go to the school disco with and the atrocities of the Rwandan genocide. Writing continued when I started to work within international humanitarian aid in my twenties. I've tried to be as honest as possible about what I witnessed as an aid worker and as a midwife, which was sometimes wonderful, but sometimes horrific and hard. Throughout this book, I've tried to portray our successes, but also face up to my own failings and naivety. The world in which aid workers often find themselves is so far outside the realms of 'normal' experience, that fear of not being understood is enough to keep many silent about what they have experienced or witnessed. I have that fear too, but I'm determined to speak out, because silence helps no one and taboos can kill. I don't expect applause. This book is simply a testimony of what I have seen and experienced, written in the hope that it might be able to do some good.

Of course, I might have remembered events differently from other people who were present. No surprise there, as no two people perceive the same event in exactly the same way, but I have contacted as many individuals as possible to get their perspective on the shared experiences we lived through.

Those recognisable in this book have given me permission to write about them. Some colleagues have specifically asked to be excluded from my writing, and I have honoured that. Others I have fully anonymised, and any description that happens to resemble someone alive today is unintentional and purely accidental.

It proved impossible to contact most of the women and patients I cared for as a nurse or a midwife in humanitarian emergencies. The sad fact is that many are dead, while others have disappeared without trace, their lives so transient and so vulnerable. To protect those still living, I've changed the identifiers of all patients in this book, and occasionally adjusted dates, time frames, place names and conversations. I recognise that in a perfect world it would be them telling their story, not me. The fact is that they are not in a position to speak out, but I am, and I want to use my privilege to help them. I had no idea how much they suffered until I saw it up close and raw.

The account of my first frontline mission – to Sudan – is based on the political situation at the time I was there in 2007. As I am writing retrospectively, I refer to it as South Sudan, but I acknowledge that it was not recognised as an independent country until 2011.

ACKNOWLEDGEMENTS

My first thank you has to be to all the women, birthing people, and families over the years who have shared their most profound and intimate life moments with me as their midwife. May you be safe, healthy and free from suffering.

I'm forever thankful for my family and friends. Writing this book has helped me to understand why I found it so hard to share the truth of my experiences at the time. Perhaps it will help them to understand, too. I hope those I love will forgive me for not being better at this sooner, and I remain grateful for all the support I've received over the years. Thank you to those who would prefer to go unnamed - I hope you know who you are and how much I love you. My family, friends and support bubble have been my lifeline.

This book would not have been possible without the help and support of the wonderful author Julia Gregson. We met in 2015, when she was researching her novel *Monsoon Summer*, about an English midwife who goes to India in 1948 to train local women in midwifery. Over many long conversations, I gradually started to tell her snippets of my own life as an aid worker, until the day came when I let her fully into my confidence. Julia was the first person I trusted with my whole story. Her words and compassion have given me great comfort over the years, and she became the 'midwife' to this book. Her insight, literary skill and sensitive questions have led us to write, laugh and cry together, and by sharing, I have started to heal some very old wounds. This book is born from our shared commitment to tell this story.

Thank you so much to Clare Alexander for your compassion and commitment to this book, and to all at Aitken Alexander Associates. Many thanks to Alexis Kirschbaum and all at Bloomsbury Publishing UK, who have worked so hard on delivering the book, despite the pandemic pressures.

A final thanks to friends and colleagues who have helped with recollections, early drafts and edits, and who have motivated me to keep writing. For those scattered across the world, I pray you all stay safe, and may we one day be reunited.

IN LOVING MEMORY OF

The woman on the plane
The baby in the dark
Baby Mary
Eve
John
Mariam
Nyawik
Aadab
Mia's baby
Amar Juaan
Judith Nicholas
Sarah Mann
David and Joan Asprey, my grandparents
Dr Catherine Hamlin
Helen Loewenstein
Baby Fatima

'If I have ever wronged you, please forgive me.'

FURTHER READING

Alison O'Connor, 'Moral Injury', *Therapy Today* (March 2021, pp. 35–7)

Bessel van der Kolk, *The Body Keeps the Score* (Penguin Books, London, 2015)

John Steinbeck *Of Mice and Men* (Penguin Books, New York, 1994)

Julia Donaldson and Axel Scheffler, *The Snail and the Whale* (Macmillan, London, 2003)

Médecins Sans Frontières, *Essential Obstetric and Newborn Care* (https://medicalguidelines.msf.org, MSF, 2019)

Primo Levi *If This Is a Man - The Truce* (Penguin Books, London, 1979)

Wallace J. Nichols, *Blue Mind: How Water Makes You Happier, More Connected and Better at What You Do* (Little, Brown, London, 2014)

FURTHER INFORMATION

For readers interested in supporting midwifery training, the Helen Loewenstein Memorial Trust (HLMT), makes grants to cover course fees and essential study expenses for student midwives in Liberia. HLMT enables talented and committed individuals, who would not otherwise have sufficient funds to train, to become qualified midwives.

The Trust has been set up in memory of Helen Loewenstein, who was Anna's friend and her midwife for the birth of Fatima. Helen, who died in 2018, was a remarkable midwife and someone who touched the lives of so many, both in the UK and Liberia.

For more details, please visit

www.hlmt.org.uk

A NOTE ON THE TYPE

The text of this book is set in Perpetua. This typeface is an adaptation of a style of letter that had been popularised for monumental work in stone by Eric Gill. Large scale drawings by Gill were given to Charles Malin, a Parisian punch-cutter, and his hand-cut punches were the basis for the font issued by Monotype. First used in a private translation called 'The Passion of Perpetua and Felicity', the italic was originally called Felicity.